# AGRICULTURE, BUREAUCRACY, AND MILITARY GOVERNMENT IN PERU

# AGRICULTURE, BUREAUCRACY, AND MILITARY GOVERNMENT IN PERU

*Peter S. Cleaves*
*Martin J. Scurrah*

CORNELL UNIVERSITY PRESS
ITHACA AND LONDON

Copyright © 1980 by Cornell University Press
All rights reserved. Except for brief quotations in a review, this book,
or parts thereof, must not be reproduced in any form without written
permission from the publisher. For information address Cornell University
Press, 124 Roberts Place, Ithaca, New York 14850.

First published 1980 by Cornell University Press.
Published in the United Kingdom by Cornell University Press Ltd.,
2–4 Brook Street, London W1Y 1AA.


International Standard Book Number 0-8014-1300-1
Library of Congress Catalog Card Number 80-14687
Printed in the United States of America
Librarians: Library of Congress cataloging information appears
on the last page of the book.

To our parents

# Contents

7

# Contents

# Tables

# Figures

# Preface

In 1969 the Peruvian military government initiated a radical agrarian reform program. As a break with the past it rivaled Fidel Castro's nationalization of U.S.-owned plantations in Cuba and Mexico's agrarian policies under Lázaro Cárdenas. When normal political liberties in Peru were suspended, the national bureaucracy assumed responsibility for land distribution. In 1973, at the beginning of our research, we hoped to learn how the reform was conceived, modified, and implemented by the bureaucracy. It soon became evident, however, that other questions needed to be answered simultaneously if the full significance of the Peruvian reform was to become apparent. How did a small group of military nationalists undertake a revolutionary program with few objective bases of support? Why did they lose their grip, and was there any way that they could have transformed their experimental program into lasting structural reform? How does bureaucratic behavior relate to national ideology and political institutions in Peru? Are current theories of administration sufficient for an understanding of bureaucracy's role in the carrying out of structural reform in times of social upheaval?

Latin America has experienced more land reforms in the

twentieth century than has any other region of the world, but few of these reforms have led to satisfactory income redistribution, political participation, and production. Reforms in some countries (for example, in Bolivia) have left disproportionate amounts of land in the hands of large owners, and in others have been aborted before being carried to completion (those in Guatemala and Chile). Cuba's reform, while successful in its objective of eliminating large landowners, organized most of the rural population in a vertical relationship with government, which allowed little participation from below. Mexico's land reform contributed to stability in rural areas, but in recent years land concentration has increased and food production has dropped, so that large imports have been needed to feed the population. The Peruvian reformers hoped to avoid each of these shortcomings. Although we do not put forth a formal theory of agrarian reform, some of the generalizations advanced on the basis of the Peruvian case can be used as reference points toward an understanding of similar efforts in Latin America, Asia, Europe, and Africa.

The subject of the military in politics has generated a large number of studies that help to explain military intervention and subsequent policies. In Peru, the coup occurred in the aftermath of economic and moral deterioration of the civilian government of Fernando Belaúnde. Many of the new regime's policies were linked to the events that justified the takeover in the first place, the armed forces' conception of national security, and development ideologies prevalent in the international scene in the 1960s. The military establishment was analogous to a political party in its penetration of the government machinery but not in its relations with civil society. The regime's search for popular support for radical reforms eventually undermined the armed forces' internal cohesion. The placement of military personnel in civilian bureaucratic roles upset traditional criteria for military promotion, and the advancement of junior officers on the basis of ideological adherence to the revolution created further strains. Much of the fascination of the presidency of General Juan Velasco Alvarado (1968–75) derived from the fact that for a long period his regime behaved in ways contrary to the objective interests of the military as an institution. Because the armed forces were permeated by obedience norms and service loyalties, however, a skillful military commander such as Velasco could lead them down political paths that they would not have otherwise followed. Under somewhat different circumstances his government might have achieved a permanent change in Peruvian economic and political institutions.

Comparative studies of bureaucracy are experiencing a revival in academic circles, and one aim of this book is to encourage new ways of interpreting administrative behavior in Third World countries. Almost all of the prescriptive literature on management is based on the historical experiences of advanced industrial nations. The unsuitableness of those norms for organizational behavior in societies with different values leads one to question the universality of conventional management theory. The experience of the Velasco regime helps to clarify the tenuous relationships among national ideology, political structure, and bureaucratic behavior. An examination of those relationships is another objective of this book.

The data gathered to treat these questions come in great part from more than 130 open-ended, confidential interviews with respondents ranging from peasants in indigenous communities to presidential advisers. The Appendix contains a methodological note and a list of these interviews, which are cited periodically in the text. This wide array of respondents provided us with extensive inside commentary on the operations of the Peruvian state along with the reactions to government initiatives of affected persons outside of official circles. In addition to the hundreds of pages of verbatim interview notes, we relied on newspaper records, published documents, scholarly papers, official statistics, published memoirs, and a limited amount of regression analysis. Some respondents also read chapter drafts and corrected factual errors. Peter Cleaves researched and prepared the first draft of the Introduction and Chapters 1, 2, 4, 5, 7, and 8, and Martin Scurrah did the same for Chapter 3 and most of Chapter 6. Each section was then surrendered to the co-author for review, and sometimes for major rewriting.

The original manuscript was researched and written from January 1973 to August 1976 during spare hours while we worked full-time for the Ford Foundation and Lima's Escuela

Superior de Administración de Negocios, respectively. During this period we received generous cooperation from many quarters. We are grateful to our employers for logistical support, to *La Prensa* of Lima for access to its newspaper files, and to the Department of Political Science at Yale University for Cleaves's 1976–77 visiting fellowship. Colleagues who provided helpful comments after reading earlier versions of the manuscript were Judith Albert, David Bayer, Alejandro Camino, Geraldo Canto, David Collier, Luis Deustua, Robert Drysdale, Anthony Ferner, Alberto Giesecke, Rainer Godau, Colin Harding, Peter Knight, Susana Lastarria, Federico León, Abraham Lowenthal, Cynthia McClintock, Vivienne Marquez, Héctor Martínez, Antonio Muñoz-Nájar, Raquel Núñez, Oscar Oszlak, Vivienne Shue, Bernardo Sorj, Alfred Stepan, Evelyn Stephens, Fernando de Trazegnies, James Trowbridge, Michael Twomey, and Ross Zucker. Luz María Montaño graciously typed the final drafts of the manuscript.

We acknowledge separately the assistance of Giorgio Alberti and Enrique Mayer, who provided wise counsel at critical stages of the research and insightful suggestions after reading long sections of the manuscript. But no errors in fact or judgment can be attributed to them or to any of the other persons or institutions mentioned here. The responsibility for the final product rests solely with us.

Final thanks are reserved for Dorothy, Geoffrey, and Rachel Cleaves and María, Cecilia, and Lucía Scurrah, whom we overly neglected while we were preparing this book. With apologies for past absences, we hope that subsequent projects will be less time-consuming. We will be fortunate, however, if our future research is as engaging as this study of bureaucratic and agricultural change in Peru.

P. S. C.

M. J. S.

*Mexico City and Lima*

# Abbreviations and Acronyms

| | |
|---|---|
| AGEPSA | Asesoría y Gerencia EPSA (EPSA Advisory and Management Office; see EPSA) |
| ANTA | Asociación Nacional de Trabajadores del Arte (National Association of Artistic Workers) |
| AP | Acción Popular (Popular Action Party) |
| APRA | Alianza Popular Revolucionaria Americana (American Popular Revolutionary Alliance) |
| CAEM | Centro de Altos Estudios Militares (Center for Higher Military Studies) |
| CAP | Cooperativa Agraria de Producción (Agrarian Production Cooperative) |
| CAS | Cooperativa Agraria de Servicios (Agrarian Services Cooperative) |
| CCP | Confederación de Campesinos del Perú (Peasant Confederation of Peru) |
| CECOAAP | Central de las Cooperativas Agrarias Azucareras de Producción (Central Office of Sugar Production Cooperatives) |
| CENCIRA | Centro Nacional de Capacitación e Investigación para la Reforma Agraria (Center for Training and Research in Agrarian Reform) |
| CIAP | Comisión Interamericana de la Alianza para el Progreso (Inter-American Commission for the Alliance for Progress) |

| | |
|---|---|
| CIDA | Comité Interamericano de Desarrollo Agrícola (Inter-American Committee for Agrarian Development) |
| CNA | Confederación Nacional Agraria (National Agrarian Confederation) |
| COAP | Comité de Asesoramiento de la Presidencia de la República (Presidential Advisory Committee) |
| COFIDE | Corporación Financiera de Desarrollo (Financial Development Corporation) |
| CONACI | Confederación Nacional de Comunidades Industriales (National Confederation of Industrial Communities) |
| CONAPS | Comisión Nacional de Propiedad Social (National Social Property Commission) |
| CORPIURA | Corporación de Desarrollo Económico y Social del Departmento de Piura (Piura Economic and Social Development Corporation) |
| CPC | Cámara Peruana de la Construcción (Peruvian Construction Bureau) |
| CTP | Confederación de Trabajadores del Perú (Confederation of Peruvian Workers) |
| DESCO | Centro de Estudios y Promoción del Desarrollo (Center for the Study and Promotion of Development) |
| D.L. | Decreto-Ley (Decree Law) |
| ELECTROPERU | Empresa Pública de Electricidad del Perú (Peruvian State Electric Company) |
| EMADI | Empresa de Administración de Inmuebles (Buildings and Real Estate Administration Company) |
| EPCHAP | Empresa Pública de Comercialización de Harina y Aceite de Pescado (Public Enterprise for Fish Meal and Fish Oil Marketing) |
| EPSA | Empresa Pública de Servicios Agropecuarios (Public Enterprise for Agricultural Services) |
| ESAN | Escuela Superior de Administración de Negocios (School of Business Administration) |
| FENCAP | Federación Nacional de Campesinos del Perú (National Federation of Peruvian Peasants) |
| FLN | Frente de Liberación Nacional (National Liberation Front) |
| FONAPS | Fondo Nacional de Propiedad Social (National Social Property Fund) |
| FPA | Fuero Privativo Agrario (Agrarian Court System) |
| FTAP | Federación de Trabajadores Azucareros del Perú (Federation of Peruvian Sugar Workers) |

| INAP | Instituto Nacional de Administración Pública (National Institute of Public Administration) |
|---|---|
| INCOOP | Instituto Nacional de Cooperativas (National Institute for Cooperatives) |
| INDUPERU | Empresa Estatal de Industrias del Perú (Peruvian State Industrial Corporation) |
| INP | Instituto Nacional de Planificación (National Planning Institute) |
| IPC | International Petroleum Company |
| MEF | Ministerio de Economía y Finanzas (Ministry of Economy and Finance) |
| MINEROPERU | Empresa Minera del Perú (Peruvian State Mining Company) |
| MSP | Movimiento Social Progresista (Social Progressive Movement) |
| ONDECOOP | Oficina Nacional de Desarrollo Cooperativo (National Office for Cooperative Development) |
| ONIT | Oficina Nacional de Integración (National Economic Integration Office) |
| ONRAP | Oficina Nacional de Reforma de la Administración Pública (National Administrative Reform Office) |
| ORDEN | Oficina Regional de Desarrollo del Norte (Development Office for the Northern Region) |
| ORDEZA | Oficina para la Reconstrucción y Desarrollo de la Zona Afectada (Office for the Reconstruction and Development of the Earthquake Zone) |
| PDC | Partido Demócrata Cristiano (Christian Democratic Party) |
| PETROPERU | Petróleos del Perú (Peruvian State Petroleum Company) |
| PIP | Policía de Investigaciones del Perú (Peruvian Bureau of Investigation) |
| SAF-CAP | Sistema de Asesoramiento y Fiscalización de las Cooperativas Agrarias de Producción (Advisory and Auditing System for Agrarian Production Cooperatives) |
| SAIS | Sociedad Agrícola de Interés Social (Agrarian Social Interest Society) |
| SERP | Sindicato de Educadores de la Revolución Peruana (Revolutionary Teachers Union of Peru) |
| SIDERPERU | Empresa Siderúrgica del Perú (Peruvian State Iron and Steel Corporation) |
| SINAMOS | Sistema Nacional de Apoyo a la Movilización Social (National System for Social Mobilization) |

SNA          Sociedad Nacional Agraria (National Agrarian Society)
SUTEP        Sindicato Unico de Trabajadores de la Educación del
             Perú (Central Educational Workers' Union)
TUC          Texto Unico Concordado del D.L. 17,716 (Unified Inte-
             grated Text of the Agrarian Reform Law)
UNO          Unión Nacional Odriísta (National Union for Odría)

# AGRICULTURE, BUREAUCRACY, AND MILITARY GOVERNMENT IN PERU

# Introduction

The Peruvian government that assumed power in October 1968
did not take the course usually followed by military regimes in
Latin America. Whereas most such governments seek stability
and pursue conservative policies, the army officers led by General Juan Velasco Alvarado (1910-78) promoted political and
social reforms aimed at shifting power from the upper classes
to the peasants, workers, and urban poor. Velasco himself was
strongly antipathetic toward Peru's traditional governing class,
the so-called oligarchy, which had declined in influence by
1968 and was disoriented. Velasco was able to weaken it further and to outflank other opponents during the greater part of
his tenure. He and his advisers, however, lacked adequate
understanding of Peruvian society, and they did not succeed in
formulating a national ideology that could generate broad support, guide the reorganization of the state, and produce a coherent set of reform policies. Instead, the military government
experimented sequentially with three state models that, for
purposes of this study, can be labeled centralism, corporatism,
and liberalism.

None of these models fits the natural contours of Peruvian
society, and the government could not fully consolidate or

legitimize its rule. The failure of the Peruvian revolution was not a unique experience. Few governments are able to mold official ideology, bureaucratic behavior, and the actions of important national institutions so as to channel the flow of political and economic goods to nonelites. The Velasco regime is attractive as a subject for the analyst because it attempted to achieve these lofty aims.

Focusing on agricultural reform and the state bureaucracy, this book attempts to draw lessons from the Peruvian experience that may be applicable to other national situations in which a large percentage of the population resides in rural areas. In 1966, 49.1 percent of Peru's economically active population were involved in agriculturally related endeavors; this sector, however, generated only 17.8 percent of national income. It seemed to many analysts that Peru's future economic development depended on breaking the yoke of a traditional tenure structure and on integrating peasants into the national political and economic markets. The importance of the bureaucracy in the process was due to the authoritarian nature of the Velasco regime. Because the Congress was in forced recess and the activities of traditional political parties were severely curtailed, most of the controversies surrounding the agrarian reform were generated by and filtered through the bureaucracy. Its size, composition, and behavior were thus important intervening variables in the outcome of the government's agrarian policies. Although other sectors of society, especially industry, were passing through similar disruptions at the time, the agrarian sector provides a particularly fertile area for development of an understanding of the military regime's ideology, structure, and accomplishments.

Chapter 1 presents an overview of the three types of political systems that have represented broad alternatives for the organization of national societies in Latin America, and which were in evidence during various stages of the Velasco regime; it probes their implications for the goals of state institutions and administrative functions, and provides preliminary data on some of the changes imposed on the Peruvian bureaucracy after 1968. The subsequent chapters are case studies of various aspects of the relationships among political structure, administrative behavior, and ideology in the agrarian sector. The order of presentation corresponds approximately to the chronology of government agricultural policy under General Velasco. Chapter 2 covers the genesis and reformulation of agrarian reform legislation over a six-year period, and documents the transition from a centralist policy-making style early in the administration to a more liberal one at the end. Chapter 3, on the Chira-Piura irrigation project, shows how the centralist approach at the dawn of the Velasco presidency affected the state's relations with regional elites, poor peasants, and international financial institutions. Chapter 4 indicates how centralist principles affected personnel management in the Agrarian Court System.

Later, when the Velasco regime chose to pursue corporatist ideals, it created official interest groups among middle- and lower-class elements, including peasants. Chapter 5 reveals that opposition to these chartered organizations was greater than anticipated, and the original intentions were soon distorted. Meanwhile, some of the policies in the centralist mode began to erode because of increased differentiation within the state and severe financial difficulties. Chapter 6 examines conflict between the Agriculture and Housing ministries over land-use policy, and between EPSA and the rest of the public sector over food subsidies. Chapter 7, on agrarian reform cooperatives, deals with the administrative implications of an overlapping and inconsistent approach to social reform. Public agencies assisting the fledging agrarian cooperatives promoted three solutions for their internal management. These proposed solutions, inclining toward liberalism, corporatism, and centralism, respectively, reflected disagreement over the nature of man and ideal social and economic arrangements in Peru. The concluding chapter summarizes our findings on bureaucratic behavior, military government, and agrarian reform in Peru.

## Early History

In the 1970s Peru's 14 million inhabitants were spread unevenly over the third largest national territory in South America. About 45 percent of its population were Indian, 40 percent were mestizos, 15 percent were white, and less than 1 percent was black or Oriental. Its per capita income was about $500 per year, but approximately 75 percent of national wealth was concentrated in the top 10 percent of the population.

Since Peru's discovery and conquest by Spaniards in the early sixteenth century, major themes in its history have been the large indigenous population, the role of the state, and civil-military relations.[1] Under the Inca empire (1438–1533), all land belonged formally to the Inca and was divided into portions for the state, for the priestly representatives of a plethora of deities, and for the populace (called *markas*). The *markas* encompassed one or more *ayllu*, or kinship lineages associated with the land, which predated Inca times. The local representative of central authorities was the *curaca*, or village headman, who sometimes was a former prince of a conquered tribe who had redirected his allegiance to the Inca.[2] Ayllu families cultivated, intermittently, their own plots, ayllu lands under common work obligations (*mita*), and state, church, and crown lands in corvée duty. The state's production was used for the military, the bureaucracy, the Inca's retainers, and the peasants when they were actually working for the state.[3]

After the 1532 conquest, official title to Inca lands passed to the Spanish crown, which authorized land grants and *encomiendas* (virtually people grants) to the conquistadores and their troops. The Spaniards were supposed to Christianize the pagans, instruct them in Iberic civic culture, and, as recom-

1. Comprehensive histories of Peru are Rubén Vargas Ugarte, *Historia general del Perú*, 10 vols. (Lima: C. Milla Batres, 1966–71), and Jorge Basadre, *Historia de la República del Perú*, 11 vols., 6th ed. (Lima: Editorial Universitaria, 1968–70). Useful one-volume texts are Luis Martín, *The Kingdom of the Sun* (New York: Scribner, 1974); Fredrick B. Pike, *The Modern History of Peru* (New York: Praeger, 1967); and Robert Marett, *Peru* (London: Benn, 1969).

2. The most widely cited source on government and customs under the Inca empire is Inca Garcilaso de la Vega, *Comentarios reales de los Incas* (Lima: Librería Internacional, 1959; originally published 1609).

3. Contrary to popular belief, state production was not used for welfare purposes. This myth was perpetuated in such books as Louis Baudin, *L'empire socialiste des Inka* (Paris: Université de Paris, 1928), but was largely discredited by John V. Murra, "The Economic Organization of the Inca State" (Ph.D. dissertation, University of Chicago, 1956), pp. 204–27, and *Formaciones económicas y políticas del mundo andino* (Lima: Instituto de Estudios Peruanos, 1975).

pense, collect and keep for themselves a portion of the Indians' royal tribute as subjects of the crown. They generally ignored the more noble of their duties and forced the Indians to labor in mining and, when precious metals ran out, in agriculture, textile sweatshops (obrajes), and personal services.[4] The abuses of the system caused scandals in Europe, and the crown supported the reforms instituted by Francisco de Toledo, who served as viceroy from 1569 to 1581. He concentrated large numbers of natives in reducciones (Indian towns), especially near Cuzco and Huancayo, and gave them land rights and authority over local matters. The reducciones also permitted the crown to monitor and tax the Indians more directly.

Over the next two and a half centuries, rural landowning families rose and fell in status and wealth, and consolidated and/or divided their property. As the encomienda system broke up, more Indian villages received title to communal lands, and these units became known as indigenous communities in the republican period and as campesino communities after 1969. Their territorial boundaries, however, were not respected by the hacendados or latifundistas (landowners). Throughout the sierra the Spanish descendants infringed on communal property through direct purchase (which was officially forbidden, except during the early years of the republic), fraudulent deeds, and forceful occupation. The communities gradually lost almost all of their rich agricultural land in the valleys and their best pastures in the highlands, and were obliged to conduct their farming or herding operations in more desolate areas.[5]

4. For a discussion of the transformations of the indigenous population during the colonial period, see Karen Spalding, De Indio a campesino (Lima: Instituto de Estudios Peruanos, 1974). The breakdown of the Indians' pre-Hispanic world view is analyzed in Nathan Wachtel, Sociedad e ideología (Lima: Instituto de Estudios Peruanos, 1973), especially pp. 82–124. Continuing patterns are described in Giorgio Alberti and Enrique Mayer, eds., Reciprocidad e intercambio en los Andes peruanos (Lima: Instituto de Estudios Peruanos, 1974).

5. For a review of Indian legislation in the modern republican period, see Thomas M. Davies, Jr., Indian Integration in Peru (Lincoln: University of Nebraska Press, 1974). Encroachment on community lands by haciendas is documented in CIDA, Tenencia de la tierra y desarrollo socio-económico del sector agrícola: Perú (Washington: Pan American Union, 1966). See also Giorgio Alberti and Rodrigo Sánchez, Poder y conflicto social en el valle del Man-

The communities generally retained some common lands, but their customs and work patterns altered over the years.[6] One feeling that community members shared was resentment against the neighboring haciendas. Campesino communities in the 1960s had not forgotten land claims dating from the seventeenth century, and after the 1969 agrarian reform the target of their grievances became the cooperatives created out of the old haciendas.

During colonial times, Lima was the administrative center for Spanish rule in South America. After Peruvian independence in 1821, the size of the bureaucracy diminished as Spanish-born administrators returned home. It did not grow significantly until after 1840, when income from the guano boom permitted the maintenance of thousands of pensioners, soldiers, and bureaucrats. In 1886 33,280 persons were on the state payroll, of whom 1,272 were civilian functionaries residing in Lima. Employment in the public sector increased to 8,095 in 1928, 24,418 in 1945, and 179,000 in 1969.[7] Until the 1960s the functions of the state were restricted to tax collection, police, justice, public works, and defense. State officials did not direct the economy, leaving the matter in private hands. Bureaucratic trends that persisted from colonial days to the twentieth century were centralism, formalism, and fiscal parasitism, including regressive indirect taxes and the channeling of public reve-

*taro* (Lima: Instituto de Estudios Peruanos, 1974); Wilfredo Kapsoli, *Los movimientos campesinos en Cerro de Pasco, 1800–1963* (Huancayo: Instituto de Estudios Andinos, 1975); and, for a perceptive discussion of rural change, William Foote Whyte and Georgio Alberti, *Power, Politics, and Progress* (New York: Elsevier, 1976).

6. Studies of the communities include Fernando Fuenzalida et al., *Estructuras tradicionales y economía del mercado* (Lima: Instituto de Estudios Peruanos, 1968); Norman Long and Bryan Roberts, eds., *Peasant Cooperation and Capitalist Expansion in Central Peru* (Austin: University of Texas Press, 1978); Gabriel Escobar, *Sicaya* (Lima: Instituto de Estudios Peruanos, 1973); Olinda Celestino, *Migración y cambio estructural* (Lima: Instituto de Estudios Peruanos, 1972); and Carlos Degregori and Jürgen Golte, *Dependencia y desintegración estructural en la comunidad de Pacaraos* (Lima: Instituto de Estudios Peruanos, 1973).

7. Carl F. Herbold, Jr., "Developments in the Peruvian Administrative System, 1919–1939" (Ph.D. dissertation, Yale University, 1973), pp. 36ff, 162; E. V. K. Fitzgerald, *The State and Economic Development* (Cambridge: Cambridge University Press, 1976), p. 42.

nues for the benefit of the elites to the exclusion of the masses, especially Indians.[8]

Peru's republican history is replete with coups and counter-coups, and the military's role in politics has been legitimized through constitutional clauses permitting it to intervene in times of national strife. In the nineteenth century, economic and social elites supported a string of military caudillos for the presidency, and only one civilian president completed his full term of office. The coherence of the military as an institution, however, was precarious. The War of the Pacific (1879–83) resulted in devastating defeat at the hands of Chile's better equipped, trained, and motivated armed forces. Surrender had a traumatic effect on the Peruvian military, which resolved never again to allow its fighting capabilities to lag behind those of neighboring countries. A more modern and better organized army did much better in its next significant confrontation, against Ecuador in 1941.[9] That victory, and the growth of professionalism within the armed forces, led to institutional coherence and autonomy for the military establishment, despite the sometimes serious conflicts between the conservative navy and the more progressive army.

## Agriculture and Rural Life in the Prereform Period

The variety of agricultural practices and tenure patterns that evolved during the colonial and republican periods makes it difficult to summarize briefly the prevailing situation in the early 1960s, when agrarian reform became a leading political issue.[10] The landholding pattern was highly skewed. Table 1 shows that in 1961, 14 percent of the landowners possessed 75.9 percent of the total area in private hands, and 83.2 percent of the independent farmers worked properties of 5 hectares or less. Peru was divided into several agricultural zones, each of

8. Herbold, "Developments," pp. 12–14.
9. See Víctor Villanueva, *Cien años del ejército peruano* (Lima: Juan Mejía Baca, 1971).
10. The best profile is Thomas R. Ford, *Man and Land in Peru* (Gainesville: University of Florida Press, 1959).

Table 1.  Land distribution in 1961

| Size of holdings (hectares) | Number of units | Percent of all units | Hectares | Percent of all hectares |
|---|---|---|---|---|
| Less than 1 | 290,000 | 34.1% | 127,869 | 0.7% |
| 1–5 | 417,357 | 49.0 | 926,851 | 5.0 |
| 5–20 | 107,199 | 12.6 | 879,385 | 4.7 |
| 20–100 | 24,628 | 3.0 | 980,058 | 5.3 |
| 100–500 | 8,081 | 0.9 | 1,624,643 | 8.7 |
| 500–1,000 | 1,585 | 0.2 | 1,065,157 | 5.7 |
| 1,000–2,500 | 1,116 | 0.1 | 1,658,636 | 8.9 |
| More than 2,500 | 1,091 | 0.1 | 11,341,901 | 61.0 |
| All holdings | 851,057 | 100.0% | 18,604,500 | 100.0% |

SOURCE: CIDA, Tenencia de la tierra y desarrollo socio-económico del sector agrícola: Perú (Washington: Pan American Union, 1966).

which included one or more production patterns.[11] On the coast, the river valleys provided excellent terrain for such industrial and food crops as sugar, cotton, rice, citrus fruits, and vegetables. Sugar and cotton were concentrated on relatively large plantations, while the other products generally came from smaller properties. In the middle sierra (2,000 to 3,500 meters above sea level), haciendas were larger than those on the coast, and because of the severe climate and steep slopes, the land was unsuited for extensive cultivation. The main products were potatoes, barley, beans, sweet potatoes, wheat, corn, quinoa, oca, milk, garlic, rye, and beef. In the high sierra (above 3,500 meters), alpaca and cattle were tended by herders on large latifundios or in indigenous communities.

Labor was always more plentiful in the sierra, where the mass of the indigenous population lived, than on the coast, which was inhabited by people of European, African, and Asian origin. Coastal farmers imported first black workers (almost all from the Caribbean), then Chinese (through the port of Macao), and finally sierra Indian labor (contracted under the

11. Peru is generally divided into four main agricultural zones: the coast, the sierra, the ceja de selva (humid mountainous region on the east slopes of the Andes, suitable for tea and coffee growing), and the jungle. See Emilio Romero, Geografía económica del Perú (Lima: Politécnico Nacional "José Pardo," 1961).

*enganche* or indenture system).[12] The sierra was overpopulated for the amount of land gainfully cultivated or grazed, and economic depression represented one of the "push" factors of internal migration.

Especially after the beginning of the twentieth century, agriculture was more capital-intensive on the coast than in the middle and high sierra, where many Indians operated outside of a money economy. The owners of large coastal farms and plantations usually had university training in agronomy or farm management. They invested in improvements, hired agronomists to maximize efficiency, and employed both permanent and temporary workers. They were also the most active members of the National Agrarian Society (SNA), an interest group that was influential with government from its founding in the nineteenth century until 1969.

The permanent workers on the coast were mechanics, millers, tractor drivers, and irrigation specialists whose numbers depended on the labor requirements of the crop during the laxest months of the year. They joined labor unions, received regular salary increases, and tolerated fewer social abuses than occurred in the sierra. Temporary workers, hired at periods of peak activity, came either from the sierra or from nearby *minifundios* (minifarms). In the sierra, campesinos paid rent to the landowner for the right to cultivate small plots for family consumption. The most common form of payment was the provision of labor to the hacienda for a certain number of days per year, followed by payment in kind and payment in cash.[13] The hacendado could rotate or take away the land at his discretion. Renters who were somewhat better off had larger parcels and more secure land tenure, and were not required to pay the hacendado in services.

These rental practices in the middle sierra gave rise to a

12. See Frederick P. Bowser, *The African Slave in Colonial Peru, 1524–1650* (Stanford: Stanford University Press, 1974); Emilio Harth-Terré, *Negros e indios* (Lima: Juan Mejía Baca, 1973); Watt Stewart, *Chinese Bondage in Peru* (Durham, N.C.: Duke University Press, 1951); and Peter F. Klarén, *Formación de las haciendas azucareras y orígenes del APRA*, 2d ed. (Lima: Instituto de Estudios Peruanos, 1976).

13. See Mario C. Vásquez, *Hacienda, peonaje, y servidumbre en los Andes peruanos* (Lima: Estudios Andinos, 1961).

pervasive image of the traditional hacienda in Peru.[14] The labor and tenure systems resulted in low productivity. The typical large landowner was both prestige- and profit-oriented, but his earnings were small compared with the economic potential of his holdings. His work force consisted of his peasant renters, whose labor he demanded most when crops needed seeding, weeding, and harvesting, just at the times they would have preferred to tend their own plots. Daily operations were in the hands of an administrator, who collaborated with a *mayor-domo* (overseer) and *caporales* (field supervisors).[15]

Symbolic incentives and negative sanctions were used for social control. Outside analysts have emphasized coercion, although on most properties positive relations, including spiritual leadership, gifts, charity, paternalism, and *compa-drazgo* (a ritual bond of obligation), were more frequent. The behavior of many hacendados, mayordomos, and caporales toward the peasants, however, was repressive. If a renter did not arrive for work, even when he was detained by a family emergency, the caporales fetched him and forced him onto the field, fined him, or even ejected him from the hacienda. Torture, hacienda imprisonment, and forced concubinage were known. The peasant could not seek recourse from the police because the hacendado had close links with the local military commanders, the subprefect, and the governor. Most peasants were not even aware of their situation. The hacendados discouraged the education of peasant children because of the likelihood that knowledge would raise their life expectations. Under these

14. Traditional relations of the factors of production in the sierra have given rise to extensive debate in both academic and leftist political circles on whether sierra agriculture was feudal, semifeudal, or simply precapitalist. As these terms are borrowed from the European context, they are not, except in the loosest sense, directly applicable to Peru. See Rodrigo Montoya Rojas's attempt to resolve the issue, *A propósito del carácter predominantemente capitalista de la economía peruana actual* (Lima: Ediciones Teoría y Realidad, 1970).

15. For the hacendado, prestige meant large land ownership. But he did not have sufficient capital to farm his land intensively. Nor would peasants work it diligently without owning it. The rental system was the rational economic response under the circumstance, but it generated only enough income to maintain the peasants barely above a subsistence level, the mayordomos and administrators at living wages, and the sierra hacendado and his family in a comfortable but not luxurious life style.

conditions, the peasant was a prompt and obedient if not an enthusiastic or productive worker.

The latifundios of the high sierra were the largest in the country, and a small number of herders could tend a great many animals over a wide expanse of territory.[16] The more wealthy herders compensated the hacienda in money or in kind per head grazed, while the poor paid in the form of labor. Many hacendados tried to improve pastures, to use advanced breeding and fattening methods, and to market their meat and wool on the coast and abroad. The dense population of the area, however, meant that they could not defend the perimeters of their haciendas against incursion by neighboring indigenous communities. Disease-ridden rams and bulls of inferior stock owned by the hacienda's own herders often impregnated finer breeds. When initial experiments at pasture and herd improvement failed, the hacendados redoubled their efforts to achieve control over their land, putting up fences and expelling herders. The battle never progressed beyond a standoff, and the arrival of the 1969 agrarian reform altered the nature of the competition.

The rural sector was highly stratified. The peasants were differentiated according to their accumulated wealth, their links to the centers of political decision making (including those inside the indigenous community), and the extent to which they hired other persons or rented out their own labor to earn their livelihoods. The major social categories were owners, permanent workers, renters, landless peasants, and members of indigenous communities. The variations in the fertility of land at different altitudes, the complexity of labor relations, and the inadequacy of statistics make it difficult to classify the peasants within these groups or to estimate the size of each group on the basis of the rural population at the time.[17]

16. For a detailed analysis of several such latifundios before the reform, see Héctor Martínez, "Tres haciendas altiplánicas: Chujuni, Cochela, y Panascachi," *Perú Indígena* 26 (1967), 96–162. The best treatment of Andean herders is Juan Martínez-Alier, *Los huacchilleros del Perú* (Lima and Paris: Instituto de Estudios Peruanos and Ruedo Ibérico, 1973).

17. Given a population of 1.5 million families, approximate figures might be hacendados 0.8 percent, middle-sized farmers 8.0 percent, stable workers 3.5 percent, renters 27.7 percent, and minifundistas and landless peasants 60.0

No study successfully captures the subtlety of the rural hierarchy of prereform agriculture. The pinnacle of the system, made up of the coastal and sierra hacendados, was more easily discernible than its base, containing minifundistas, temporary workers, landless peasants, and renters.[18] The middle-sized farmers, who generally produced a food crop for profit, occupied the place just below the hacendado on the wealth and prestige scale. Permanent workers on the coast had more favorable life chances than almost all renters in the sierra. Minifundistas obtained their land through inheritance, purchase, or communal rights, and often worked temporarily for latifundistas, middle-sized farmers, and wealthy renters at certain periods of the agricultural calendar. Owners of plots smaller than required for family subsistence, as well as destitute campesinos, were considered landless peasants. But some landless peasants who worked part-time on the coast for relatively high wages were in a more favorable economic position than some sierra renters. Most renters, in turn, were better situated than permanent workers in the sierra, which explains why sierra Indians resisted abandoning their traditional plots in exchange for salaries. The large number of workers who depended on the hacienda economically but maintained cultural ties to the indigenous community complicated the picture even more. Although prosperous renters were better off than landless peasants, their occasional participation in low-status roles in the indigenous community mitigated these differences.

---

percent. Montoya, in *A propósito*, agonizes over data from the 1961 census but is unable to come to definite conclusions on the size of these social categories.

18. The terms in Spanish and Quechua describing segments of the peasantry and relations among them are diverse and abundant. See David Chaplin and Huga Vega, *A Glossary of Peruvian Land Tenure and Rural Labor Organization Terminology* (Madison, Wis.: Land Tenure Center, 1972). For instance, a campesino in service to the hacendado (disparagingly known as the *gamonal*) was a *peón* or *colono*. If he paid in service and lived in the central sierra, he would be called a *feudatario, yanacona,* or *pongo* (when his labor was domestic); if he paid in kind, an *apacero, medianero,* or *partidario;* if he paid in cash, an *arrendire,* who might subrent to an *allegado*. On the coast, permanent workers were *trabajadores permanentes;* renters in cash, *yanaconas;* and temporary workers, *eventuales, jornaleros,* or *golondrinos*. In the high sierra, *huacchilleros* were herders (*huaccho* is Quechua for orphan), and those who paid in kind, *yerbajeros*. See also José Matos Mar, *Yanaconaje y reforma agraria en el Perú* (Lima: Instituto de Estudios Peruanos, 1976).

The rural population tended toward individualism and intraclass competition. Despite the ayllu tradition of commonality of ownership and tasks, the commitment of sierra inhabitants to collective enterprises weakened over the years. The increasingly precarious economic base of the indigenous communities contributed to dyadic relationships. It was to the Indian's advantage to accept the tutelage of the hacendado for the right to cultivate some of "his" land, even if that land had once belonged to the community. In the middle sierra, upward mobility involved renting a larger plot, employing field hands, and purchasing a small parcel. In the high sierra campesinos attempted to enlarge their herds through savings or gifts from the hacendado. Inside indigenous communities, social and economic differentiation was based on ownership of cattle, sheep, or alpaca, preferential land assignments, and water rights. On the coast, permanent workers occasionally sublimated strong individualistic drives through union membership.

Pre-1969 agriculture was hardly characterized by ferocious struggle between large landowners and the mass of campesinos. While exploitation of surplus was ubiquitous, the hacendados and the commercial middlemen were not the only beneficiaries of the system. Peasants competed among themselves to raise their economic and social position. When a peasant improved his lot, he often adopted a more lordly attitude toward his former peers. The peasant mobilization during the 1960s joined these classes in some areas into a temporary alliance against the hacendados, which blurred divisions. Social competition surged to the forefront again in the post-reform period, to the disappointment of activists and theoreticians who hoped that eliminating the hacendados would permanently eradicate injustice and inequality in rural Peru.

## Events Leading Up to the Agrarian Reform

Peruvian intellectuals in the nineteenth century who wrote on agrarian issues and political leaders in the early twentieth century denounced the traditional latifundio as one of the country's most serious ills.[19] José Carlos Mariátegui, the founder of the Peruvian Communist Party, described the landholding pattern as feudal and felt that a revolution would be necessary to return the haciendas to communal ownership.[20] Víctor Raúl Haya de la Torre, who in 1924 founded the APRA party (Alianza Popular Revolucionaria Americana), included land reform as an essential part of his platform.[21] The SNA also advocated reform, but through government subsidies for new seeds, fertilizers, vaccines, and machinery rather than land distribution.

After 1950 the momentum for reform picked up considerably. Peasants migrated to cities, returning with a greater sense of self-worth, and mine workers in rural areas unionized. The governing class was increasingly unable to prevent labor unions, peasant movements, the APRA, and other middle- and lower-class political parties from gaining strength. By the 1960s politics involved a relatively broad segment of the population, and the military and church began to define institutional goals that were no longer synonymous with those of the upper class.[22] The immediate forerunners of the 1969 agrarian reform law were the Pedro Beltrán–led Commission for Promoting Small and Middle-Sized Urban and Rural Property (1960); Hugo Blanco's successful farmers' union movement in La Convención and Lares valleys, near Cuzco; the presidential election campaign of 1963; the guerrilla movement in the central sierra

19. Most notably, Manuel González Prada (1848–1919). See his *Horas de lucha* (Lima: Ediciones Futuro, 1964), pp. 199–213. His influence on Mariátegui and Haya de la Torre is treated in Eugenio Chang-Rodríguez, *La literatura política de González Prada, Mariátegui, y Haya de la Torre* (Mexico City: Andrea, 1957).

20. José Carlos Mariátegui, *Seven Interpretative Essays on Peruvian Reality*, trans. Marjory Urquidi (Austin: University of Texas Press, 1971), pp. 16–76.

21. Víctor Raúl Haya de la Torre, *Política aprista* (Lima: Amanta, 1967; originally published 1933), pp. 17–18, 88–89. See also Harry Kantor, *El movimiento aprista peruano* (Buenos Aires: Pleamar, 1964), pp. 147–57, and Robert J. Alexander, ed., *Aprismo* (Kent, O.: Kent State University Press, 1973), pp. 88, 182–83.

22. Carlos A. Astiz, *Pressure Groups and Power Elites in Peruvian Politics* (Ithaca: Cornell University Press, 1969); also François Bourricaud, *Power and Society in Contemporary Peru*, trans. Paul Stevenson (London: Faber & Faber, 1970).

in 1965; and the agrarian reform law passed by Congress during the presidency of Fernando Belaúnde Terry (1963–68).

Beltrán, editor of the influential Lima newspaper *La Prensa*, was an important figure in civilian president Manuel Prado's government from 1956 to 1962. His commission, which met periodically over two years, was convoked in the spirit of the Alliance for Progress and represented the first official recognition of inequalities in the rural sector. Prado, however, delayed in presenting an agrarian reform proposal to Congress and did not push for its passage. The initiative was aborted when the military ousted Prado and closed Congress in July 1962.

The army officers intervened mainly to prevent the presidential election of Haya de la Torre. The military had detested APRA since July 1932, when APRA insurgents near Trujillo captured and executed a number of officers and soldiers. The subsequent massacre of APRA followers cemented the mutual enmity, which had had important repercussions on Peruvian history.[23] Soon after the 1962 abortion of Haya's presidential plans, the military found itself confronted by a serious peasant movement in the tea- and coffee-producing valleys near Cuzco, organized by the Trotskyite Hugo Blanco. The response was a policy statement, "Twenty Criteria for Agrarian Reform," and subsequently Decree Law 14,444, which was a special agrarian reform program for the embattled region.[24] These concessions calmed the agitation and convinced some military officers that they could resolve rural conflict where civilians had failed.

The presidential campaign of 1963 was contested by the APRA, the conservative UNO (Unión Nacional Odriísta, led by the former dictador General Manuel Odría, 1948–56), and Belaúnde's Acción Popular (supported openly by the Christian

23. See Guillermo Thorndike, *El año de la barbarie* (Lima: Nueva América, 1969), and Víctor Villanueva, *Cien años del ejército peruano*, for details of these events.

24. See Blanco's own account of the movement, *Land or Death*, trans. Naomi Allen (New York: Pathfinder Press, 1972). Also Eduardo Fioravanti, *Latifundio y sindicalismo agrario en el Perú*, 2d ed. (Lima: Instituto de Estudios Peruanos, 1976); Howard Handelman, *Struggle in the Andes* (Austin: University of Texas Press, 1975); and Wesley W. Craig, Jr., "Peru: The Peasant Movements of La Convención," in *Latin American Peasant Movements*, ed. Henry A. Landsberger (Ithaca: Cornell University Press, 1966), pp. 274–96.

Democrats and tacitly by the Movimiento Social Progresista, a group of respected intellectuals and civil servants), as well as leftist groups. Each of these groups proposed its own brand of agrarian reform. Barely a month after Belaúnde won the election, his Christian Democratic minister of agriculture, Enrique Torres Llosa, submitted a far-reaching agrarian reform law to Congress. Each political party added pet clauses, removed objectionable provisions, and made political hay while debating its merits. The staunch opposition of the SNA to a comprehensive measure enervated its clauses. In 1964, Belaúnde signed a halfhearted bill for agrarian reform, Law 15,037.

The Peruvian military, which had overtly backed Belaúnde and his development program in the 1963 election, reentered the picture in 1965 when three bands of rural guerrillas attempted to set up permanent bases in the central sierra.[25] Although the guerrillas were amateurs, easily contained and routed, the experience unsettled the Peruvian army, which concluded that its responsibilities for maintaining national security were at odds with the prevailing land-tenure system. Army officers who later played important roles in the government of General Juan Velasco Alvarado (1968–75) felt that the malaise in agriculture also extended to other realms of economic and political life.

On the civilian side, the executors of Law 15,037 and its supposed beneficiaries became increasingly frustrated. The law did little more than make some landowners pay salaries to their workers and guarantee renters tenure rights. Two of its provisions virtually prohibited radical agrarian reform. The first exempted the large sugar plantations because they were efficiently managed. The other permitted landowners to keep much more land than the hypothetical limit of 150 hectares. Owners of farms that were publicly registered firms could multiply the unexpropriable limit by the number of shareholders, who were often family members or ficticious persons. Other

25. One of the guerrilla leaders, Héctor Béjar, described the debacle in *Peru 1965: Notes on a Guerrilla Experience*, trans. William Rose (New York: Monthly Review Press, 1970). Béjar was recruited into a SINAMOS executive position under Velasco. For the other side of the story, see General Armando Artola Azcárate, *Subversión* (Lima: Editorial Jurídica, 1976).

aspects of Law 15,037 perpetuated the minifundio and subjected expropriation to lengthy judicial appeal. As land-value
disputes worked their way up to the Supreme Court, hacendados could influence judgments through personal connec-
tions, favors, and bribes. The small amount of funds budgeted
by Congress for expropriation reduced the reform's potential
impact. Even under ideal conditions, expropriation required
fifty-one steps and a minimum of twenty-two months. The failure of Law 15,037 helped to make *effective* land reform a policy
imperative by late 1968. Organized peasant sectors felt betrayed.
The military feared a renewal of insurgency in the countryside.
The Christian Democratic and Communist parties were clamor-
ing for change. Teams of civil servants, thoroughly cognizant of
the shortcomings of Law 15,037, committed themselves to a
more radical reform.

Agriculture was not Belaúnde's only difficulty. He had also
promised industrial development and a better life for Peru's
urban masses, goals that were not being realized. The congressional alliance between his party, Acción Popular, and the
Christian Democrats faced a numerically larger bloc of delegates from UNO and APRA. As a staunch defender of constitutional procedures, Belaúnde was outflanked by this opposition,
and he became increasingly preoccupied with the Amazonian
highway and jungle colonization as cure-alls for national problems.[26] After a devaluation in 1967 and a debilitating split in
the Acción Popular leadership, the Belaúnde government appeared to be even less in control. Its inability to solve a tax and
property claim against the International Petroleum Company
and the prospect of an APRA victory in the 1969 presidential
elections prompted the military to intervene in October 1968.

## The Revolutionary Government of the Armed Forces

The Velasco regime called itself the Revolutionary Government
of the Armed Forces, and in the context of past Peruvian poli-

---

26. Jane S. Jaquette analyzes the Belaúnde regime in *The Politics of Development in Peru* (Ithaca: Cornell University Dissertation Series, 1971).

tics and other military regimes in Latin America, its "revolutionary" tag was not misplaced. Historians describing events after 1968 are likely to attribute importance to the social background of the president. Born in 1910 on the outskirts of Piura, Velasco (or El Chino, as he was affectionately known after the coup) came from humble origins. His father was an untitled "medical helper" who dispensed drugs and advice to the town's poor and competed for patients with the local herb healer. One of eleven children, Velasco suffered from long spells of melancholy. Admitted into the army as a trooper, he passed the examination for the Chorillos Military School a year later, graduated with honors in infantry skills, married into an upper-middle-class family, and became commander in chief of the army and president of Peru. Velasco's personal history was remarkable for a country with a rigid social hierarchy. Years later, members of the oligarchy could not understand why he harbored hatred for them and a system that had allowed him such an extraordinary rise in social status.[27]

Although difficult to describe in conventional ideological terms, Velasco's political instincts after the coup were more radical than those of most senior officers in the three branches of the armed services. The military adhered to the revolution in pursuit of national security; Velasco went further and pushed Peru to the forefront of the unaligned bloc. Most officers wanted planned economic development and industrialization; Velasco promoted state ownership of the means of production and restrictions on the liberty of the industrial bourgeoisie.[28] The armed forces sought simply to gain greater prestige among the country's social elites; Velasco wanted to eradicate the oligarchy and all vestiges of its hegemony. The military wished to generate patriotism among the Indian masses; Velasco was prepared to experiment with mass mobilization on a semipermanent basis.

27. For biographical data, see Alfonso Baella Tuesta, El poder invisible (Lima: Editorial Andina, 1976), pp. 94–97, and Guillermo Thorndike, No, Mi General (Lima: Industriagráfica, 1976), p. 42.

28. A description of the rise of the industrial bourgeoisie is contained in Baltazar Caravedo Molinari, Burguesía e industria en el Perú, 1933–1945 (Lima: Instituto de Estudios Peruanos, 1976).

Velasco did not limit himself to interpreting the interests of the Peruvian military. To govern, he relied on a core coalition and a looser support coalition. The core coalition, nicknamed the Earthquake Group, was made up of Velasco and four colonels who planned and executed the 1968 coup and who were personally loyal to the president. These four colonels were Leonidas Rodríguez Figueroa (the first head of SINAMOS, a public agency for mass mobilization), Jorge Fernández Maldonado (minister of energy and mines), Enrique Gallegos (who rented the apartment where the coup was planned and was later minister of agriculture), and Rafael Hoyos (the youngest member, who later became minister of food).[29] No major policy was undertaken without the knowledge of these officers, who had easy access to the president's inner chambers. Civilians at times could gain proximity to this governing circle by offering expertise on specific problems, but no civilian was called upon to advise on the full range of issues facing the military government.

The support coalition included army, air force, and navy officers whom Velasco entrusted with the execution of the re gime's policies. The most important were José Graham Hurtado and Arturo Valdez Palacio (both on the president's advisory committee, COAP), Pedro Richter (minister of the interior), Javier Tantaleán (fisheries), Rolando Gilardi (air force), Jorge Barandiarán (agriculture), Enrique Valdez Angulo (agriculture), Luis Barandiarán (air force general and minister of commerce), and Luis Vargas Caballero (navy admiral and minister of housing and navy). Over time, some members of the support

29. The designation Earthquake Group stemmed from the fact that Fernández Maldonado, the oldest colonel in the core coalition, graduated from Chorillos Military School in 1943, and his graduating class dubbed itself Earthquake. Although the name is appropriately descriptive of the Velasco regime, the president had graduated in 1934, Rodríguez Figueroa in 1945, Gallegos in 1946, and Hoyos in 1948, each in a class with a different nickname. See Baella, *El poder invisible*, pp. 69ff. Velasco's press secretary, Augusto Zimmerman, provided details on the coup in *Objetivo: Revolución peruana* (Lima: El Peruano, 1974). The pecking order of the generals was leaked by official sources in "France-Presse detalla crisis política en el Perú," *Expreso*, June 14, 1974, p. 3. In 1974 the regime claimed that its policies had been guided all along by the *Plan Inca: o, Plan de Gobierno Revolucionario de la Fuerza Armada del Perú* (Lima: La Cabrera, 1974).

coalition (Richter, Graham) became part of the core coalition; one (Tantaleán) developed close personal bonds with Velasco; and others (Vargas Caballero, the Barandiaráns, Valdez Angulo) were disposed of for political reasons.[30] Civilians committed to the government's objectives and appointed to high posts, such as Carlos Delgado, Augusto Zimmerman, and Guillermo Figallo, were within this group during much of the period. Several other civilians drifted in and out of Velasco's less intimate circle and were influential in the evolution of his presidency. By participating in the revolution, the members of the support coalition saw some of their ideological preferences implemented and improved their chances for professional advancement. In return, the military officer appointed to senior posts were expected to secure the allegiance of the rest of the armed forces, whose enthusiasm for the revolution faltered as the government radicalized. The risk for the direct participants was that they were vulnerable to dismissal if political conditions warranted. In the face of this uncertainty, some of them sought their own fortunes while in office.

This intricate meshing of contacts was important for Velasco because his regime had the backing of few organized elements in the society at large. Among the groups that supported him were some government-formed labor unions, the Communist Party, civilian technical specialists (técnicos) in the bureaucracy, and, in most matters, the Christian Democratic Party. In verbal opposition were the APRA, Acción Popular, the Maoist political parties; the teachers' union, SUTEP; many student factions; the industrialists' interest group; the SNA; and, before their expropriation, the two most important Lima newspapers.

Although the new government defined itself from the begin-

---

30. Francisco Moncloa, in Perú: ¿Qué pasó? (Lima: Horizonte, 1977), pp. 42–48, prefers to categorize these military men as revolutionaries, developmentalists, and conservatives. The revolutionaries formed the core coalition, and the developmentalists and conservatives comprised the support coalition during the early years of the Velasco regime. See also George D. E. Philip, The Rise and Fall of the Peruvian Military Radicals, 1968–1976 (London: Athlone Press, University of London, 1978). For a statement on coalitions in Latin America, see Eldon Kenworthy, "Coalitions in the Political Development of Latin America," in Sven Groennings et al., The Study of Coalition Behavior (New York: Holt, Rinehart & Winston, 1970), pp. 103–33.

ning in progressive terms, the weight of traditional paradigms was such that its first major piece of legislation, agrarian reform, was received with considerable shock. Under Velasco Peru became the first Latin American country since Cuba to expropriate efficiently operated plantations, many of them foreign owned. The government's activist, anti-imperialist foreign policy and subsequent legislation in the industrial area gave further evidence that this was not the sort of military government Peruvians had been accustomed to, or the sort of military government prevalent in other South American countries.[31] During its first three years, the regime followed policies that strengthened the state, weakened regional elites, and centralized decision making in the hands of Velasco and his advisers.[32]

The main characteristics of the regime's foreign policy were nationalism, anti-imperialism, and nonalignment. The government, which chose the mild-mannered and intelligent generals Edgardo Mercado Jarrín and Miguel de la Flor to denounce imperialism at international gatherings, did not shy away from confronting the United States on numerous opportunities. The Velasco regime nationalized the International Petroleum Company, the Cerro de Pasco Corporation, W. R. Grace and Company sugar properties, the Marcona Mining Company, and many smaller concerns, and abided by strict regulations for the entry of new foreign capital consistent with Decision 24 of the Andean Pact. The foreign policy also displayed pragmatism when the government, through the Greene Agreement, compensated several expropriated U.S. companies and thus qualified for more international loans.

31. For several in-depth articles on the programs of the Velasco regime, see Abraham F. Lowenthal, ed., *The Peruvian Experiment* (Princeton: Princeton University Press, 1975). The compendium edited by Henry Pease and Olga Verme, *Perú 1968–1973*, 2 vols. (Lima: DESCO, 1974), contains rich data on the progression of events after Velasco assumed office.

32. Those centralizing trends encouraged some observers to conclude that Velasco was a communist dictator. The president of Peru's government in exile, Julio Vargas Prada, included in his book *Destierro* (Lima: Editorial Atlántida, 1976) such chapter headings as "Velasco: Marxist without Knowing It," "The Historical-Materialism of the Revolutionary Government," and "The Soviets Are on the Way." See also the comments by James D. Theberge, Jr., *New York Times*, August 6, 1974, p. 32.

The Industrial Law placed enterprises in four categories, assigned basic industries to the state's domain, and excluded private and foreign capital from important production. It also delegated responsibility to the bureaucracy for economic development. The Industrial Communities Law (D.L. 18,384) imposed a profit- and ownership-sharing scheme on all large manufacturing industries (and later fishing, mining, and telecommunications concerns). The underlying philosophy was that if workers were gradually made co-owners of the firm and given a place on the board of directors, they would be less alienated and less likely to foment industrial disputes. Nationwide, class conflict between workers and capitalists would disappear and production would increase. These assumptions were not borne out in practice but the law did oblige many private industrialists to negotiate an unprecedented array of grievances with their labor force. A final reform in the industrial realm was social property, a new type of ownership and self-management.[33] Velasco frequently claimed that social property would become more dynamic and more important than any of the other three forms of officially recognized property: home crafts and small industries, state property, and private property reformed via the workers' communities.

After three years of energetic leadership in the centralist mode, during which he instituted educational reform and policies favorable to Lima's shantytown dwellers, Velasco became increasingly concerned about the lack of overt popular support for his government. He consulted frequently with the civilian intellectual Carlos Delgado in an attempt to imbue his revolution with greater ideological coherence.[34] Previously the regime had been satisfied simply to describe its approach as neither communist nor capitalist. Later presidential speeches stressed the division of society into functional groups (called *sectores*) and the need for organic harmony among them. Many

33. See Peter T. Knight, *Perú: ¿Hacia la autogestión?* (Buenos Aires: Editorial Proyección, 1974).
34. Delgado assembled much of his philosophical and polemical writings in *Revolución peruana* (Lima: Libros de Contratiempo, 1975). For a prejudiced view of Delgado's participation in the military government, see Baella, *El poder invisible*, p. 324.

government actions affecting the lower and middle classes represented attempts to reconcile conflicting social groups in organizations created by the state. The government created a teachers' union and a fishermen's union, and intervened in the National Confederation of Workers' Communities in an attempt to restore order. Two of its most dramatic endeavors in the corporatist direction were the creation of SINAMOS, or the National System for Social Mobilization, and the expropriation of the national newspapers.

SINAMOS was formed in 1972 by the joining of agencies from several ministries with the objectives of proselytizing for the revolution and rewarding those who supported it.[35] The agency was organized along the lines of functional groups: union members, youth, the peasantry, and shantytown dwellers. SINAMOS' subagency for rural affairs was instrumental in founding the National Agrarian Confederation (CNA), which claimed to be the interest group for the campesinos. With the creation of the CNA, the old National Agrarian Society was forcibly dissolved. In 1974 the government nationalized the major newspapers with the aim of turning them over to the "organized sectors" of society. Thus *El Comercio* represented the peasantry, *La Prensa* the industrial workers, *Expreso* the educators, *Correo* the professionals, and *Ojo* the intellectuals. The government later conceded that these groups were not sufsufficiently integrated to have legitimate representatives, and the newspaper editors were appointed by presidential decree.

Instead of increasing support for the government, SINAMOS and the newspaper expropriation probably helped to undermine it. Many military men, preferring control to mobilization, were uncomfortable with SINAMOS' purpose, and the agency met strong resistance among workers and students, groups that had already been well organized along traditional political lines. The Communists and Christian Democrats were cool to the idea of government-formed unions and interest groups competing with their grass-roots organizations. The three

35. See Henry A. Dietz, "Bureaucratic Demand-Making and Clientelistic Participation in Peru," in *Authoritarianism and Corporatism in Latin America,* ed. James M. Malloy (Pittsburgh: University of Pittsburgh Press, 1977), pp. 413–58.

branches of the armed forces had shown remarkable unity during the initial years of the regime, until plans to expropriate the press produced a serious schism. The minister of the navy, Vargas Caballero, was forced to resign when he opposed the action.[36] President Velasco's governing capacity appeared to be impaired by a nearly fatal aneurism that required the amputation of one leg in 1973. His decisions became more secretive, arbitrary, and irrational; his tolerance for criticism, even in the mildest form, disappeared.

The government program had proved to be too ambitious. The Velasco regime pursued goals of economic nationalism, industrialization, national security, income distribution, and social mobilization. Specific policies in each realm, however, worked at cross-purposes with policies in other realms. Incentives for importation of capital goods to spur industrialization were incompatible with the social objectives of the industrial communities. A firm's investment in foreign machinery precluded the need for new labor and reduced the distribution of profits to the workers, who could not use part of those profits to increase their share of ownership in the firm. Subsidies for food consumption in urban areas contributed to income distribution but undermined the ability of the agrarian cooperatives to make a profit. Heavy arms purchases and the building of an oil pipeline catered to the military's concept of national security but mortgaged the country's financial future for projects of questionable economic value. The multitude of programs gave new functions to the state, nearly to the point of overloading it. Many public officials, however, used the power of the traditional bureaucracy to manipulate lower-class organizations that were supposed to become autonomous. In the end, the Velasco government was beset by contradictions. It called for

36. According to Moncloa, in *Perú: ¿Qué pasó?*, the radicals progressively eliminated the conservatives, the last of whom was Vargas Caballero. The alliance between the radicals and developmentalists, however, did not last long. When the economic crisis became acute and internal pressures mounted, the developmentalists switched allies and eliminated the radicals. Moncloa argues that the radicals and developmentalists could stick together as long as it was unclear whether the structural reforms would lead to capitalist modernization or to socialism. Once the radicals demonstrated that they were prepared to go beyond capitalism (via a predominant social property sector, for example), the alliance crumbled.

national unity when its internal ranks were split; insisted on civilian morality while lieutenant colonels managed an influence network rivaling that run formerly by senators and congressmen; proposed solutions on behalf of the dispossessed masses without consulting them; opened a draft law to public debate and then deported some of its critics; and still claimed to be a revolutionary government seeking full popular participation.

The decisive factors in Velasco's downfall were the factionalization of the army and a deteriorating economic situation in 1974 and 1975, which the government had papered over with an artificial exchange rate, heavy borrowing, and extensive rhetoric. Rioting and looting in downtown Lima in February 1975, sparked by a policemen's revolt, left more than eighty dead and undermined Velasco's claim that he was representing the country's disadvantaged groups. La Misión, a group of corporatist-leaning military officers, felt it could manage the country more effectively than the progressive officers originally in the core coalition. General Francisco Morales Bermúdez, leading an "institutionalist" alternative, became increasingly alarmed by Velasco's dogmatic opposition to the resolution of a territorial dispute being negotiated by Peru and Chile, and felt the army should return to its original functions. Morales Bermúdez, former finance minister and then prime minister, executed the putsch on August 30, 1975, obtaining even the reluctant support of Leonidas Rodríguez, the commander of the Lima military garrison, who acted to thwart the pretensions of La Misión.[37]

Foreign capitalists and upper-middle-class entrepreneurs

37. The core coalition expected that one of its members would inherit the presidency. Velasco's physical incapacity, however, sparked the presidential ambitions of some members of the support coalition, most notably Javier Tantaleán, who had become a personal friend of Velasco's. Tantaleán had organized the Movimiento Revolucionario Laboral among fishermen who worked for his ministry. According to *No, Mi General*, a *roman réaliste* by Guillermo Thorndike (editor of the government newspaper *La Nueva Crónica*), Tantaleán's main allies were Pedro Richter (minister of the interior), Pedro Sala Orosco (labor), Alberto Jiménez de Lucio (industries and tourism), Rudecindo Zavaleta (SINAMOS), and Eduardo Segura (SINADI, the national news and communications system). Known as La Misión and promoting a line that Thorndike labels "neo-fascist," the group had little support within the military itself and no members led troops at the time of the Morales Bermúdez coup.

were relieved by the Morales Bermúdez succession, but he disappointed them initially by making a pretense of continuing the main lines of Velasco's policies. Before the end of the first year of his administration, however, he had dismissed Rodríguez, Fernández Maldonado, and Graham, and briefly jailed Tantaleán; changed the industries law, making it easier for investors to avoid setting up workers' communities; abandoned an aggressive stance against economic imperialism; began to hedge on support for Decision 24; downgraded the importance of social property; removed food subsidies and froze wages; and heavily devaluated the sol. Soon afterward he announced a return to elected government.[38] While some of these policy shifts appeared to be necessary to avert economic collapse, it was clear that many of Velasco's innovations had come to an end. The agrarian reform, however, had made great strides. Nearly all large haciendas had been expropriated by the time Velasco left office, and agrarian reform was to be one of his administration's lasting contributions.

38. Presidential elections held on May 18, 1980, were won by former president Fernando Belaúnde Terry, the candidate of Acción Popular, who received over 40 percent of the vote. His main rivals were Armando Villanueva del Campo, of APRA (27.5 percent), and Luis Bedoya Reyes, of the Popular Christian Party (11 percent). Factionalism damaged the chances of candidates on the Left (Hugo Blanco and Genero Ledesma), and abstentions reached approximately 35 percent. Belaúnde's inauguration was scheduled for July 28, 1980.

# Chapter 1

# Political Systems and the Administrative Sciences

To carry out structural change, the Velasco regime needed to reorganize the state apparatus and to imbue it with new goals and hierarchical norms. Ideally, the public sector's allegiance and performance would reinforce the regime's revolutionary initiatives in agriculture, industry, education, and popular mobilization. The military government, however, vacillated on the type of bureaucratic structure it wished to promote, and failed to comprehend the importance of consistent administrative behavior for the achievement of its wider political goals. By adopting one set of ideological principles and then another, the regime failed to promote a standard doctrine for the guidance of administrative activities. Bureaucratic forms and procedures actually multiplied under the military government, and though the public administration was generally sympathetic to the goals of the revolution, it was relatively ineffective in helping to achieve them.

## New Directions in Comparative Administration

Much of the literature on comparative administration is narrow in its focus or assumptions. In the early 1960s, the "develop-

ment administration" school argued essentially that poor
societies could not progress until their bureaucracies
modernized their procedures and functions.[1] Fred Riggs took
the analysis one step further by arguing that much of the blame
for inept bureaucracies could be laid at the feet of confused
administrators torn between tradition and modernity. Their
values, reflecting those of society itself, were ill suited to the
responsibilities of national leadership.[2] By implication, the
model of a desirable bureaucracy for both development administrators and Riggs was the Western European or North American.

Even today, normative standards for Third World bureaucracy continue to be drawn from ideal administration in the
developed world. Why is this so? First, the fact that the industrialized societies are better off materially seems to provide
compelling reasons for attempting to copy their procedures.
The United Nations and government administrative reform
agencies have adopted organizational guidelines from the rich
countries for implementation in the Third World, thus reinforcing their claim to universality.[3] Second, the most thoughtful
writing on organizational sociology is based on cases and systematically collected data from industrialized countries. What-
ever their national origins, students of administration are almost obliged to use the referents of Western bureaucracy to study

1. Representative studies of development administration are Ferrel Heady
and Sybil L. Stokes, eds., *Papers in Comparative Public Administration* (Ann
Arbor: Institute of Public Administration, University of Michigan, 1962), and
Martin Kriesberg, ed., *Public Administration in Developing Countries*
(Washington: Brookings Institution, 1965).

2. Fred Riggs, *Administration in Developing Countries* (Boston: Houghton
Mifflin, 1964).

3. See, for example, United Nations Technical Assistance Administration,
*Problemas relativos a la organización y administración de empresas públicas
en el sector industrial* (New York, 1958); United Nations, *Aspectos adminis-
trativos de la planificación* (New York: CEPAL, 1968); Fondo Monetario Interna-
cional, Banco Interamericano de Desarrollo y Centro de Estudios Monetarios
Latinoamericanos, *Manual de presupuestos por programas y por realizaciones*
(Mexico: CEMLA, 1968); Peru, Instituto Nacional de Administración Pública,
*Procesos administrativos* (Lima: Dirección Nacional de Personal, 1977); Wil-
burg Jiménez Castro, *Administración pública para el desarrollo integral*
(Mexico: Fondo de Cultura Económica, 1971); Irving Swerdlow, *The Public
Administration of Economic Development* (New York: Praeger, 1975).

administration in the Third World. Third, several concepts that have proven their worth in northern industrial countries also can be applied successfully to Third World bureaucracy. Examples are resources, structure, goals, and environment.[4] A general statement that seems to be valid regardless of cultural milieu and historical epoch is that bureaucrats with ambitions (goals) and variable personal qualifications (resources) operate within a role set (structure). Similarly, administrative units carry out specific tasks with legal and budgetary support in interaction with particular reference groups (environment). At every level of organizational life, these variables help to determine the behavior of individuals, the activities of administrative units, and their level of efficiency and effectiveness.

Unfortunately, by their very generality these concepts do not provide well-defined images of bureaucracy in specific settings. They exist independent of history, social class, philosophy, or political structure. Thus they do not explain systematic differences in bureaucratic behavior between countries, and within the same country over time. An important advance in distinguishing among patterns of administration under varying circumstances will occur when students concentrate greater attention on two interrelated variables, ideology and political system. By "ideology" we mean a political philosophy that presents an integrated interpretation of the nature of man, the course of history, and good and evil, and suggests casuistic norms. Aside from other functions, these intellectual constructs suggest parameters for the structure of society, the goals of public organizations, and internal management. Political philosophies gain ascendency when they legitimize the privileged standing of influential national actors in a way that

4. See Warren I. Ilchman and Norman P. Uphoff, *The Political Economy of Change* (Berkeley: University of California Press, 1969); Mayer N. Zald, ed., *Power in Organizations* (Nashville: Vanderbilt University Press, 1970); Chester I. Barnard, *The Functions of the Executive* (Cambridge: Harvard University Press, 1938); William Foote Whyte, *Organizational Behavior* (Homewood, Ill.: Richard D. Irwin, 1969); Michel Crozier, *The Bureaucratic Phenomenon* (Chicago: University of Chicago Press, 1964); James D. Thompson, *Organizations in Action* (New York: McGraw-Hill, 1967). The utility of these concepts is discussed in Peter S. Cleaves, *Bureaucratic Politics and Administration in Chile* (Berkeley: University of California Press, 1974).

is plausible to nonelites. The process of ideological hegemony can occur gradually as the social structure evolves, or suddenly when a new group rises to power. The political system is a set of voluntary and enforced relationships between the central state apparatus (typically consisting of leadership and public organizations) and society, or the classes, groups, and individuals that in varying degrees contribute to, receive benefits from, and challenge the workings of the state.[5]

Often ideological prescriptions are highly correlated with the functions of national political institutions. In the United States and England, the relative equilibrium among social classes and

---

5. Scholars have been concerned over proper definitions of "state" and "society" in practically all intellectual periods from classical times to the present day. For useful introductions to the terms' philosophical, ideological, and empirical roots, see Leon H. Mayhew, "Society," in *International Encyclopedia of the Social Sciences*, ed. David L. Sills (New York: Free Press, 1968), vol. 14, pp. 577–586; Frederick M. Watkins, "State: The Concept," in *International Encyclopedia*, vol. 15, pp. 150–57; J. P. Nettle, "The State as a Conceptual Variable," *World Politics* 20:3 (July 1968), 559–92; and Roland Maspétiol, "L'apport à la théorie de l'Etat des méthodes phénoménologiques et structuralistes," *Archives de Philosophie du Droit* (1970), especially pp. 282–86. In the modern era, Marx devised probably the most suggestive definition of the state (the oppression of one class by another), but his failure to systematize his ideas left his students to quibble over their meaning. A sampler of the scores of articles on the theme would include John Sanderson, "Marx and Engels on the State," *Western Political Quarterly* 16:4 (December 1963), 946–55, which lists the philosophers' several conceptions of the state, and Frank Cunningham, "Marxism and the State," *Revolutionary World* 6 (1974), 21–30, which contrasts the pluralist with the Marxist approach to the concept. In the debate over whether state and society are one and the same, Henry Zentner sides with those who argue they are interdependent in "The State and the Community: A Conceptual Clarification," *Sociology and Social Research* 48:4 (July 1964), 414–27; as does Otto Heinrich von der Gablentz, in "Staat und Gesellschaft," *Politische Vierteljahresschrift* 2:1 (March 1961), 2–23. Harold Laski uses the concepts of state and society pragmatically in *The State in Theory and Practice* (London: Allen & Unwin, 1935), pp. 8–17 *passim*. "We find ourselves living in a society with other men; that society, in relation to all other forms of human association, is integrated into a unity we call a state; as a state, its affairs are administered by a body of persons we call the government." One of the "fundamental axioms of political science [is] that we must distinguish sharply between state and government. The latter is but the agent of the former." "Yet it must be said at once that the distinction between state and government is rather one of theoretical interest than of practical significance." "The state in daily fact is a power-organization relying upon its legal title to coerce for the ultimate enforcement of its will; and . . . in the last resort, the armed forces of the state are the instrument of this enforcement."

economic groups during the period of national consolidation created an excellent foundation for liberalism. The wide swings among economic and political models in Southern European countries were due to the absence of a powerful coalition in favor of a single ideology, much less one based on liberalism. In Latin America, the three ideologies that have competed with each other since the beginning of the nineteenth century have been liberalism, corporatism, and centralism. Their relative weight has been determined by the power of groups espousing them. Liberal advocates of federalism held office after independence, but in most countries they relinquished center stage soon afterward to a conservative brand of centralism. Pure corporatist ideologies are uncommon, but the values of hierarchy and obligation traditionally propagated by the church and the military have given a corporatist hue to much oratory and subnational political organization, as recent writings have emphasized.[6] Centralism in the modern period has typified some countries' development strategy, most notably Cuba's.[7]

No single ideology is universally accepted in the region today, and proponents of each are found even in the most repressive countries. Each philosophy has implications for a society's subsystems, such as labor unions, political parties, and interest groups, and for various processes, such as leadership styles and the rights and obligations of citizenship. Each also suggests ideal management practices and distinctive ways to organize the state. Competition over these approaches disrupted Peruvian society during the period studied in this book, and had

6. Howard J. Wiarda, "Toward a Framework for the Study of Political Change in the Iberic-Latin Tradition: The Corporative Model," *World Politics* 25:2 (January 1973), 206–35; Philippe C. Schmitter, "Still the Century of Corporatism?" in *The New Corporatism*, ed. Frederick B. Pike (South Bend, Ind.: University of Notre Dame Press, 1974); Howard J. Wiarda, ed., *Politics and Social Change in Latin America* (Amherst: University of Massachusetts Press, 1974); and James M. Malloy, ed., *Authoritarianism and Corporatism in Latin America* (Pittsburgh: Pittsburgh University Press, 1976). Kalman Silvert wrote widely on this theme, most explicitly in *Man's Power* (New York: Viking Press, 1970) and, with Leonard Reissman, *Education, Class, and Nation* (New York: Elsevier Scientific, 1976).

7. See Claudio Véliz, "Centralism and Nationalism in Latin America," *Foreign Affairs* 47:1 (October 1968), 68–83.

profound consequences for the status of agricultural elites, unmobilized peasants, and the administrators of agrarian reform enterprises.

### Liberal Bureaucracy

In Latin America and elsewhere, the liberal political system is characterized by a large number of articulate interest groups, a relatively high degree of national integration, a moderately small state sector, and political and economic decentralization. Political power is dispersed within the state, among political groupings with specific goals, and sometimes even among regions. Except in periods of widespread legitimacy (e.g., at ascension), the regime does not enjoy a power advantage that enables it to implement its policy preferences virtually uncontested. The body politic consists of numerous actors conscious of their goals and capable of forming coalitions to pursue them. The regime, with its variable stocks of legitimacy, finances, and skills, is obliged to cater to certain clients and win their support in order to legislate and implement its policies. Nonofficial actors in alliance with bureaucratic elements can distort regime preferences; sometimes opponents can completely overwhelm the government's stated aims, an outcome not proscribed by the rules of the game and certainly not fatal to the system.

When conflict occurs in the liberal system, the state tends to mediate between and reconcile adversaries. It promotes economic development through incentives for savings, investment, and consumption, and nation building by ensuring that potentially disruptive marginal groups gradually achieve economic or legal access to national power. When enough groups feel threatened by a monopoly of power in a few hands, and when these groups are sufficiently well organized to make their interests felt, the conditions are propitious for the installation of a liberal system, complete with an appropriate ideology and formalized in some sort of written constitution. This system requires for its maintenance officially sanctioned power fragmentation, high national integration, and a low value on hierarchy. It is usually associated with capitalist social formations.

In Latin America, Locke's and Jefferson's veneration of the

individual is of no instrumental value to the military discipli-
narian or the union organizer. But it does strike a resonant
chord with the entrepreneur who feels he has overcome unfavorable odds and "made it on his own." He is often joined by
middle-class professionals who at least value their own spe-
cialness, if not necessarily that of persons lower on the social
scale. Chile under the 1925 constitution probably came closest
to the integrated liberal type. Many other countries with the
trappings of liberal constitutions, such as Peru before 1969,
qualify less fully because of the small number of autonomous
groups in the body politic and the convergence of
socioeconomic and political power within the same elite.

Bureaucratic recruitment, attempts at coordination, and
policy-making styles can often reinforce a centralist, corporatist, or liberal political system. In any society, an individual's recruitment into the bureaucracy generally depends on the
degree to which employers believe his skills and resources will
further their goals for the organization. Promotion is affected by
the individual's performance in the eyes of organizational
superiors. Technical skills usually govern employment and
promotion at the lower and middle levels of bureaucracy in the
liberal system because they can increase the organization's autonomy in an atmosphere of relative power equality.

Because political pressures emanating from outside of the
liberal state structure can overwhelm the regime's ability to
enforce conformity, multiple policy arenas emerge and goal
diversity sometimes permeates the bureaucratic echelons.
When policy makers adjust for peculiarities in the task environment, they often count on client support to defend their
actions before superiors, even while proclaiming formal allegiance to the political regime in power. Dispersal of power
makes coordination haphazard, leading some apologists of the
system to elevate "muddling through" to a universal value.
Students of the liberal system do not search for coordinating
mechanisms in agencies set up to oversee the whole system,
but in innumerable incremental adjustments and compensa-
tions performed by the bureaucratic units themselves. Policy
ideas can spring from any of a number of autonomous units
interested in the relevant issue area, such as the executive,

legislature, bureaucratic agency, interest groups, and even the judiciary. One of the normative attractions of the liberal system is the liberty accorded individuals to promote causes that do not necessarily correspond to the perceived interests of the state.

The preceeding comments are familiar to the reader knowledgeable about bureaucracy in countries with a relatively integrated liberal approach to political life. Many of the early writers on development administration abstracted the most benign aspects of liberal organizations into prescriptive guidelines for the creation and management of organizations in all countries, regardless of their history or political system.[8] The error of this approach would be manifest if the roles were reversed, and advocates of corporatism or centralism recommended an overhaul of United States administrative practices based on their own historical and organizational experiences.

## Corporatist Bureaucracy

In the ideal corporatist state, individuals with similar functional activities are supposed to participate politically through amorphous grass-roots organizations that selectively filter demands upward to the predesignated state agencies. The structure of these organizations and their exchange relations with the state and with their constituents serve as obstacles to coalition formation, as in the liberal system, or to the creation of a class-based political party, which is often the dominant force underpinning the centralist state. One goal of the corporate system is deliberately to link marginal social groups to national political and economic structures, from which they benefit materially and psychologically but in which they wield little effective power. Lack of mobilization among the lower

8. Members of the Comparative Administrative Group of the American Society of Public Administration endlessly debated whether administrative growth should be encouraged in poor societies in the absence of countervailing institutions. The risks were perceived to be bureaucratic authoritarianism and a divergence from the Anglo-Saxon model of democracy based on a small state. For a discussion of the issues involved, see Ramesh K. Arora, *Comparative Public Administration* (New Dehli: Associated Publishing House, 1972), pp. 88–95, and Fred W. Riggs, Introduction to *Frontiers of Development Administration*, ed. Riggs (Durham, N.C.: Duke University Press, 1970), pp. 1–37.

levels of society, along with gratitude for the marginal advantages accruing from the system, results in a relatively tranquil political environment when the system operates as designed. The system organizes and legitimizes patron-clientelism within a paternalistic value structure.[9]

The corporate state is patterned on a column-and-lintel arrangement in which the bottom of each column penetrates and is penetrated by functional economical or social organizations. Near the top, peak interest groups interact frequently with bureaucratic leaders. Intrasectoral conflict (workers versus industrialists, teachers versus the Ministry of Education) is resolved within the column, while intersectoral disputes are adjudicated at the top, where elites who worked their way up one or several of the hierarchies and who share similar values meet regularly to keep the organic whole in equilibrium. They can do so as long as political interaction is contained within the sectors and coordination problems are sufficiently simple to be managed by the highest ranking political elites.

The corporate system's latent function of achieving harmonious integration of the society sets the stage for clientelism in both the hiring and the transferring of individual administrators. Technocrats, especially those noted for their bargaining skill, often dominate administrative leadership. At the middle levels, technical competence is less important than the size and composition of the individual's following and the degree to which his incorporation into the administrative structure guarantees his followers' continuing support for the system. The individual's relationship with both superiors and subordinates is characterized by reciprocal exchange of the positive and *quid pro quo* variety, including values of prestige, economic advantage, and information. At the lower levels, bureaucrats obtain positions through access to "contacts," and maintain them by demonstrating loyalty to their clientele networks.

The corporatist system is less penetratable by nonofficial political actors than the liberal system. Policies are generated

9. Jorge Tapia-Videla describes organicist bureaucracy in "Understanding Organizations and Environments: A Comparative Perspective," *Public Administration Review* 36:6 (November/December 1976), 631–36.

by sectoral elites with close links to peak interest groups or state-chartered mediating organizations "representing" popular sectors. These public and private elites decide questions of allocation and redistribution in their functional areas. Only when the scope of the policy threatens to cause social conflict or to impinge on the domain of parallel hierarchies is the issue decided in the multisectoral lintel, where the relevant actors are precommitted to abide by the decision adopted. In this model, coordination is often aided by information flow within clientele networks. Relevant actors look for cues as to which policies require cooperation (those sponsored by or important to persons within the same clientele network) and which can be ignored (those undertaken by competing groups or contrary to the interest of the bureaucrat's following).

Many of the symbols used by contemporary authoritarian regimes in Latin America can be traced back to Plato, Aristotle, and Thomas Aquinas. These attempts by regimes to endow teleology with form and substance do not necessarily prove that a corporatist tradition is exclusively embedded in these nations' political cultures. They indicate rather that powerful groups that have thrust themselves to the forefront find that corporatist-like symbols and institutions help to legitimize and prolong their rule. Both military and civilian regimes have been carriers of corporatist ideologies, and their chances for success appear to be greatest in the presence of predominantly peasant populations, highly institutionalized pillars of society founded on vertical principles (such as the church and the military), a small middle class, a relative absence of organized interest associations, and recent social upheaval or economic collapse.

The Mexican state and its alter ego, the Institutional Revolutionary Party ( PRI), are often cited as classic examples of the corporatist system in Latin America, despite the strains that have appeared in the Mexican body politic in recent years.[10]

10. Robert Scott says of Mexico:
    Internal Policy concerning each sector's interests was made and implemented by means of the pyramidal sector organization but, given the realities of the political and social environment, rather than moving from the grass roots up, policy decisions usually

Peru's most typically corporatist agency during the Velasco period was SINAMOS (the National System for Social Mobilization), which was founded in 1971 with charismatic leadership and instructions to gain support for the regime among peasants, workers, students, and professionals. It is worth noting, however, that just as one should not be deceived into believing that a country such as Somoza's Nicaragua was a liberal democracy because it had a congress, it is a mistake to conclude that Peru exemplified the corporatist state simply because of the existence of one or two corporatist-like institutions.[11]

*Bureaucratic Centralism*

The centralist system is characterized by singleness of purpose and a high degree of social monitoring. When the state is controlled by a hegemonic coalition (bureaucracy, military, party), few political resources are available for use by opposing autonomous groups in pursuit of their interests.[12] The state

---

emanated from the bureaucracy and leadership of the sector, filtering down through the hierarchy to the rank and file. Decisions of the central sector authorities were, of course, always subject to the approval of the president. In practice, conflicts among the sectors—or even within a sector, if the question was serious enough—were settled by the PRI's National Executive Committee, which usually meant by the president himself. [Robert E. Scott, *Mexican Government in Transition* (Urbana: University of Illinois Press, 1959), p. 134]

See also Merilee S. Grindle, *Coalition and Clienteles* (Berkeley: University of California Press, 1977). For discussion of the Portuguese case, see Lawrence S. Graham, *Portugal* (Beverly Hills, Calif.: Sage, 1975).

11. James Malloy's "Authoritarianism, Corporatism, and Mobilization in Peru," in *New Corporatism*, ed. Pike, pp. 58–84, exemplifies this point; Malloy's thinking is further developed in his *Authoritarianism and Corporatism in Latin America* (Pittsburgh: Pittsburgh University Press, 1977), pp. 3–19. Carlos Delgado describes his conception of the agency in "SINAMOS: La participación popular en la revolución peruana," *Participación* 2:2 (February 1973), 6–25.

12. In *State and Revolution* (New York: International Publishers, 1932), Lenin describes several characteristics of the bureaucratic-centralist state, which in his conception corresponds to the transitional stage from capitalism to communism. A central state is formed (pp. 60–61). Bourgeois enemies of the government are pursued and suppressed. Social property of the means of production replaces private ownership (pp. 77, 79). Commandeering from above prevails and control is severe (p. 80). All citizens become workers and members of one state party (p. 83), representing the "dictatorship of the proletariat," which audits state financial affairs and corrects deviant behavior. The rele-

welcomes these groups into the fold when they give unequivocal support to its policies, but it is impatient with them
when they protest too energetically or present themselves as
counterelites.[13] Control is effected through a large bureaucracy,
with centralized decision making and little penetration by
political actors who are not members of the governing coalition. The relative autonomy of the state tends to be high.[14]
Economic development is dependent on state-controlled investment. A system with a rapidly growing bureaucracy, consistent unity in the outlook of the governing coalition, and a
heavy emphasis on enforced social control is probably moving
toward the centralist mode. When large segments of the society

---

vance of these ideas for the later evolution of the Soviet system is treated in
Wolfgang Weichelt, "Das Wesen des sozialistischen Staates" [The Essence of
the Socialist State], *Staat und Recht* 23:10 (October 1974), 1629–47, and in L.
G. Churchward, "Contemporary Soviet Theory of the Soviet State," *Soviet
Studies* 12:4 (April 1961), 404–19.

13. Guillermo A. O'Donnell argues in *Bureaucratic-Authoritarianism* (Berkeley: Institute of International Studies, 1973) that many Latin American states
are upheld by a coalition of foreign capital, the bureaucracy, and the national
bourgeoisie, and protect their interests in great part by excluding the participation of popular elements. Elaborating on this theme, O'Donnell views "cor-
poratization" as a technique used by bureaucratic-authoritarian regimes to
penetrate, weaken, and control potentially unruly popular groups. See his
"Corporatism and the Question of the State," in *Authoritarianism and Corporatism*, ed. Malloy, pp. 47–87.

14. Our use of the concept of autonomy of the state relates to the degree to
which the state is able to articulate policies that do not correspond to interests
of powerful economic or social groups in civil society. For a fuller discussion,
see below, pp. 132–35. State autonomy in the liberal system is reduced, subject
as the state is to the influence of dominant social classes and international
actors. The greater autonomy of the corporatist state stems from its attempt to
absorb other sectors of society. While it is true that bureaucratic fiefdoms may
become dependent on classes and groups in the society at large, the state's
function of harmonizing these interests within the state apparatus—rather than
allowing their reconciliation to occur in the society and be imposed on the
state—gives it greater autonomy in the corporatist model than in the liberal
model. In the centralist state, those groups that are incorporated are also assimilated, and those that are not assimilated are either neutralized or eliminated.
For this reason, the stable centralist state displays greater autonomy than either
the corporatist or liberal type. Nicos Poulantzas, incidentally, would have
taken exception to this description of corporatist systems. He believed state
autonomy declines in neocorporatism because institutionalized assemblies of
interests "cooperate under the leadership and neutral arbitration of the
technico-bureaucratic administration." See his *Political Power and Social
Classes* (London: NLB, 1973), pp. 267–68.

are unmobilized and opposing elites are comparatively weak, the state can maintain a placid environment through highly visible, relatively mild authoritarian measures. But when dissatisfied elements articulate demands that the state cannot accommodate without moving toward a more liberal system, the result is often a high incidence of coercion aimed at the crushing of opposition.

In the centralist system, much emphasis is placed on the middle- and lower-level bureaucrat's internalization of institutional and regime goals, and his ability to serve those goals without wasting time in analyzing their rationale. The sage bureaucrat interested in mobility expends considerable effort in discerning the exact meaning of decisions issued from above, and implements them precisely with only cursory examination of the degree to which they fit the situation. High-level management must be well versed in the system's ideological precepts as well as personally loyal to those in power who are responsible for policy making. Usually operating in secrecy, governing elites make judgments on the nature of the problem, check them with specialized members of the dominant coalition, and dictate orders downward. Attempts at coordination are very explicit. Monitoring agencies aim at reducing duplication and preventing administrative units from exercising too much discretion. The institutional expressions of this control are strong planning and budgeting agencies, frequently complemented by intelligence networks linked to the national security apparatus, and an elaborate party structure. While the need for such monitoring is self-evident in the view of leadership, often these institutions' resources are insufficient to do a thorough job. As a result, the very existence of the monitoring agency may constrain bureaucratic units from seeking more direct means of coordinating their output with that of complementary organizations.

In Latin America, working classes have found Marxist philosophy conducive to their aims because it posits their eventual predominance in the society and calls their employers "exploiters." As interpreted by Lenin and Gramsci, Marxist philosophy also assigns a role to committed intellectuals in the vanguard party, who act as the brains of the workers' movement. In Peru, these ideas have found fertile fields in the mining and capital-intensive industrial sectors, among intellectuals at the heads of unions and leftist political parties, and with university students, who tend to empathize with the downtrodden and conclude that lower-class organization is the most promising way to achieve social justice. These organizations insist on ideological purity, strong discipline, and hierarchical relations. This centralist approach has characterized Cuba's political system since 1959.[15]

Advocates of corporatism and Marxist centralism question liberal political philosophy of the English and North American variety. But classes that would normally impose a centralist state upon gaining power prefer to compete for power in a liberal system because of its nominal defense of pluralism. They may even defend liberalism because it does not challenge their power base, as does corporatism, which they detest. The same rule applies to corporatist-leaning groups that combat Marxism. When they are relatively weak, proponents of both systems see liberalism's tolerance of proselyting as an advantage, although this advantage can be neutralized when opponents eat away at their strength.

### Management Correlates of the Three Systems

"Administration" is not wholly dependent on the nature of the social system. It attains a degree of autonomy through the casuistic principles that various administrative theories propagate. Executives are supposed to do $X$, $Y$, and $Z$; bureaucrats are to be hired according to criteria $P$, $Q$, and $R$; decentralization or centralization is to be pursued because of $A$, $B$, and $C$; and bureaucratic ethics embody $H$, $I$, and $J$. Students of administration may recognize the shades of well-known theorists in the ideal management practices subsumed under the three types we have been discussing. These patterns are summarized in Table 2.

The classical bureaucratic approach, symbolized by such writers as Frederick Taylor and Max Weber, is suitable for the centralist system. It emphasizes the vertical integration of man-

15. See Jorge Domínguez, *Cuba: Order and Revolution* (Cambridge: Harvard University Press, 1979).

Table 2. Focus, characteristics, and values of three public administration approaches

| Theories and theorists | Empirical focus | Characteristics | Values maximized |
|---|---|---|---|
| Classic bureaucratic approach<br>Taylor<br>Weber | Organization, production group, government agency, bureau, work group | Hierarchy, control, authority, chain of command, unity of command, centralization | Efficiency, economy, effectiveness |
| Human-relations approach<br>Mayo<br>Bennis<br>Argyris | Individual and work group, supervisor/worker relations, behavior change | Interpersonal and inter-group relations, shared authority, consensus, communications, motivation, sanctions | Worker satisfaction, personal growth, individual dignity |
| Public-choice approach<br>Zald<br>Mitchell<br>Ostrom<br>Buchanan<br>Tullock | Organization and client relations, decentralized overlapping structures, public sector as market | Bargaining, decentralization, antibureaucratic stance, application of economic logic to problems of service distribution | Competition, citizen options or choices, equal access to services |

SOURCE: Adapted from H. George Frederickson, "The Lineage of New Public Administration," Administration and Society 9:1 (May 1977), 115.

agers and workers within a strict chain of command in pursuit
of productivity and efficiency.[16] In Peruvian agriculture,
bureaucratic centralism was reflected in the early implementation of the agrarian reform legislation and the administration of
the agrarian court system. The human-relations approach is
more concerned about individual self-fulfillment within a
bureaucratic structure and positive relationships with fellow
workers and managers. Extrapolated to a national level, the
implication is one of corporatism.[17] In Peru, human-relations
principles that stressed consensus and conflict avoidance were
consistent with the regime's expectations for the political behavior of state-chartered interest groups and those production
enterprises molded into the social-property sector. The
public-choice approach calls for deconcentration, group unity,
interest articulation, allocation of system benefits through
market-like mechanisms, and political liberalism.[18] The Velasco regime's decision-making style on issues affecting
middle-sized farmers and its tolerance of intrabureaucratic
competition were suggestive of the public-choice model. Each
of these management approaches involves a distinctive conception of human nature, rooted in a strain of political philosophy.[19] Taylorism assumes that human beings are slothful; the
human-relations school, that they are compassionate but op-
pressed by social structures; and the public-choice model, that

16. For the origins of "scientific management," see Frederick W. Taylor,
*Shop Management* (New York: Harper, 1912).

17. Elton Mayo, *The Human Problems of an Industrial Civilization* (Boston:
Graduate School of Business Administration, Harvard University, 1946). As
suggested by the title of Mayo's book, the human relations school (with its
modern manifestations of work participation and self-management) is generally seen as a response of modern capitalism to apathy and low productivity in
vertically integrated organizations. Although Mayo and his followers never
defended corporatism per se, consistency exists between the symbols of the
human relations school and the precepts of an ideal corporatist system. Thus in
Peru it is not accidental that social property and *autogestión* were promoted
most energetically when the Velasco regime was passing through its corporatist phase.

18. For representative contributions to this literature, see Mayer N. Zald, ed.,
*Power in Organizations* (Nashville: Vanderbilt University Press, 1970).

19. Dwight Waldo discusses this subject in detail in *The Administrative
State* (New York: Ronald Press, 1948). A short but imaginative attempt to link
modern public administration with classical political theorists is William G.
Scott and David K. Hart, "The Moral Nature of Man in Organization: A Comparative Analysis," *Academy of Management Journal* 14:2 (June 1971), 241–55.

their passionate defense of self-interest is moderated by reason. As we shall learn later in this book, these philosophical biases were manifested in the efforts of public-sector agencies to oblige agrarian reform cooperatives to conform to one or another mode of internal management.

In summary, rules for bureaucratic behavior are related to types of political systems and prevalent ideologies. Very seldom, however, is there a neat correspondence among bureaucracy, type of political system, and ideology. Because social formations contain classes and groups with variable power, beliefs, and relations with the public sector, national systems are very mixed. So is bureaucratic behavior. In some countries the full range of administrative trends described earlier may be found in public organizations of varying goals, resources, and environments. Some Latin American agencies perform more efficiently than organizations in the industrialized world, while others reflect traditionalism. Because of complex overlapping and social fragmentation, organizations and management styles with opposing characteristics exist side by side in many Latin American societies.

Such diversity certainly characterized Peruvian bureaucratic behavior. While most political leaders are willing to tolerate ambiguity of this kind, the revolutionary finds such a potpourri of relationships unacceptable. He may attempt to "rationalize" his society according to the precepts of one or another model. The success of the venture depends on the power of the regime, of the allies it can muster, and of the opposition elements in civil society which need to be overcome. In the case of Peru's Revolutionary Government of the Armed Forces, President Juan Velasco Alvarado first followed a centralist mode, based on the hierarchical authority of a military government, and then flirted with corporatism. Ironically, the main legacy of his rule has been more equally distributed power in Peru, especially in rural areas, and more favorable conditions for liberalism, a philosophy he scorned.

## State Growth and Coordination

In 1968 the public bureaucracy was ripe for reform. The absence of modern budgeting and planning mechanisms, the predominance of omnibus, multifunctional ministries, and disruptive antagonism between the executive and legislative branches made the Peruvian bureaucracy during the last months of Belaúnde's regime perhaps the most chaotic and unwieldy in Latin America. Civilian bureaucrats interviewed soon after the coup recalled the sad state of affairs under Belaúnde. They told a disheartening tale of executive impotence in the face of an irresponsible Congress, and a constitutional framework that facilitated corruption and blocked policy innovation.[20] Many of them had become fed up with the reigning pluralistic system of "checks and balances."[21] Finally, the national budget, considered by many specialists as being the key to rational public policy making, had become a bad joke.[22]

While the coup of 1968 was precipitated by Belaúnde's unsatisfactory resolution of the La Brea y Pariñas (International Petroleum Company) dispute, deeper reasons for the overthrow lay in the moral and administrative bankruptcy of the country's dominant elites and parliamentary system of government. The military regime, with strong support from civilian técnicos, placed heavy emphasis on ideological and political unity, and

20. One functionary commented in July 1970, "Congress intervened in the budgetary process by legislating new stadiums, schools, hospitals, and other political goods. This was not grass-roots representation but simply the case of a senator, or one of his relatives, who wanted to make some money. The result was to dot the country with stadiums holding 20,000 spectators in towns of 2,000 people and large hospitals standing empty with no one to administer them. Of course, this tendency exists more or less all over the world. But here, during those years, it reached gargantuan proportions" (interview no. 5).

21. Another added, "The Congress refused to bring decentralized agencies under control because it wanted to keep the executive weak. For the same reason, it would call ministers before it to answer spurious questions, to the point of taking so much of their time that they could not do their jobs. Then Congress would ridicule them for neglecting their administrative duties" (interview no. 2).

22. "On paper, of course, the budget was balanced. The executive accomplished this by inflating revenue estimates (ten percent here, seven percent there) and underestimating expenditures. Everybody recognized that the final figures bore little resemblance to reality. In 1968, the government ran terrific deficits and began cutting back projects. The Congress was ecstatic. Many congressmen crowed that Belaúnde was a dreamer with no conception of basic economics" (interview no. 1). See also Pedro-Pablo Kuczynski, *Peruvian Democracy under Economic Stress* (Princeton: Princeton University Press, 1977), and Naomi J. Caiden and Aaron B. Wildavsky, *Planning and Budgeting in Poor Countries* (New York: Wiley, 1973).

initiated a series of reforms in the postcoup period which transformed the public sector. Before, the bureaucracy was characterized by the rampant penetration of private parties into public decision making, budgetary fragmentation, overlapping functions, reduced size and economic activity, and little executive control. Afterward, it was notable for relatively well-defined sectors, centralized administrative processes, dynamic growth, and absorption of an ever greater percentage of the GNP. Practically overnight the regime implemented a number of administrative measures widely practiced in other Latin American countries but only nascent in Peru.

The military junta that ousted Belaúnde had a number of priorities, such as the transformation of the industrial, agrarian, and natural resources sectors. To facilitate the coordination of these basic reforms, the regime considered as absolutely essential the breakup of the unwieldy Ministry of Development and Public Works. This reform was effected with considerable fanfare in 1969 and initiated a movement toward functional specialization broken only by the creation of SINAMOS, the multisectoral political mobilization agency, in 1972. Figure 1 shows that the state's organizational chart evolved in the following way:

- Left intact: Prime Ministry, Ministries of Labor, Education, Health, Finance, War, Navy, Aviation.
- Formed from the Ministry of Government and Police: Interior (1969), Transport and Communications (1969).
- Formed from the Ministry of Development and Public Works: Transport and Communications, Energy and Mines (MEM), Industry and Commerce (MIC), Housing (1969).
- Split into two ministries: Agriculture and Fishing (1969) and Industry and Commerce (1974). Agriculture further split in early 1975 into Agriculture and Food.

Starting with eleven ministries in 1968, the government had expanded to seventeen in early 1975, plus several national offices with ministerial rank (largely a prestige distinction) under the presidency.

An important motive behind this disaggregation was the desire to create governable units identified with fundamental re-

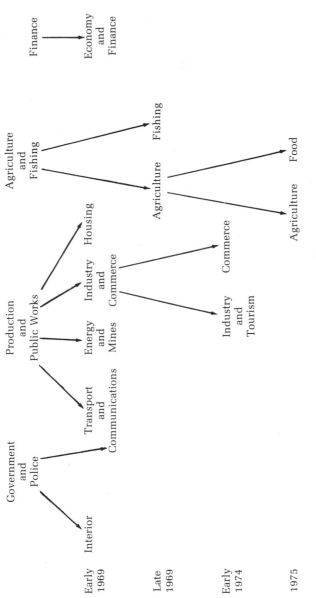

Figure 1. Ministerial reorganization, 1969–75 (SOURCES: *Expreso*, April 25, 1969; Decree Law 18,026 [December 16, 1969]; Presidencia de la República, *Compendio de leyes orgánicas de la Presidencia de la República y sectores de actividad pública* [Lima: Instituto Nacional de Planificación, 1972].)

gime goals and susceptible to budgetary and planning guidance. Sectorialization was the first step in a continuing reform that significantly increased the state's role in the economy and facilitated new planning, budgeting, and social control. These reforms coincided with reduced private-sector investment, decreased interest-group activity, and fewer resources for local government. Table 3 demonstrates the growth of the public sector from 1965 to 1977, measured in terms of governmental expenditures as a percentage of GNP, government investment as a percentage of gross national investment, absolute total employment of the public sector, local government resources, and expenditures of the National Accounting Office, Budget Bureau, Ministry of Finance (MEF), and police.[23] While the state structure spread like an accordion, many semi-autonomous agencies were brought under the authority of the central ministries, their liberal statutes annulled, and their earmarked taxes canceled. By 1974 these fiscal reforms had been gradually consolidated and the MEF was emphasizing monetary and investment policies for the country's financial institutions. Reformed agencies included the Superintendency of Banks, the Lima Stock Exchange, and the Industrial, Mining, Agriculture, Housing and National banks. These remarkable figures, especially those dealing with state expenditures as a percentage of GNP, investment, and local government resources, are testimony to the rapid growth of the Peruvian state and its new potential for dominance in the society.[24]

Simultaneously, the influence of the National Planning Insti-

23. The authors are indebted to Alejandro Camino for gathering much of the statistical data presented here.

24. For statistics of other countries, see Clement H. Moore, "Authoritarian Politics in Unincorporated Society: The Case of Nasser's Egypt," *Comparative Politics* 6:2 (November 1974), 199. Werner Baer, Isaac Kerstenetzky, and Annibal V. Villela, "The Changing Role of the State in the Brazilian Economy," *World Development* 1:11 (November 1975), 31, estimate that expenditures as a percentage of GNP reached 50 percent in Brazil by 1969. See also Celso Lafer, "Sistema político brasileiro: Balanço e perspectivas" (mimeo, Getulio Vargas Foundation, 1973), pp. 36–38. It is almost impossible to evaluate these data, however, because the figures are not necessarily informed by the same methodology. If "state size" is to become a useful political economy concept, analysts must first agree on the proper statistical measure with which to scale public-sector orders of magnitude.

Table 3. Growth and control in the public sector, 1965–77 (with adjustments for inflation where applicable)

| Year | Public sector as percentage of GNP[a] | State investment as percentage of GNI[b] | Number of public employees, centralized and decentralized sectors | Local government resource index[c] | General comptroller expenditure index | Finance Ministry expenditure index | Budget Bureau expenditure index | Investigative police (PIP) expenditure index |
|---|---|---|---|---|---|---|---|---|
| 1965 | 18.8% | 26.3% |  | 100.0 | 100.0 | 100.0 | 100.0 | 100.0 |
| 1967 | 24.3 | 21.5 | 270,000 | 35.5 | 119.3 | 108.2 | 90.3 | 114.4 |
| 1968 | 24.7 | 27.5 |  | 33.4 |  |  | 102.3 | 111.8 |
| 1969 | 25.2 | 31.7 |  | 20.6 | 114.4 | 152.9 | 135.7 | 85.6 |
| 1970 | 25.0 | 35.1 | 304,176[d] |  |  | 168.1 | 159.7 | 123.0 |
| 1971 | 27.3 | 32.3 |  |  | 118.5 | 156.1 | 134.6 | 119.9 |
| 1972 | 32.9 | 35.5 |  |  | 118.5 | 156.1 | 134.6 | 119.9 |
| 1973 | 39.1 | 38.0 | 401,100 | 14.5 | 126.7 | 212.8 | 481.5 | 194.6 |
| 1974 | 45.4 | 43.4 | 427,700 | 14.5 | 126.7 | 212.8 | 481.5 | 194.6 |
| 1975 | 46.2 | 48.7 | 455,600[e] |  | 117.8 | 246.9 |  |  |
| 1976 | 46.2 | 49.7 | 523,000 |  | 102.8 | 230.3 |  |  |
| 1977 | 49.9 | 45.3 | 577,000 |  | 107.0 | 285.9 |  |  |

[a] The public sector includes central government, social security, and state enterprises, as calculated by the Central Bank. Deduction of intrasystem transfers would reduce these figures from 3 to 6 percentage points. The figures included here provide a composite picture of the importance of the Peruvian state in terms of the total resources at its disposal. For example, although the banking system and EPSA (the food-distribution agency) add little to the GNP, their activities are crucial for management of the national economy.

[b] Unpublished statistics, Banco Central de Reserva.

[c] Ministerio de Economía y Finanzas, Presupuestos generales de la Republica (Lima: Dirección General de Presupuesto Público, 1960–74). After 1974, the MEF ceased to provide budgetary data on local governments.

[d] Angel Núñez Barreda, Los recursos humanos en el sector público peruano (Lima: INAP, 1974).

[e] Características del empleo estatal, 1970–1975: Investigación final del censo II (Lima: CPND, INP-UNI, OIC-IPL, May 1978), Appendix 7. Includes central government, decentralized institutions, local government, social security, and public enterprises.

tute (INP) rose significantly. Before 1968, Belaúnde, who had considerable confidence in his own grand design for the country's development, had systematically ostracized the INP from policy formation and given no support to its attempt to monitor policy implementation. In 1966, many professional planners, completely demoralized, left the Institute and were replaced by political appointees.[25] With the military government, however, the situation turned around dramatically and the INP became one of the most important agencies in the Peruvian public sector. From 1969 to 1971 its budget increased by 25 percent in real terms. It hired staff with new technical skills and it established sectoral planning offices in all of the high investment ministries. Each year's Annual Operating Plan gave the INP authority to approve budgetary entries, an important requisite for effective short-term planning.[26] INP officials helped to set original budgetary ceilings (in association with the Budget Bureau), order sectoral projects by priority (both at the ministerial level and with Finance's Department of Economic Affairs), and approved all modifications in sectoral investment.

The state's self-monitoring seemed to parallel greater government surveillance over the society as a whole. The creation of SINAMOS to supervise popular support for the government, the elimination and disenfranchizing of some interest groups (the Sociedad Nacional Agraria, the Sociedad Nacional de Industrias), the expropriation of the national press, the enhanced status of military intelligence, and the frequent deportations of political spokesmen were cases in point.[27]

25. Interview no. 3. See also Juan Chong Sánchez, "El proceso de planificación social en el Perú," *Estudios Andinos* 3:1 (1973), 29–55; Daniel R. Kilty, *Planning for Development in Peru* (New York: Praeger, 1966); Robert E. Klitgaard, "Observations on the Peruvian National Plan for Development, 1971–1975," *Inter-American Economic Affairs* 25:3 (Winter 1971), 3–22.

26. E. V. K. Fitzgerald, *The State and Economic Development* (Cambridge: Cambridge University Press, 1976), pp. 80–90.

27. From 1962 to October 1968, for example, the government deported only one person; from 1969 to August 1975, the number of deportees was 70. By order of frequency, they were journalists, political party activists, union leaders, social scientists, and priests. Deportation is a mild measure of repression compared with the number of persons killed in political violence or imprisoned for political activities. Figures on those phenomena, unavailable officially, were probably low until the February 1975 disturbances, in which 86

While partial raw data might indicate that Peru was heading irrevocably toward rigidly centralized control, that trend was not universal or necessarily helpful in predicting bureaucratic behavior. If the government were bent on creating a command economy with extensive social control, one would not expect to find in Table 4 a *decline* in absolute terms in the budgets of the Ministry of the Interior (1965 budgetary index of 100 reduced to 81.6 in 1975) and SINAMOS (100 in 1971 to 57.6 in 1975), and an increase in the resources of the National Planning Institute of only about two index points from 1971 (99.7) to 1974 (102.0).[28] Indeed, even though INP resources spurted upward again in 1975, it is obvious that the Planning Institute was not asked to exert full control over state growth. Over the years, its relations changed vis-à-vis regime leaders, the public enterprises, and the state financial institutions (COFIDE, National Bank, Industrial Bank, and so on). At first it molded sectoral investment schemes to a national plan; later it relied more on expert economic analysis and persuasion to try to influence investment patterns and avoid *faits accomplis*.

Factors influencing this change, besides the very magnitude of planning tasks implied by an enlarged state apparatus, were problems of enforcement within some of the sectoral ministries (due in part to inconsistencies between military rank and formal lines of authority) and the civilian makeup of the INP staff. Even though a sectoral planner might convince a minister of the value of the INP's coordinating directive, the minister's difficulties in managing his subordinates made the INP's advice inapplicable. The INP was basically a civilian organization in a military government, and although it was led by a general, it

---

persons were reported killed in Lima. With the advent of the Morales Bermúdez government, a new wave of arrests and deportations occurred, and at least 22 were killed in a general strike in June 1978.

28. The explanation for the reduction of Interior's budget (Table 4) and the increase in the PIP expenditures (Table 3) is that investigative police activities increased markedly under Velasco while the salaries of the national police force (Guardia Civil) were held steady or even declined when adjusted for inflation. The breaking point occurred in February 1975, when the Guardia Civil's strike for higher wages provoked a serious confrontation with the army and a breakdown of authority led to rioting in downtown Lima. The government subsequently granted pay hikes to the policemen and stamped "Confidential" on the budget of the Ministry of the Interior.

Table 4. SINAMOS, INP, and Ministry of Interior expenditure
indexes, 1965–78

| Year | SINAMOS expenditure index | INP expenditure index | Ministry of Interior expenditure index |
|---|---|---|---|
| 1965 | | | 100.0 |
| 1967 | | 100.0 | 110.8 |
| 1968 | | | 102.7 |
| 1969 | | 75.9 | 72.9 |
| 1970 | | 89.8 | 107.6 |
| 1971 | 100.0 | 99.7 | 99.2 |
| 1972 | 100.0 | 99.7 | 99.2 |
| 1973 | 83.1 | 102.0 | 81.6 |
| 1974 | 83.1 | 102.0 | 83.6 |
| 1975 | 57.6 | 111.1 | 84.3 |
| 1976 | 52.7 | 104.3 | 87.9 |
| 1977 | 39.9 | 109.5 | 69.6 |
| 1978 | 23.5 | 89.7 | 70.5 |

SOURCE: Ministerio de Economía y Finanzas, *Presupuestos generales de la República* (Lima: Dirección General de Presupuesto Público, 1965–78).

could not depend on the military hierarchy to enforce its directives. Policy coordination depended more on self-restraint and negotiation among the sectors (often in board meetings of state agencies including representatives from many sectors) than on uncontested rules handed down from above.

In summary, as the state grew, the number of agencies increased, and so did the disparity of their interests. In most cases, the Planning Institute influenced policy deliberations, but only as one of several actors. Final decisions emerged from the interaction of dynamic state enterprises and ministries, which strengthened their bargaining positions by drawing on the skills and resources of private firms, outside consultants, foreign financiers, and men of military ascendancy. They negotiated agreements one by one, making marginal alterations in plans in light of new realities, in a process similar to mutual adjustment. It is important to note that while political interaction among private actors used to determine resource distribution under Belaúnde, political competition under Velasco was very much confined within the state, with official agencies calling the shots. Bureaucratic politics displaced the previous mode of national politics, and those private economic interests that could still exert influence knew that they needed to ally themselves with elements of the bureaucratic or military hierarchy if their preferences were to be implemented.

## Personnel Practices

Civil service codes are usually written on the assumption that all candidates who fulfill objective prerequisites for a particular post (age, work experience, minimal training, and so forth) are evaluated equally. Peruvian Law 11,377 (1950), governing personnel policies in the centralized and decentralized sectors, is no exception, since it attempts to reward technical skills and performance. It has been long recognized, however, that the norms of a Weberian "legal-rational" bureaucracy, on which the law is premised, are inconsistent with modal patterns within Peruvian administration, and that the government's civil service commissions traditionally have been too weak to correct deviations.[29] For example, the law states that all jobs are to be filled by public competition, and provides for publicity on openings, a review of the candidates' qualifications, written tests (for lower-level slots), and personal interviews. Some offices, however, limit competition to people already employed by the agency, and many hold no formal competition whatsoever. A standardized job classification is supposed to determine salary scales but few agencies abide by it. Pertinent aspects of Peruvian personnel practices are the incidence of clientelism, confianza, "technification," and, during the Velasco period, the relationship between military promotion and the civilian bureaucracy, especially at the middle and upper levels.

### Lower-Level Personnel

At the auxiliary and nonprofessional levels of the Peruvian bureaucracy the formal way to obtain a position is through

29. Jack W. Hopkins, "Comparative Observations on Peruvian Bureaucracy," Journal of Comparative Bureaucracy 1 (1969), 301–20.

inscription and competition, but these positions seldom are
announced publicly and those are not the only steps necessary
to secure employment. The rule covering almost all cases is
that "recommendations" have preponderant influence.[30]

Recommendations can come from inside the ministry, from
another ministry, or from outside the public sector altogether.
In the first case, an employee of the ministry learns simultaneously of the existence of an opening and of his friend's or relative's search for a job. He makes the linkage by informing the
hiring office of the good qualities of his friend. Second, persons
lucky enough to have acquaintances in key positions, such as
personnel manager, plague them for assistance in finding a job.
The high unemployment rate makes for heavy competition, and
aspirants recognize the need to enlist support from all quarters.
A personnel manager often prefers not to lobby with his counterparts in other ministries because a favor received one day is
invariably followed by a counterrequest the next. But usually
the pressure is too great to resist. Third, and most common,
candidates secure positions via recommendations from persons
outside the public sector who happen to know the hirer. Previously, such influence came mainly from the legislative
branch of government; after 1968 it grew out of personal contacts with military or civilian elites in upper-level posts. Here
the influential party visits or telephones the vice-minister or
agency head to inform him of the availability of a talented
friend or relative. This step, which paves the way for employment, often precedes any direct contact between the interested
party and the hiring agency. Ultimately, the candidate who
mobilizes the most impressive array of recommendations is the
successful applicant. These arrangements—the details of
which are known only to the vice-minister, the personnel manager, the agency head, and the candidate—are difficult to

---

30. A study of Peruvian bureaucracy by Gabriel Ochoa R. et al. contains the
following comment: "When we asked about the efficiency and trustworthiness
of formal recruitment methods, a high percentage of the members, including
those in offices specializing in personnel selection, believed that these were
facades, and that in daily practice personnel selection was influenced by
third-person intervention and other nonlegal factors" (*Estudio diagnóstico
sobre funcionamiento organizacional de la administración pública peruana*
[Lima: Instituto Nacional de Administración Pública, 1974], p. 87).

document, but extremely frequent. If we assume that half of public service jobs are in the bottom range of the hierarchy and that virtually all of them are filled in this manner, the system has directly benefited approximately 200,000 Peruvian families.

Employment based on recommendations implies reciprocal obligations, which spread the indirect social effects of the pattern. First, the candidate has to be well known to the recommender because the latter (often called a *patrón*) is partially responsible if the worker does not do well in the job. The favored candidate then owes loyalty (or a favor) to the inside or outside person who intercedes on his behalf. It is common to hear in the corridors of the ministry statements to the effect that "I got a job at the ministry because X helped me out." The agency head, who needed to hire someone anyway, now has a worker whose performance is guaranteed by a third party. While the loyalty of the employee to his new boss is insufficient to cancel all the favors received, it appears that the mutually discharged obligations are mechanisms for creating *confianza* (trust), which enables the transactions to continue (see Figure 2). Subsequently, the hirer can ask a favor of the person whose recommendation he followed. Thus multiple mutually reinforcing inducements perpetuate the pattern.

The worker wanting a raise can follow one of several routes. He can wait for a statewide salary increase in his grade, compete for a vacancy higher in the organization, or *mover un poco* (jockey a bit) to receive special consideration in the next budget allocation. For help in this procedure he may solicit the intervention of his original sponsor or of another contact who carries influence with the minister or vice-minister. Talking with his boss is not necessarily the first step, but whether because of friendship, influence, or merit, the candidate's superior has to argue for the raise in the yearly review of the biannual budget.

The budgetary law says that all salary increases should be justified in writing, but such written reports are not made in practice. The ministerial budget commission discusses possible raises when it considers new equipment, materials, and personnel. If one of the commission members is not on good terms with the agency head, he will challenge the raise even

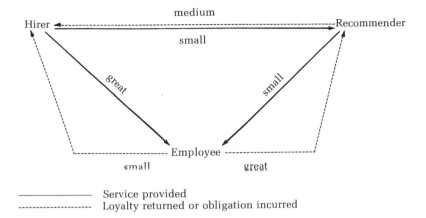

Figure 2. Reciprocal obligations in the hiring of lower-level personnel

when the person deserves it. On the other hand, a boss may recommend a raise of S/4,000 per month, and the worker through skillful behind-the-scenes maneuvering will receive S/8,000. While it is true that raises have been granted as a result of an objective evaluation of attendance, dedication, and performance, the pervasive feeling in the lower levels of the bureaucracy is that the most competent and talented persons are not necessarily those given greatest remuneration. One personnel manager observed, "Previously, a person got a raise by appealing to a deputy or senator in the Congress. There has been some change in practice, but I would say that we are still a long way from perfection. We at least appear to be going in the right direction."[31]

### Technical Specialization

The ascendency of technocrats in the Peruvian public sector under Velasco was cited by government spokesmen proud of the competence of the reformed Peruvian state and analysts finding traces of corporatist tendencies in the military regime. No empirical studies have dealt with this phenomenon in Peru,

31. Interview no. 45. Also interview no. 46.

and the national personnel office does not have statistics on the technical qualifications of public employees. Our independent survey found that five ministries—the Prime Ministry, Interior, Foreign Relations, Education, and Labor—did not hire many technocrats and did not promote them to high positions. Another group—Agriculture, Energy and Mines, Finance, Industry, Health, Housing, Transport, Fishing, Commerce, and the National Planning Institute (INP)—did employ the services of assorted agronomists, engineers, economists, medical doctors, architects, biologists, M.B.A.s, and planners. Unfortunately, these ministries had not assembled information over time which would provide a running account of their "technification." Moreover, because of several governmental structural reforms and general archival disorganization, it was practically impossible to reconstruct personnel lists for specific ministries in past years.

To measure high-level "technification," our procedure was to limit the analysis to the number of leadership appointments (agency heads, vice-ministers, advisory posts) occupied by technocrats in 1974, and to compare selected sectors between 1974 and 1963 (the first year of the Belaúnde regime). The comparison was possible after we came across a relatively complete listing for 1963. Table 5 indicates that, if we assume that military personnel trained in one of the applied sciences (civil engineering, mechanics, communications) can be considered technocrats in their own right, the incidence of technocrats did increase over the eleven-year period, even strikingly. President Belaúnde was an architect and over 50 percent of his appointees in the relevant ministries were technical specialists too. Nonetheless, the percentage of technocrats in important posts under Velasco increased by about half over the decade, to 75 percent in 1974. The figure is impressive, and one is tempted to conclude that an important change occurred in the "technification" of the Peruvian state elite.

Technification was not limited to the elite but extended throughout the middle levels of relevant state agencies. Moreover, middle-level technocrats did not remain in one functional area but moved laterally into positions located in other sectors. Indeed, the expansion of the Peruvian bureaucracy represented

*Table 5.* The "technification" of the bureaucratic elite, 1963–74

| Measures of technification | 1963 | 1974 |
|---|---|---|
| Number of upper-level posts | 70 | 104 |
| Number occupied by military | 1 | 35 |
| Number occupied by civilians | 69 | 69 |
| Number occupied by civilian técnicos | 38 | 43 |
| Percent filled by civilian técnicos | 54.3% | 41.3% |
| Number occupied by military or civilian técnicos | 39 | 78 |
| Percent filled by military or civilian técnicos | 55.7% | 75.0% |

SOURCE: "Principales funcionarios de la administración pública," *Perú* (Lima: Latinoamericano, 1963); personnel sheets issued by public-sector agencies.

a veritable boon for middle-level technocrats. Salaries skyrocketed. Newly created ministries raided sister sectors with abandon. The universities (in some cases, private enterprise too) were depleted of skilled professionals. Elegant devices circumvented restrictions on hiring, and technocrats content with their tasks used lucrative outside offers to negotiate favorable pay hikes where they were.

The fact that most mobile technocrats were hired by contract meant that they had less job security than permanent employees but were better paid. During Velasco's regime, cabinet ministers received salaries and fringe benefits equivalent to about $1,100 per month. Since no one lower in the hierarchy should have earned more than the minister, the Finance Ministry habitually limited all remunerations in the centralized sector of government to about $890 per month. Exceptions had to be approved by the Council of Ministers. Ministries abided by this rule for the "permanent" appointees. They resorted to contractual arrangements to hire "temporary" expertise routinely approved by the Council, even though the salaries of these technocrats often exceeded that of the minister himself. Regulations said that temporary employees were not to exercise executive functions or undertake long-term assignments, but in some cases contract personnel were appointed as agency directors. Some ministers followed the practice of paying permanent appointees out of the current account of the budget, and giving contracts to those persons paid from the capital account. These latter assignments were supposed to be of short duration and highly specific—for example, to design an oil pipeline in the jungle or a new building for the ministry. "You will note, however, that in the case of practically every personnel law in Peru, exceptions are made one by one and no regulation covers one hundred percent of the cases. Exceptions even exist in the case of persons contracted for special projects. A person hired to work on a program in Puno has carried out routine functions in our ministry since the day he arrived."[32]

There was less evidence that personal relations intervened in the hiring of middle-level technocrats than in the case of auxiliary personnel, because the former's skills were scarce and agencies competed to obtain them. The national personnel office (located in the National Institute of Public Administration, INAP) believed that about 60 percent of the positions open to engineers, architects, economists, and accountants were filled through public competition and 40 percent by merit promotions. A closer look at the agencies, however, revealed a more diverse panorama. Legal directives said that almost all jobs were to be filled through competition, but the personnel director and agency head decided on their own procedures. Sometimes the agency head tried to locate the person he needed directly and advertised for the position only if the search failed. For a similar job, another bureau might automatically call a public competition. And there were cases in which competition was called, candidates presented themselves, and then a professional recommended by an influential outside party arrived. The competition was canceled and the "fair-haired boy" was hired on the spot.

### Confianza

The ubiquitous term *confianza* (trust) governs all appointments in the upper reaches of the Peruvian bureaucracy. *Confianza* is seldom defined in generic terms, but rather through empirical examples covering a full spectrum of relationships: the friend who is *cumplido* (keeps his word); the subordinate who performs well and transmits valuable information to his boss; the supervisor who doesn't stab you in the back or bad-

---

32. Interview no. 43.

mouth you in the presence of others; the janitor who respects others' property and avoids reading private papers on your desk; the civilian vice-minister who unwaveringly supports the goals of the Revolutionary Government of the Armed Forces. *Confianza* usually goes beyond personal relationships between two parties and is reinforced by a network of reciprocal obligations with outside parties, tied together by kinship, common schooling experience, political activity, economic entrepreneurship, or ideological commitment over a relatively long period of time.

More civilian appointments to senior policy-making posts come from outside of the ministry than from internal promotion. Many superiors prefer to bring in an outsider in whom they have *confianza*. By importing talent they avoid jealousies among those who would have been neglected had an internal candidate been chosen. The aspirant assists his case when he takes advantage of personal links with politically influential actors, such as an uncle who is an army general or Supreme Court justice. Many persons have sought to build up these relationships through marriage and social contact, and those who do not do so suffer the consequences. "Persons at the middle level tend to depend on their technical skills for promotion. Maybe that's why they remain at the middle level."[33]

The Velasco regime assumed that the appointment of military men to important posts furthered its control over the public sector. Table 6 shows that in mid-1975, all ministers were military men, as were 6 of 14 vice-ministers, 33 of 48 sectoral advisers, 30 of 91 major agency heads, and the presidents of 16 of 38 state industries. Military men also were the directors of the six major independent bodies with coordinating or executing tasks in the society (COAP, INP, SINAMOS, ORDEZA, the National Intelligence Service, and ONIT).[34] Ministries and important agencies in turn were distributed among the three branches of the armed services, with the army's domain including nine nondefense ministries and five of these six independent bodies.

33. Interview no. 41.
34. COAP coordinated the president's staffwork and the regime's legislative process; ORDEZA was the earthquake relief agency; ONIT was the office that dealt with Andean economic integration.

Table 6. Military vs. civilian control of the bureaucracy, mid-1975

| Indicator of control[a] | Civilian | Military |
|---|---|---|
| Minister | 0 | 14 |
| Vice-minister | 8 | 6 |
| Ministerial adviser[b] | 15 | 33 |
| Head of major centralized agency | 61 | 30 |
| Head of state industry | 22 | 16 |
| Percent of investment | 42% | 58% |
| Head of SINAMOS zone | 2 | 9 |
| COAP staff | 0 | 16 |

[a] Figures summarize data from the 14 core civilian ministries and their dependencies. They do not include the ministries of War, Aeronautics, and the Navy.
[b] Figures unavailable for the ministries of Housing and Commerce.
SOURCE: Personnel sheets issued by individual ministries.

By no means, however, was the civilian bureaucracy simply an ersatz military machine. In actual numbers, military officers represented less than 0.1 percent (one-tenth of 1 percent) of the 450,000 persons employed by the Peruvian public sector.[35]

What was the degree of overlap between military promotion and performance in the civilian bureaucracy? Practically all officers were guaranteed some administrative experience in the *military* ministries. In the army, for example, all officers (except doctors) graduated from the Chorrillos War College (Centro de Instrucción Militar del Perú) and, after reaching the rank of captain, eventually had to fulfill administrative functions in the Ministry of War (Estado Mayor). At each stage of their careers—major, commander, colonel, and general—officers were expected to spend two or three years in a regional or the national Estado Mayor, or approximately one-fourth of their thirty-five-year tenure. Classroom achievement, troop leadership, and performance in administrative functions each played

35. Civilians again began to be appointed to ministerial posts after the Morales Bermúdez coup. We estimate that approximately 400 military officers held decision-making posts in the civilian bureaucracy at any one time during the Velasco and Morales Bermúdez regimes. Luigi Einaudi reports that there are about 5,000 officers in the Peruvian armed forces (3,500 in the army), in "U.S. Relations with the Peruvian Military," in *United States Foreign Policy and Peru*, ed. Daniel Sharp (Austin: University of Texas Press, 1974), pp. 15–56.

a part in the individual candidate's promotion. Though an officer might advance with high points in academic endeavors and
organizational skills, he would not ascend to the rank of general on those qualities alone. In the normal course of events,
promotion evaluators gave the nod to officers with proven
capacity in the field, where their ability to plan, act, and control
was immediately evident in the discipline and *esprit de corps*
of the troops.[36]

While top-quality performance of an aspiring officer in the
field was more important for his promotion than his administrative competence in one of the defense ministries, relevant
experience in the *civilian* bureaucracy *was* helpful for promotion. This fact was due to the inevitable intermeshing of national politics with military promotion when the military regime was in power. First, the regime was not oblivious of the
symbolic effect of military promotions at the highest level of
government. The brigadier general with ministerial rank who
was made general of division was riding high less because of
his peacetime military accomplishments than because his
political performance was satisfying to the regime. At times the
government found it necessary to expedite the promotion (or
the forced retirement) of some generals in order to reaffirm
publicly its attitude toward certain policies. From the military
point of view, these considerations were extraneous to the traditional role of the armed forces but necessary in light of their
mission in national reconstruction and development. Ministers, agency heads, and presidents of state industries were
viewed more as political than military appointments and nontraditional promotion criteria for active officers were accepted.[37]

A more delicate matter pertained to promotion criteria for the

36. Carlos A. Astiz and José Z. García, in "The Peruvian Military: Achievement, Orientation, Training, and Political Tendencies," *Western Political
Quarterly* 25:4 (December 1972), 667–85, argue that "achievement" is not a
good predictor of promotion. We contest their belief that achievement can be
measured only on the basis of academic performance, since discipline and
leadership are criteria just as important, if not more so, in military circles. See,
for example, Thomas D. Morris, "Merit Principles in Military Officer Personnel
Administration," *Public Administration Review* 35:5 (September/October
1974), 445–50.
37. Interview nos. 46 and 47.

multitude of military advisers at the right hands of the ministers and agency heads. These junior officers obtained their positions not necessarily because of their objective qualifications, but because of the luck of the draw (that is, they were well known to the senior officer, who in this case turned out to be the minister or head of the state enterprise). The general who was partially responsible for the direction of government, at the command of numerous financial and organizational resources, and recognized by the informed public was able to lobby for his protégés more successfully than his counterpart of equal rank stationed at a jungle outpost near Tingo María. During the Velasco regime, this practice caused increasing dissension in the ranks.

The appointment of military officers to almost all crucial bureaucratic posts did not transform the bureaucracy into a centralized, disciplined command network, and the inconsistencies between the military and administrative hierarchies occasionally upset formal policy-making processes. Relationships between important public agencies and the minister often depended on whether the minister truly outranked all of his administrative underlings, be they retired or active military personnel. (Rank is determined by seniority as well as by grade.) If he did not, or if one of his civilian executives had a special relationship with another military officer with undisputed ascendency, the minister's possibilities for controlling and monitoring his sector were attenuated. Senior officers in the Ministry of War preferred not to get involved in these nonmilitary matters. "Conflicts of hierarchy in the civilian bureaucracy are political questions, not discussed in the Ministry of War, and resolved in the upper levels of government with the president, the ministers, and other important officers in policy-making posts."[38]

In summary, recruitment and promotion patterns during the military regime were mixed. At the lower levels, clientelistic considerations predominated, and the historical absorption by bureaucracy of lower-class elements unemployable in the economy as a whole lent stability to the political system, such

38. Interview no. 47.

as one might expect in a corporatist system. The competition for such favors and the obligations they entailed helped to undermine the creation of "class consciousness," justifying the complaints of Marxist critics. Simultaneously, Peruvian technocrats were able to sell their services to the highest bidder, somewhat as in a free-enterprise market. Usually they won their positions and salaries because of technical skills and experience, although clientelism also played a part in individual cases. At the upper levels, commitment to the goals of the sector or regime, plus technical competence, were predominant influences in both civilian and military appointments, together with personal loyalty, especially in the case of junior military officers. These criteria for appointment and advancement were suggestive of a centralist approach to personnel management.

## Peruvian Policy Making

Between 1968 and 1977, Peruvian governments passed more than four thousand laws. Major policy initiatives under Velasco were in the spheres of foreign affairs, agriculture, economic growth, industrialization, natural resources (including fisheries and forests), the mass media, and property. Some of these initiatives overlapped and all were relatively specific in terms of implementing legislation. Under Morales Bermúdez, important decrees related to devaluation, foreign policy, economic measures pertaining to wages and prices, a restructured industrial community, and military hardware purchases and reorganization.[39] Despite this multitude of potential case studies, social scientists have conducted little research into the policy-making process, or on the individuals of various institutional bases who wielded the greatest influence on policy formulation within these regimes. Our findings are that policy making was generally more centralized under Velasco than under Morales Bermúdez.

The principal policy-making actors were the members of the President's Advisory Committee (Comité de Asesoramiento de

39. Charles T. Goodsell summarizes important features of the Velasco regime in "That Confounding Revolution in Peru," *Current History* 68:20 (January 1975), 20–23.

la Presidencia, or COAP), the sectoral ministries within their own domains, ministries advising on policies in other sectors, and "miscellaneous individuals." COAP was made up of about sixteen middle-level officers (colonels, captains, and below) and acted as the president's personal staff on policy-related matters. Each officer specialized in one sector of state activity. While some of the most fundamental policies affected the ministries of Agriculture (agrarian reform) and Industry (industrial community, nationalization of private property and the like), the ministry with the greatest influence on policies originating elsewhere was Economy and Finance (because of the tax, budgetary, and foreign currency implications of each). "Miscellaneous individuals" are those persons and groups occasionally consulted by COAP or the ministries because of their specialized expertise (civilian economists, lawyers, agronomists, anthropologists) or political power. Under Velasco political groups that often received advance word of pending legislation were Communist Party–led labor unions or government-created interest groups. Under Morales Bermúdez, members of the industrial bourgeoisie and the international financial community were frequently included in policy-making discussions. Cabinet sessions were used to debate controversial policy or explain routine initiatives on the verge of being adopted.

The regimes, considered together, displayed four policy-making patterns. First, policy decisions originated in COAP, on instructions from the president and his closest advisers, and, after a cabinet session, the legislation was promulgated as a *fait accompli*. This procedure was used extensively by Velasco but not by Morales Bermúdez. Examples include the 1969 press law, the 1968 administration law, and the 1969 agrarian reform law. The affected publics were not privy to the deliberations on any of these laws and were virtually obliged to acquiesce.

Second, policy suggestions originated in the ministries and were submitted to COAP and the president for approval, without consultation with representatives of other governmental and nongovernmental jurisdictions. Examples were the laws governing currency and the banks, devaluation, the 1974 press expropriation, and urban land reform, and laws in the industrial sector. Again, Velasco was more likely than Morales Bermúdez to use this more restricted policy-making procedure.

Third, initial drafts originated in the ministries and then were circulated by COAP to other governmental agencies and to preselected individuals for comments before the final legislation was formulated. This "coordination" procedure, described in Directive 3 of 1969, was recognized as the modal policy-making form because the vast majority of laws abided by it. Most of the laws passed under Velasco were of little import, however, except for those instituting industrial communities, the nationalization of the fishing industry, and SINAMOS.

Fourth, "coordination" could also involve submitting the measure to broader public or private scrutiny. Under Velasco, concerned citizens sent written observations to the local press (which published some of them) in the cases of the laws governing jungle native communities and social property. The educational reform at one point involved a constituent assembly of the educational sector which was supposed to put the finishing touches on the law. Morales Bermúdez took account of the expressed interests of influential actors in both the local and the international economic scenes (such as industrialists, the World Bank, and the International Monetary Fund) in the specifics of several of his policy initiatives. Morales Bermúdez consistently followed this open approach (which also involved closer collaboration with various elements of the armed forces than had been the case under Velasco), while Velasco at the beginning operated in relative secrecy, with little input beyond his immediate entourage.

The thrust and content of Velasco's policies emerged from a diagnosis of Peru's socioeconomic problems and its world position. The analysis, molded by civilian intellectuals influenced by international currents of thought, was picked up by the military in the 1960s. The underlying principles were that Peru's underdevelopment stemmed from disproportionate economic and political power in the hands of the upper class (*la oligarquía*), lack of national integration (especially of the Indian masses), a weak state, and international economic dependence, most notably on the United States. These views permeated the higher levels of the army, informally through social and professional contacts with civilian elites and formally through a program of courses at the Center for Higher Military Studies, the CAEM. It was solidified by the military's 1965 experience in fighting guerrillas, and by its acceptance of the thesis, which gained currency during the Indochinese War, that internal security was precarious as long as the country was underdeveloped.[40] In 1974 the regime published the Plan Inca, which it claimed had been prepared, circulated, and agreed upon by a select group of officers before they roused President Belaúnde from his bed in October 3, 1968, and placed him on an airplane to Buenos Aires. The Plan Inca contained broad outlines of the regime's action program, including almost all of the major policies listed above.

The regime's ideological bias toward a strong state and its apparent commitment to reform Peru's class structure were suitable preconditions for centralized policy making. Secrecy and political surprises were endemic in the early years of the Velasco regime, when its hegemony was unassailable and it could operate with considerable autonomy, without regard to the preferences of powerful economic actors at home and abroad. If the Velasco groups knew fairly well in advance what it wanted accomplished, why did it bother at all with "coordination" of any of its main legislation? The answer is that it attempted to use the policy-making process as a means of perfecting the laws and unifying military and civilian support for its program. Over time the policy-making style moved perceptibly from one of secrecy toward fuller public debate. The regime showed a trend toward airing its structural reforms more and more widely before instituting them, a pattern that appeared to be correlated with a curve of declining control and influence.

When the Velasco group was sufficiently confident about the passivity of potential opposition and quick action was essential, policy was decided in the inner circles of government and implemented rapidly. When legislative initiatives required confidentiality and high technical expertise and were the ex-

40. Alfred C. Stepan discusses at length the maturation of the military's outlook in *State and Society* (Princeton: Princeton University Press, 1978).

clusive domain of one ministry, they were drafted in the sector and approved by the president on the advice of COAP. The regime followed Directive 3 when potential opposition was of such magnitude that countervailing opinions had to be completely aired, or when the law required collaboration of a number of ministries or groups for its implementation. By ostensibly sharing authority, the directive allowed the regime to co-opt both bureaucratic representatives and civilian elements whose support (or neutrality) was needed to enable the government to proceed with its plans.

Table 7 lists in chronological order fifteen major reforms of Velasco and six reforms of Morales Bermúdez and indicates the process used to draw them up, from highly centralized to sectoral review and "coordination" with full public debate. As the Velasco government aged but failed to generate broad popular support for its policies, it opened its decision-making style to a wider circle of actors outside of the core coalition. The inconsistency in this general pattern is that, especially in the last months of his tenure, Velasco tried to compensate for his weakening position through the persecution of his opponents, in acts decided behind closed doors and often unknown even to other members of the core coalition.

Under Morales Bermúdez, state ideology shifted considerably in a liberal direction, and no major policies were drafted without regard for the interests of powerful national and international actors. The high autonomy and lower power that under Velasco proved increasingly problematic was followed by low autonomy and low power under Morales Bermúdez, a more "natural" congruence. The latter government responded to multiple pressures in its exchange rate and its economic, industrial, property, labor, and foreign policies, and justified its consensual approach as one representing national interests. The inevitable result was that specific policies favored the groups helping to formulate them and many of the benefits enjoyed by nonhegemonic elements under Velasco evaporated. The trend was reflected eventually in the military's decision to return to representative government, announced in the Plan Tupac Amarú.

Table 7. Major policies pursued under Velasco and Morales Bermúdez, by means of formulation

| Means of formulation | Velasco | | | | | | | | | | | | | | | Morales Bermúdez | | | | | |
|---|---|---|---|---|---|---|---|---|---|---|---|---|---|---|---|---|---|---|---|---|---|
| | Foreign policy | Administrative reform | Press and mass media | Agrarian reform | Currency and banks | General industries | Industrial communities | SINAMOS | Education | Fishing nationalization | Social property | Press expropriation | Devaluation | Jungle native communities | Urban land reform | Devaluation | Foreign policy | Social property | Industrial policies | Labor policies | Plan Tupac Amaru |
| President and advisers | X | X | X | X | | | | | | | | X | | | | | X | | | | |
| Ministry and COAP | | | | | X | X | | X | X | | | | X | X | X | X | X | | | | |
| "Coordination" | | | | | | | X | | | X | X | | | | | | | X | X | X | X |
| "Coordination" and private-sector input | | | | | | | | | | | X | | | | | | | | | | |

92

# Conclusions

Ideology, political system, and bureaucratic behavior are dynamically interrelated. During the period of social upheaval in Peru after 1968, the links between ideology and political system and between political system and bureaucratic behavior were more discernible than those directly between ideology and administration, in part because a new Peruvian political system was never consolidated. The most accurate explanation of the administrative practices described here is based on variable power rather than on the confrontation of opposing political philosophies. Personnel, planning, and policy-making patterns were manifestations of the goals of relevant individuals and organizational actors, the resources at their disposal, and constraints posed by elements in their working environments. Under the Peruvian military regime personnel practices in regard to unskilled jobs were clientelistic; upper-level positions were filled on the basis of the candidates' commitment to regime objectives; and, in the hiring of professionals, technical and experience criteria usually prevailed. The military government made an effort to improve coordination by streamlining the functions of the various ministries. Likewise, it strengthened the authority of the National Planning Institute to enforce intersectoral coordination, especially with respect to public investment. Much coordination in the Peruvian public sector, however, took place through a process of mutual adjustment among various public and private actors, not just central planners and ministerial authorities. The regime's policy-making style varied according to its relative immunity to the pressures of important economic and social classes.

The relationship between ideology and administration is clear in two situations. The first occurs when a political system is shaped by the interests of dominant classes that refer to a chosen philosophy in articulating and legitimizing governing bodies. These institutions over time reward bureaucratic behavior that strengthens the system and reaffirms the ideology. In such circumstances, the overall system is well integrated and functions much like one of the representative types introduced at the beginning of this chapter. Clearly this was not the case in Peru during the period studied.

The role of ideology is also manifest when revolutionary leadership faced with a fragmented society makes use of a political philosophy to guide and restructure social relationships. In this case, the easiest task for leadership is to announce and reiterate the preferred ideology to the community at large. Analysts must be careful not to confuse the utterances of political leaders with the way the society usually operates.[41] A serious challenge for the regime is to conform institutional relationships to the ideological mold. An even more difficult assignment is to make bureaucratic behavior functional for the operation of the system and supportive of the professed ideology. Policy-making styles are most sensitive to changes in public philosophy and institutional relations, while personnel practices are most resistant.

Peru under military rule manifested this second series of characteristics. After Velasco had assumed power, the initial objectives of his regime were to gain control of the state and make it predominant in Peruvian society. Strong centralist trends were in evidence from 1969 to 1972 and they had an impact on structural reform and the content of policy. When the Velasco group became concerned about popular support, corporatism characterized the polity and new organizations were premised on the values of harmony and integration. Because of other pressing concerns, however, the regime attempted only halfheartedly to make administrative behavior throughout the public sector conform to centralist or corporatist principles.[42] With the arrival of the Morales Bermúdez regime, a more pluralistic governing style emerged, and the

---

41. Linn A. Hammergren astutely points out that jumping to conclusions after reading political speeches is a common failing of students of corporatism. See "Corporatism in Latin American Politics: A Reexamination of the 'Unique' Tradition," *Comparative Politics* 9:4 (July 1977), 443–61.

42. Chapter 4, on the agrarian courts, traces an administrative experiment in the centralist mode. In 1974, INAP, the administrative reform agency, devised an imaginative proposal to recast municipal governments along corporatist principles, but by the time the draft project was complete, the Velasco government was no longer in a position to execute it. See also Victor Neyra, *Elementos de administración participante* (Lima: Centro SINAMOS, 1974).

country set its sights on returning to electoral democracy. This rapid sequence of official philosophies, each of which left its mark on the bureaucracy, helps to explain the lack of regularity in Peruvian administrative practices.

These global trends were evident in the agricultural sector. Chapter 2 shows how the Velasco government gradually opened up policy making related to land reform as it lost its initial momentum and faced greater challenges.

# Agrarian Policy Making

During 1969 and 1970, the government was able to promulgate
and execute agricultural legislation without taking direct account of the preferences of the affected parties. Successes depended on threats of force rather than on voluntary compliance
with legal dictums. Over time the government incorporated
more opinions into agrarian policy making, and relied on material rewards and persuasion to induce compliance. The
policy-making style responded to the power and unity of the
government coalition relative to its opponents in the society at
large.

## The Background

The Peruvian agrarian reform was facilitated by the existence of
a committed minority, with a relatively well-developed action
plan, which previously had lacked the means for carrying out
its preferences. The ideas of such exponents of reform usually
dissipate when opportunities for execution are remote. In Peru,
the plan's implementation was abetted by an overlap in the past
professional and life histories of advisers in the Ministry of

Agriculture and members of the military coalition. These persons faced and eventually overcame several of the trade-offs inherent in any comprehensive agrarian reform measure.

## The Policy Makers

Among the most important policy makers were Benjamín Samanez, director of the Agrarian Reform Agency in the post-1969 period; Guillermo Figallo, president of the Agrarian Court System; Pedro Alibert, adviser to the Agriculture Ministry during the Velasco regime; Eduardo Morán, vice-minister of agriculture; General Leonidas Rodríguez Figueroa, a principal figure in the government's core coalition; and Carlos Delgado and Generals Jorge Barandiarán, Enrique Valdez, Arturo Valdez, and Luis Barandiarán, all members of the support coalition. Some of these persons, such as Figallo, Samanez, and Alibert, participated continuously in formulating or advising on agricultural policy from the 1950s on. Others, such as Morán, Generals Leonidas Rodríguez and Arturo Valdez, and President Velasco himself, intervened at specific instances with new ideas, technical skills, or political power after 1968. In citing these names, we do not intend to attribute historical outcomes to the decisive behavior of a few individuals. Yet had some of these persons not risked defeat earlier over matters of principle, the reform would not have emerged in the form it did.

One of the earliest participants in agrarian policy debates was a sympathizer of the Christian Democratic party. Pedro Alibert worked as a staff lawyer to the Beltrán Commission and helped to prepare the draft law submitted to Congress by President Manuel Prado Ugartech. Later, under the 1963 military junta, he helped to draw up "Twenty Criteria for Agrarian Reform" and Decree Law 14,444, the measure that distributed land in La Convención Valley. Belaúnde appointed him to the post of director general of expropriation, where he stretched the letter of Law 15,037 to its limits. When he refused to sanction force to protect expropriated land from peasant invasion, Belaúnde transferred him to a government research center, where he proselytized young ministry functionaries in favor of a more radical reform.[1] He and Minister Enrique Torres Llosa were sacked after Torres issued an expropriation decree for the large, U.S.-owned Cerro de Pasco pasturelands without presidential approval. Alibert later emerged as a high-level adviser to the Agriculture Ministry under the Velasco military regime.

Benjamín Samanez headed the agrarian zone office responsible for La Convención Valley during most of Belaúnde's presidency. A man of modest family origins, he sympathized with the complaints of Hugo Blanco's followers and felt divided loyalties in confronting their demands. At the time, he worked closely with the then colonel Leonidas Rodríguez, a fellow native of Cuzco assigned to the local military zone. After the coup, Samanez, who was of leftist persuasion but not an activist in any political party, was appointed director general of agrarian reform and later promoted to vice-minister of agriculture.

The lawyer Guillermo Figallo was born in Piura, as was President Velasco. His roots in agriculture sprang from his mother's side of the family: his maternal grandmother was a *comunera* (full member of an Indian community). Both his paternal grandfather and great-grandfather were lawyers, and young Figallo's studies at San Marcos University leaned toward law and the land. His 1946 jurisprudence thesis—on agrarian cooperatives—was well ahead of its time.[2] Figallo later joined the Social Progressive Movement, and after Belaúnde's election he worked in the National Agrarian Council, gaining stature as an accomplished agrarian legal expert.[3] Figallo spent the first

1. Young technicians passing through Alibert's center had ample opportunity to discuss the expropriation of the Fundo Algolán, one of the most blatant failures under Belaúnde's administration. This large sheep hacienda, surrounded by indigenous communities in the high sierra, was operating relatively efficiently when it was purchased by the Agrarian Reform Agency, soon after the passing of Law 15,037. The hacienda was divided into three parts, one for the workers and two for nearby indigenous communities. Conflicts erupted, land invasions and parceling occurred, and soon almost all of the 207,000 hectares had been fragmented into family-sized pastures inappropriate for efficient large-scale herding.

2. For Figallo's biographical data, see *La Prensa*, August 23, 1967, p. 3.

3. The National Agrarian Council was supposed to be the central committee of Belaúnde's land reform. Comprised of representatives of several public agencies and private institutions, it directed the agrarian reform process, rec-

six years of the military government as president of the new Fuero Privativo Agrario (the Agrarian Court System). Though not directly involved in day-to-day operations of the agrarian reform, he had a hand in drafting all major legal dictums affecting the agrarian sector from the first law onward.

These men were known to the military officers who executed the coup of October 3, 1968. Samanez and Leonidas Rodríguez both came from Cuzco and shared in the traumas of the Convención rebellion. Figallo was a close acquaintance of Rodríguez's and had family ties with Velasco Alvarado. Colonel Enrique Gallegos, another cuzqueño, had a command post in the 1965 antiguerilla campaign, maintained contact afterward with civilians interested in agrarian reform, and became minister of agriculture in 1974. Three of these policy makers were lifelong acquaintances from the same city, and came to be known as the Chiclayo Friendship Group. Carlos Delgado (later to become the top-ranked civilian in SINAMOS), air force general Luis Barandiarán Pagador (later minister of commerce), and his brother Jorge (army general and military government's second minister of agriculture) contributed to the final text of D.L. 17,716. Figallo, Samanez, and Alibert had made their views known in social gatherings and academic forums attended by both military and civilians. After 1968 these civilians used their contacts with the core army officers to lobby for a comprehensive agrarian reform.

### Technical and Social-Class Factors

An inadequate organizational structure, untrained personnel, an unfavorable land/person ratio (see Table 8), and the difficulty in determining beneficiaries were constraints that the agrarian policy makers faced. The ministry's organizational chart under Belaúnde contained several autonomous agencies operating under an ambiguous chain of command.[4] Landown-

---

ommended changes in the law, and supervised the activities of the National Office for Agrarian Reform. Because the council met but once a month, had a very small staff, and gave voice and vote to persons with interests adversely affected by the stated intentions of the reform, it was not an effective agency.

4. For a description of the agrarian bureaucracy under Belaúnde, see Ernst R. DeProspo, "The Administration of the Peruvian Land Reform Program," Ph.D. dissertation, Pennsylvania State University, 1967.

Table 8. Agricultural land per person in eight Latin American countries, c. 1970 (in hectares)

| Land/person ratio | Peru | Colombia | Brazil | Chile | Ecuador | Mexico | Bolivia | Argentina |
|---|---|---|---|---|---|---|---|---|
| Arable land/person ratio (national population) | 0.19 | 0.17 | 0.28 | 0.49 | 0.50 | 0.53 | 0.59 | 1.02 |
| Pastureland/person ratio (national population) | 2.14 | 0.81 | 1.15 | 1.14 | 0.39 | 1.44 | 5.90 | 6.20 |
| Arable land/person ratio (rural population) | 0.39 | 0.43 | 0.63 | 2.03 | 0.80 | 1.23 | 0.87 | 3.71 |
| Pastureland/person ratio (rural population) | 4.40 | 2.04 | 2.61 | 4.74 | 0.62 | 3.49 | 8.60 | 20.65 |

Source: Derived from United Nations Food and Agricultural Organization, *Production Yearbook* (Rome: FAO, 1971–72); United Nations, *Demographic Yearbook* (New York: Department of Economic and Social Affairs, Statistical Office, 1970–71).

ers had been able to exacerbate coordination problems inherent in the system and usually delayed expropriation indefinitely. Under Velasco these autonomous agencies were reorganized under a centralized ministry, and the Agrarian Reform Agency became the focal point of activity.[5] The Velasco agrarian reform law made expropriation an administrative rather than a judicial procedure, and coordination improved.

A new organizational doctrine helped to compensate for the past lethargy of some agrarian bureaucrats. Under Belaúnde, middle-level bureaucrats realized that lax enforcement of the law would not jeopardize their careers. Under Velasco, the impetus in favor of reform, especially after 1970, changed the outlook of many functionaries, who cooperated fully with the effort. Those who did not were dismissed. For many field posts, the government recruited recent university graduates in the social sciences and other professionals who favored radical reform. Conservative elements in the ministry were thus outflanked and the expropriational zeal of some of the new recruits proved to be more of an administrative and political problem than bureaucratic foot-dragging.

Peru's 1,285,220 square kilometers of territory include only about 30 million hectares of arable land (23.3 percent of the total). In 1969, 3.7 percent (1.1 million hectares) of this land was irrigated, 10 percent (3 million hectares) was cultivated, and about 90 percent (27.1 million hectares) was in pastures.[6] Approximately 11 percent of arable land was owned by the indigenous communities.[7] In 1969 the Ministry of Agriculture calculated that 8.8 million hectares were eligible for reform as being inefficiently exploited, under absentee ownership, or too large.[8] Policy makers felt that perfectly equal distribution

5. Douglas E. Horton discusses the modifications in the agrarian bureaucracy in *Land Reform and Reform Enterprises in Peru* (Madison, Wis.: Land Tenure Center, 1974), pp. 53–57.

6. CIDA, *Tenencia de la tierra y desarrollo socio-económico del sector agrícola: Perú* (Washington, D.C.: Pan American Union, 1966), chap. 1. Because of deficiencies in past agricultural censuses, these figures are probably overestimated but do represent the information available to policy makers at the time.

7. Horton, *Land Reform*, p. 26.

8. Wayne R. Ringlien, "Some Economic and Institutional Results of the Agrarian Reform in Peru," *Land Tenure Center Newsletter* 38 (October–December 1972), 7.

among rural families would not be feasible because there was not enough land to go around. Eventually, new lands would need to be brought into production via irrigation and colonization projects, while some spillover of population into the cities would take place. Meanwhile, it was necessary to classify rural producers and determine how to distribute land among them.

The main rural actors were owners, renters, permanent workers, landless peasants, campesino communities, and subclasses of each category.[9] The owners included (1) latifundistas whose properties ranged from large to huge, (2) owners of "middle-sized" farms of 15 to 150 hectares on the coast, and (3) minifundistas on plots providing a livelihood at subsistence level or below. As described in the Introduction, the renters worked under any one of a score of social relations of production and were widely differentiated in terms of wealth and life opportunities. The distinctions among permanent workers were blurred by their common membership in farm unions. The landless peasants, either poor members of campesino communities or children of minifundistas, were a volatile force in the countryside but relatively unorganized in 1968. Finally, the campesino communities were treated as integrated units encompassing their total membership. The government did not intervene in their internal affairs even though most community property was cultivated privately, some members were the equivalent of absentee owners, and land was unequally distributed. The communities were brought into the agrarian reform via the SAIS (Agrarian Social Interest Society), an innovative form of cooperative organization to be discussed in Chapter 7. The government had difficulty assigning individuals to categories because peasants often qualified under the criteria of several and presented themselves as members of classes most likely to benefit from the reform.

Policy makers were torn between a short-term reform em-

9. Solon Barraclough estimates that in 1961, 1,124,500 rural families were divided into the following socioeconomic categories: operators of large-scale estates (0.9 percent), operators of medium-sized estates (2.1), administrators of large and medium-sized estates (1.0), operators of family-sized small holdings (7.6), operators of sub-family-sized small holdings (61.7), and landless workers (26.7, of whom some 17.8 percent were renters and 8.9 percent wage laborers). See "Agricultural Policy and Land Reform," *Journal of Political Economy* 78:4 (July–August 1970), 920; also Horton *Land Reform,* p. 22.

phasizing productivity and one emphasizing redistribution, or some mixture of both. A concern with productivity would extend the law's benefits to efficiently managed, large-scale operations, and would favor owners of modernized plantations, middle-sized farmers, and more established renters. A policy of redistribution would accrue to the advantage of permanent workers, peasant communities, poorer renters, and landless peasants. The choices involved in allocating rewards and sanctions to these groups were at the heart of the policy-making process. Our analysis of the drafting of D.L. 17,716 shows that docisivenoss at a critical point permitted civilian functionarios to execute an administrative coup, neutralize the productivity bias of the National Agrarian Society, and help some military men to substantiate their revolutionary predilections. The second case, the parceling controversy, combined the initial naiveté of policy makers, the protest of permanent workers, and the timely support of President Velasco to set the agrarian reform on a firm course. Third, agrarian policy makers achieved their objective of reducing the size of the largest individual farming unit permitted in Peru from 150 to 50 hectares. This issue aroused the most dangerous threat to land distribution in Peru, and required the military regime to engage in a delicate balancing act to keep its support coalition intact.

## The Velasco Agrarian Reform: Decree Law 17,716

Of the reforms undertaken by the Peruvian military government, the agrarian measure is generally considered to be the most significant. Despite the law's scope and significance, little is known of its genesis and no study has analyzed D.L. 17,716 as a policy-making event. Its drafting was conducted in almost total secrecy, and few people even in the military knew the identity of its authors. This section has been prepared on the basis of extensive interviews with many of the principal participants.

### The Benavides Draft

On October 3, 1968, Velasco telephoned General José Benavides, commander of the 5th Military Region in Iquitos, to inform him that the armed forces had deposed Belaúnde, and to ask for the support of his military region. Benavides was instructed to come to Lima to discuss with other top officers the formation of a new government. Benavides's appointment as minister of agriculture reflected the regime's desire to gain broad army support for the coup instigated by the officers in Velasco's entourage. Benavides was qualified for a ministerial post by his command of army, navy, and air force officers in the jungle region and his status as the son of a former president (and a relative of former president Belaúnde) and as one of the highest ranking army officers. Benavides had had no previous agricultural experience but he did have friends and relatives who were property owners or engaged in agribusiness.

In November 1968 Minister Benavides took the first steps toward fulfilling the regime's public promise of replacing Belaúnde's agrarian reform law. He appointed a commission to prepare a draft of the new law for submission to the Council of Ministers. The commission was made up of government functionaries and technocrats from the private sector whom the minister knew and trusted. Among its members were Juan Bazo of the Banco Agropecuario; Jacoa Sender, the young rector of La Molina Agricultural University; Agustín Merea, vice-minister of agriculture and an agronomist specializing in irrigation; Benjamín Samanez; and Guillermo Figallo. In commission meetings, the technocrats argued that the creation of farms averaging 150 hectares on the coast would enable owners to achieve economies of scale with the use of tractors. They also felt that a new water code was as important as the agrarian reform law and spent much time debating its regulations. Samanez and Figallo took more radical positions than the others on most issues, and until April 1969 fought their battles isolated from potential allies in civilian and military circles.

Despite his family background and social contacts, Benavides attempted to strike a fair balance both in his decisions as agriculture minister and in the final piece of recommended legislation. He carried out the expropriation of the Cerro de Pasco landholdings (which had been pending since Torres Llosa's dismissal) even though the manager of the company, Alberto Benavides, was his cousin. His approach in the commission was to gather opinions and suggestions from all sides (including the SNA, which he visited to explain, in general terms, the import of the law) in order to arrive at draft legislation that represented the mainstream of opinion.

Though he leaned toward the leftist position of Samanez and Figallo in wording many of the clauses, his arbitration did not improve the progressives' position, because the law became a series of compromises. The commission unanimously agreed that church and military lands would be expropriated almost in their entirety, but Figallo and Samanez could not persuade other commission members to favor redistribution over productivity. They discussed their objections with the minister, but since Benavides operated on the basis of majority vote, he did not interfere on major issues, including the decision not to expropriate the agroindustrial sugar plantations. At that point Samanez and Figallo were disillusioned and on the verge of withdrawing from the proceedings.

They made a final attempt to express their views to the highest level of government just before the draft law was to be presented to the Council of Ministers. At this time President Velasco's closest advisers were in the COAP, including General José Graham and Colonels Leonidas Rodríguez, Arturo Valdez, Jorge Fernández Maldonado, Pedro Richter, and Aníbal Mesa Cuadra (all of whom would later become generals). Figallo and Samanez requested an appointment with Rodríguez and expressed their dissatisfaction with the Benavides draft. Rodríguez said, "Let's bring Graham in on this." The two civilians succeeded in convincing both Rodríguez and Graham that the Benavides law did not represent a commitment to profound agrarian reform. Not only was it a continuation of the previous law, in some clauses it was a step backward. The four men then planned a scenario leading to the cancellation of the Benavides draft and the establishment of a mandate to begin anew, but in a way that would not lead to a polarization in the cabinet. The formula was to challenge the assumptions of the Benavides draft in the Council of Ministers, to argue the need for a more extensive piece of legislation, and to rewrite the law under the auspices of the COAP, where a more radical position would predominate.

After President Velasco agreed to the plan, the COAP circulated the Benavides draft to the various cabinet ministers in preparation for the Council of Ministers meeting. Seeking additional outside opinion, it invited Eduardo Morán, a Christian Democrat engineer working at the INP, to discuss the matter with them at the presidential palace. Morán brought with him a memorandum outlining the economic and political preconditions for a successful agrarian reform which he had used for teaching purposes at San Marcos University. Navy Captain Aurelio Masías, Arturo Valdez, and Leonidas Rodríguez were pleased with these ideas, and Masías and Morán worked late on the eve of the Council of Ministers meeting to write a summary statement to be approved privately by the president and read aloud by Rodríguez. At the council meeting, Vice-Minister Merea was responsible for arguing the case for the Benavides draft. While Figallo and Samanez looked on in disagreement, he eulogized the moderate legislation being proposed. One of the questions asked afterward was how the law would affect the minifundio; in his lengthy answer, Merea stated that irrigation would solve the problem of small holdings. The progressive civilians waited for the blow to fall.

The tone of the council meeting changed dramatically. In smart military manner, Colonel Rodríguez asked for the floor. Graham barked out, "The chair recognizes Colonel Rodríguez." Rodríguez began reading the summary statement that Masías and Morán had drafted earlier, characterizing the projected law as conservative and benefiting large landowners. During the riposte Benavides was visibly shaken but did not comment. After Rodríguez finished, Graham argued that a law as important as agrarian reform could not be drafted in just one ministry but should be coordinated with activities in other sectors. He proposed that a special committee be formed in the COAP to write a new law, and with the support of President Velasco, this recommendation was approved.

### The COAP Committee

The new drafting committee formed by the COAP was made up of Colonels Arturo Valdez and Leonidas Rodríguez, Captain Aurelio Masías, Eduardo Morán from the INP, and Figallo,

Samanez, and Merea from the Ministry of Agriculture. As a result of a cold and disapproving attitude toward Merea, plus the embarrassment of his earlier setback, he was rarely invited to attend the COAP meetings. Even though Benavides remained as agriculture minister for several more months, COAP succeeded in excluding the participation of traditional interests in the discussion, which was carried out in almost complete secrecy.

Near the beginning of June 1969 a cabinet crisis developed over food shortages, and the ministers of the interior and agriculture argued over prices and productivity. The verbal confrontation was a pretext designed to induce the resignation of Minister Benavides, who returned to the army on June 11.[10] His successor was General Jorge Barandiarán Pagador, then head of the military region of Puno, who brought with him as advisers his brother, General Luis Barandiarán Pagador, and Carlos Delgado, a sociologist working at the INP. Although Jorge Barandiarán reportedly arrived at his post hesitant to be a party to radicalism, his brother and Delgado were able to convince him of the need for far-reaching reform, including the expropriation of the efficient sugar plantations.

After June 11, 1969, the pace of work at the COAP increased. Throughout the meetings the approach had been to work on the basis of the best aspects of Law 15,037 and modifications to it proposed by the political parties in Congress at the twilight of the Belaúnde regime.[11] New ideas included a heavy emphasis on cooperatives and a particular system for assessing the value of, paying for, and servicing the land debt. Luis Barandiarán introduced a modification permitting the transfer of agrarian reform bonds into capital investment for new industrial projects. At the last minute Guillermo Figallo suggested the creation of the Agrarian Court System as a way of handling agrarian disputes. An important item of debate in the COAP meetings was the unexpropriable limit (or the largest permissible landholding under individual ownership). Samanez and Figallo

10. Velasco was known to have staged disputes between ministers at cabinet meetings to induce resignations (interview no. 52).

11. See Partidos Políticos AP-DC, UNO, APRA, y CCP, *Reforma agraria peruana: Cinco proyectos de ley* (Lima: Editorial Tesis, 1963).

had tried to reduce the ceiling from 150 to 50 hectares, but lost the argument when others maintained that 150 hectares was sufficient to wipe out the SNA. Moreover, the fixing of a lower limit might undermine support for the whole package when military men realized that they had relatives with medium-sized properties above 50 hectares.[12]

Leonidas Rodríguez, who helped to orient the team politically, maintained constant contact with President Velasco. Rodríguez assured the group that the law could be as revolutionary as necessary to get the job done. On June 20, 1969, the group received the order to have the final version of the law ready by June 23; afterward none of the drafters except Luis Barandiarán left the presidential palace. Because the government was still unsure of its support, he talked with Lima-based army officers to explain that the upcoming agrarian reform law was not a communist initiative but a nationalist reform.

The civilians in the COAP commission were barred from full participation in the Council of Ministers meeting. After putting the final touches to the draft, they prepared the ministers' rebuttals to possible objections in the meeting, which began at 3 P.M. on June 23 and lasted until 6 A.M. on June 24. Arturo Valdez was responsible for the general presentation and Luis Barandiarán explained the plan to convert agrarian bonds into

---

12. Thomas Carroll compares the Belaúnde and Velasco laws in "Land Reform in Peru," *AID Spring Review Country Paper* (Washington: Agency for International Development, 1970). See also John Strasma, "The United States and Agrarian Reform in Peru," in *United States Foreign Policy and Peru*, ed. Daniel Sharp (Austin: University of Texas Press, 1972), pp. 156–205. Whereas Belaúnde permitted the maximum size of private property along the coast to slide significantly above 150 hectares, the Velasco law adhered strictly to the 150-hectare ceiling. In the sierra, the 1969 limits on irrigated land went from 15 to 55 hectares (depending on the province) and limits on pastureland depended on the size needed to support 5,000 sheep. The two laws also allowed different compensation schedules. Whereas the Technical Body of Appraisers established values under Belaúnde, the hacendado's declaration of value for tax purposes was the principal measure of land value under Velasco. Cattle were compensated at market value and fixed assets at book value. The maximum cash payment for land under Belaúnde was about U.S. $7,500, and under Velasco about $2,200; for capital stock, unlimited under Belaúnde, and $22,000 under Velasco. The remainder of the payment in both cases was in bonds, 6 percent over eighteen years under Belaúnde, 6 percent over twenty years under Velasco.

industrial projects.[13] The civilians, kept on standby to treat other aspects of the law, remained in the presidential palace (where they watched cowboy movies). From time to time Arturo Valdez came into the room to say that things were going smoothly. Much of the cabinet discussion treated the same points that had caused debate inside the COAP. Late in the session, however, Housing Minister Vice-Admiral Luis Vargas Caballero complained that the law seemed to limit unduly the expansion of urbanization into rural areas. Verbal concessions were made on this point, which later caused Agriculture problems

The ministers had received a draft of the law only a few hours before the session, a procedure designed to keep the text of the law out of the hands of its enemies. Although it was stamped "Top secret," the SNA did obtain a copy and discussed the draft simultaneously with the ministers.[14] The SNA, however, did not count on the presence of government intelligence agents in its own meeting. Thus, word leaked back to the Council of Ministers that the SNA was planning to subvert the law and make it inoperable. The ministers immediately voted to make sabotage of the agrarian reform an offense subject to the military code of justice.

After President Velasco's address announcing the law to the

13. The possibility of transferring agrarian bonds into industrial development ceased when the regime decided that it would use government investment for industry. This change in policy helped to defuse leftist critics, who felt that the bond transfer policy would help to consolidate the rural oligarchy as an industrial renter class. Nonetheless, after the expropriations were almost completed, various peasant organizations took strong exception to the existence of the agrarian debt to the former landowners. Since cooperatives had to repay the government for the adjudicated value of their holdings (five year's grace period, twenty years to pay), they felt that they were recompensing the former exploiting class. The government responded unsympathetically because it felt that a debt burden would encourage the cooperatives to work harder, and the installment payments themselves would ease the government's internal deficit. The dispute dissipated with time. First, the total debt for most former haciendas was low because landowners had undervalued their properties before 1969 to reduce their tax burdens. Second, inflation considerably lowered the real value of the cooperatives' payments. For the opposite point of view, see Juan Quispe, "La deuda agraria: Un escollo para los reformistas," *Debate Socialista* 4 (November 1974), 2–26.

14. See the treatment of the commission's work in *Oiga*, June 27, 1969, p. 9.

country, Javier Silva Ruete, who had twice been minister of agriculture under Belaúnde, called to remind Morán that it was imperative to take over the sugar industries as soon as possible, or their current owners would sell sugar futures and divide the cash on hand. Silva, Morán, and Oscar Espinoza (a young professional at the INP) met to write a draft law covering the expropriation of the sugar industries. Since COAP members were physically exhausted from the past days' events, no one was at the presidential palace to meet them but Velasco Alvarado himself. He was swayed by the argument and called on Jorge Barandiarán to take immediate action. A day later army troops forcibly entered and occupied all sugar plantations.

## Conclusions

This first part of the agrarian reform saga underscores two conditions for rural transformation: an ideological commitment to comprehensive reform by policy advocates and access to power to execute their ideas. The collaboration of civilians and military had begun much earlier; the fact that radical military men were in government helped to shape the law that emerged. The secrecy surrounding the work in the COAP permitted the government to control more easily the law's initial impact. But the surprise of D.L. 17,716 was not in its clauses, many of which had been proposed previously by one or another political party; it was that these clauses were adopted by a military government, and that they were imposed with a dramatic stroke of coercion, demonstrating that the government meant business. Under Belaúnde's law, the government expropriated only 0.37 million hectares of land. With D.L. 17,716, the regime promised to expropriate almost 9 million hectares, thus stripping the oligarchy of the rural basis of its economic power.[15]

## Land Parceling

### Title IX

Title IX of D.L. 17,716 permitted large property owners to subdivide their farms into smaller, nonexpropriable units as

15. Velasco's speech was indicative of the seriousness with which he took the the agrarian reform. See *El Comercio*, June 25, 1969, p. 4.

long as all labor legislation had been respected. The subsequent controversy over land parceling exemplified the unintended consequences that flowed from incentives in the original law and the speed with which they were corrected. The issue brought into play large and medium-sized property owners, organized peasants, ministry officials (some of whom at the lower levels allegedly accepted bribes to falsify records), and President Velasco. The resolution of the conflict resulted in tighter, more coherent agrarian reform legislation than the original D.L. 17,716.

How did such a liberal clause find its way into D.L. 17,716? First, the concept of parceling had been inherited from Belaúnde's law and was justified in the COAP on a cost-benefit basis. If landowners divided their own property, the government would save time and money. Second, at the beginning of the Velasco regime, many Agriculture officials believed that parceling, together with machinery, seeds, fertilizers, and irrigation, would increase productivity by transferring land from large propertyholders to peasants who cultivated middle-sized and small units. On August 20, 1969, Minister Barandiarán even gave a speech in Paracas, in which he encouraged landowners to parcel in order to facilitate the agrarian reform. Third, Samanez and Figallo conceived of Title IX as a safety valve for conscientious and production-oriented farmers, but not one that would let large landowners escape agrarian reform completely. In the rush to prepare the law, they left Title IX largely in unfinished form; the by-laws, once written by ministry lawyers, proved to be more liberal than the law itself. In the end, the drafters of D.L. 17,716 admitted that they were naive to believe that upper-class hacendados would abet agrarian reform by sponsoring the responsible partition of their own land.

### The Response of Latifundistas, Peasants, and the Agriculture Ministry

Latifundistas meeting in the SNA were already searching for loopholes when the Council of Ministers was discussing the law in the presidential palace. Title IX was a perfect opening. The former owner could divide his land among immediate family and close friends; although land titles were spread about, the farm's administration and profits could remain in the same hands. Or the owner could sell his land in plots of from 20 to 30 hectares to persons with ready cash, turning a profit, but not necessarily benefiting the wage laborers or renters who cultivated the land. In the months of July, August, and September 1969, approximately two hundred partitions took place in Ica, Lima, Nazca, and Chincha, and were duly approved by the zonal offices of the Agrarian Reform Agency.

Skeptical campesino unions had adopted a wait-and-see attitude toward D.L. 17,716. On July 1, the National Federation of Peruvian Peasants (FENCAP, affiliated with both the Communist Party and APRA) announced conditional support for the law, saying that it incorporated many of FENCAP's positions but excluded peasants from representation in the agrarian reform agencies. The Confederation of Peruvian Workers (CTP, linked to APRA) warned that the regime might try to break up the coastal agrarian unions and noted that the government had not yet specified when it would transform the agroindustrial complexes into cooperatives. The Federation of Sugar Workers (also APRA-led) came out against the nationalization of the agroindustrial complexes, believing that the government would make them state enterprises. The APRA party itself complained that D.L. 17,716 appeared to contain clauses aimed at suppressing unions, which APRA labeled "reactionary, unconstitutional, and unjustified."[16] There were also rumblings that Velasco's law did not represent an improvement over Belaúnde's law in terms of workers' rights. While some of the articles suggested that workers would obtain plots free of charge, the government had shown no signs of proceeding in such a manner.

After August 16, 1969, when the Council of Ministers approved the by-laws for Title IX and parceling began in earnest, peasant dissatisfaction on the coast increased markedly. At the farm level, fifteen permanent workers were required to form a union. With partition, a farm's laborers were assigned to numerous parcels, reducing their unit membership below the

16. *El Comercio*, June 28, 1969, p. 2; *Expreso*, June 29, 1969, p. 2, and July 6, 1969, p. 4; *La Tribuna*, July 1, 1969, p. 9, and July 7, 1969, p. 8; and *La Prensa*, July 1, 1969, p. 2, and July 12, 1969, p. 2.

legal minimum and eradicating the union. Organized peasants saw that Title IX was sabotaging their interests and they reacted. The first protest took place in Cañete, where peasants filled the town plaza to denounce the measure. Dissatisfaction soon spread to other coastal regions. By means of published letters, strikes, and rowdy assemblies, they attempted to pressure the government into agreeing that parceling was a mockery of the law.

The workers' protest brought the issue to a head in the Ministry of Agriculture. At the time, Samanez was pointing out that the intent of the law was ambiguous, giving seemingly equal priority both to middle-sized individual holdings and to large cooperatives. Such a joint policy could not be carried out in practice, because, to be viable, both forms of ownership would need all the land available. Also, Title IX was vague about how workers actually gained title to parcels distributed by landowners. Minister Barandiarán asked Samanez and Figallo to draw up a new law clarifying the transfer of possession. They took advantage of the opportunity to reaffirm that redistribution in the countryside could be achieved only through cooperatives and associative enterprises.

The new law was perfected by the COAP, but, because of its urgency and sensitivity, it was not circulated to other ministries for comment. Approved by the Council of Ministers on November 26, 1969, D.L. 18,003 required owners who wished to parcel their land to assign a family-sized plot to each permanent worker on the farm as part of a "multifamily community" under common worker ownership. This provision removed all incentive for landowners to parcel among family members or to sell smaller plots to wealthy buyers.[17]

### *Illegal Parceling and the Valdez Commission*

After the promulgation of D.L. 18,003, no new partitions were approved *legally*, not because the Agrarian Reform

---

17. On the coast, the area equivalent to a family agricultural unit varied between three and a half and four and a half hectares. In the sierra and *ceja de selva*, the area was one-tenth on the maximum holding. We are grateful to Fernando de Trazegnies for this clarification. Alberto Bustamante has compiled a useful indexing of the agrarian reform laws in *Legislación sobre reforma agraria y cooperativas agrarias* (Lima: DESCO, 1974).

Agency deliberately rejected all such requests, but because parceling gave the owner no financial advantage over expropriation. Nonetheless, the peasant unions claimed that preventing future partitions was not enough; all past actions should be canceled as well. Landowners who had already divided their property prepared for a fight and some of those who had not taken timely advantage of the original version of Title IX attempted to compensate for their neglect. Landowners bribed local officials to backdate registries, to give the impression that they had abided by the law before it was changed.[18] As cases of fraud arrived at the desk of Benjamín Samanez, he began annulling both illegal and legal partitions, on the grounds that administrative decisions made by officials at a lower level can be reviewed and reversed by their superiors.[19]

The most renowned case of parceling involved the Fundo Huando, a highly profitable 1,347-hectare citrus farm north of Lima.[20] The owner, Antonio Graña Elizalde, allotted the main section of the farm, 287 hectares of orange orchard, to himself and his son. Former laborers received 299 hectares; former white-collar workers, 396 hectares; and independent purchasers, 365. Together with the Grañas, they added up to sixty-three owners for the Fundo Huando. The case was complicated

---

18. Agriculture proved that many of the deeds were backdated because the contracts were written on serial-numbered official paper printed after the law was changed. For the trial of some of the public functionaries implicated, see *La Prensa*, February 26, 1973, p. 9.

19. Agrarian reform officials also had economy-of-scale motives for annulling partitions. It was much more difficult to expropriate several parcels than one large latifundio. After a property was parceled legally, sections might still be liable for expropriation, so the Agrarian Reform Agency found it expeditious to annul the whole partition.

20. The Fundo Huando case is discussed in Ramón Zaldívar (pseud.), "Agrarian Reform and Military Reformism in Peru," in *Peasants, Landlords, and Governments*, ed. David Lehmann (New York: Holmes & Meier, 1974), pp. 43–44; Fernando Eguren López, *Reforma agraria, cooperativización y lucha campesina* (Lima: DESCO, 1975), pp. 64–65; and Colin Harding, "Land Reform and Social Conflict in Peru," in *The Peruvian Experiment*, ed. Abraham F. Lowenthal (Princeton: Princeton University Press, 1975), pp. 220–53. See also *Siete Días*, February 12, 1971, pp. 6–7; *La Prensa*, February 21, 1971, p. 4; and February 25, 1971, p. 3; *El Peruano*, February 20, 1971, p. 5; *El Comercio*, February 22, 1971, p. 3; *Expreso*, December 22, 1971, p. 3, and June 25, 1972, pp. 8–9; *Unidad*, August 9, 1973, p. 11, "Huando Socialista."

by the fact that the plots assigned to former workers, at a cost of between $500 and $1,000 per hectare with ten years to pay, were distributed among only 50 of the farm's 500 workers. On January 7, 1971, Hugo Blanco, the Trotskyite who had had so much success in La Convención Valley and whom Velasco had recently released from prison in a Yuletide amnesty, arrived at Fundo Huando. With the support of the excluded workers, he agitated for cancellation of the Huando partition.

The Agrarian Reform Agency eventually did annul the measure. In justifying the action on February 20, 1971, Samanez argued that the Graña family had not submitted all of the formal documents needed for parceling; that the agency needed to investigate the workers' protests over noncompliance with labor legislation; that only 10 percent of the permanent workers on the farm had received plots; and that, although workers made up 75 percent of the new owners, they received only 22 percent of the land. Because the Agrarian Reform Agency wanted to give land to those who worked it, the central office in Lima overruled the local zonal office.

What Samanez failed to mention, however, was that the subdivision was carried out before promulgation of D.L. 18,003 and conformed to the terms of Title IX. The conflict intensified as the owners of Fundo Huando gained allies. Beneficiaries of parceled land elsewhere in Peru complained that they had received their plots before the promulgation of D.L. 18,003 and that the Peruvian Constitution stated categorically that laws could not be retroactive. Middle-sized farmers in Cañete argued that the government could not start "correcting the errors" of public administrators months after they occurred. They added: "Is it possible that because agrarian reform officials continually change their minds, Peruvians can no longer have confidence in governmental authority?" In mid-1971 the Ica Farmers' Association claimed there was widespread uncertainty about the regime's final plans. "Stop using pretexts to justify expropriations. Tell us if you are going to take us over or not!" Finally, the SNA dug up a curious contradiction in Samanez's past: In June 1962, as a private agrarian consultant, he had assessed the value of a certain farm near Cuzco at S/16 million; in December 1963, after becoming regional head of the Institute of Agrarian

Reform and Colonization, he valued the same farm at
S/900,000.[21]

Agrarian Reform officials felt sufficiently threatened to seek
the support of Velasco. In a press conference on February 24,
1971, the president backed them by saying that if the government committed an injustice, it would correct it. The cries of
anguish of the former owners of Fundo Huando, however, were
of little consequence. If the law went against the Constitution,
the statutes of the revolutionary junta would simply overrule
the Constitution.[22] Two quotes, from a lower-level agrarian reform official in Ica and a policy maker in Lima, appropriately
capture the swirl of controversy at this time.

> We agrarian reform officials feel like a slab of meat between two
> pieces of bread. From above the landowners attack us, calling us
> communists, agitators, and worse. Below us, impatient peasants
> don't understand our work plans or technical limitations. They
> often accuse us of being in cahoots with their bosses.[23]

> You must remember that we were under pressure from an-
> tagonistic forces. The peasants did not like Title IX because the
> farms were being divided up among former owners and the agrar-
> ian reform was turning into a myth. Also, middle-sized prop-
> erty owners said that expropriation solely on the basis of labor
> code violations was arbitrary. Others, allied with army officers,
> wanted to preserve parceling at the same time that we were
> attempting to outlaw it. The cabinet wanted to know whether the
> law had been correctly applied. After the Agrarian Reform
> Agency had annulled several partitions, members of the Council
> of Ministers asked, "How could that Sr. Samanez proceed in such
> a reckless fashion?" On the other hand, the Fundo Huando case
> was crying out for justice. Finally President Velasco said, "What
> we need is a cold analysis of the situation."[24]

To gain additional information, the cabinet asked an army
general, Enrique Valdez Angulo, to form a commission to de-

---

21. For the public debate on this controversy, see *La Prensa,* July 4, 1970, p.
7; February 17, 1971, p. 4; April 1, 1971, p. 14; May 16, 1971, p. 15; May 29,
1971, p. 2; June 2, 1971, p. 3; June 13, 1971, pp. 1 and 2; June 17, 1971, p. 3; and
June 19, 1971, p. 8; *El Comercio,* November 25, 1970, p. 4; June 8, 1971, p. 9;
June 20, 1971, p. 6; June 21, 1971, p. 5; and June 29, 1971, p. 24; *Expreso,* May
18, 1971, p. 7; June 10, 1971, p. 4; and June 18, 1971, p. 6; and *Ultima Hora,*
February 25, 1971, p. 11.
22. *La Prensa,* February 25, 1971, p. 3.
23. *Expreso,* March 3, 1971, pp. 16–17.
24. Interview no. 84.

termine whether the Agrarian Reform Agency was operating in good faith. Valdez had been working in SAF-CAP, the government's special agency overseeing the expropriated sugar cooperatives.[25] Except for Valdez and an air force representative, all other members of the commission were civil servants, including General Counsel Alcides Roca from the Agrarian Reform Agency. In January, February, and March 1971, the commission concentrated on eight subdivisions registered in the Cañete Valley before D.L. 18,003 had been passed. It examined labor practices before the agrarian reform and the distribution of land under the parceling agreement. The commission concluded that some partitions were in clear violation of the law, while others were legal under Title IX. In the former case, the partitions could be easily nullified and the latifundios expropriated. In the latter case, partitions might be nullified if the government concluded that the former property owners should have deposited social security payments for the medical and retirement insurance of their permanent workers. The commission's recommendation was that the government should expropriate all farms that had been illegally parceled, either blatantly in defiance of the law, as in the first case, or "unethically," as in the second.

In March 1971, the Council of Ministers met in morning and afternoon sessions to discuss the final report. The commission had not lobbied among individual cabinet members before the meeting and did not know what the ministers' final decision would be. Nor had Valdez talked previously with the president, but Velasco's sympathies were soon evidenced by the supportive tone of his questions. Valdez explained that Title IX had not consolidated small and middle-sized properties because latifundios supposedly parceled were still under the ownership of one family and managed by one administrator. At Velasco's urging, the Council of Ministers canceled all partitions, whether legal or illegal. This ratification of the decision of the Agrarian Reform Agency represented a significant personal

25. General Enrique Valdez Angulo is the minister discussed in Chapter 6 who was arrested and imprisoned for his alleged corruption in the EPSA case. See *Correo*, December 12, 1975.

victory for Benjamín Samanez. The disillusioned owners of divided properties were powerless to resist the takeover of their land, soon afterward, by Agrarian Reform agents. But middle-sized farmers who did not lose their farms interpreted the regime's behavior toward the parceling issue as a cue that the government was radicalizing the reform. Forewarned, they would be better prepared to oppose future offensive thrusts.

### Conclusions

Peasant protests helped to crystallize the view of agrarian policy makers that reform should favor cooperative enterprises over individual ownership. While ministry officials encountered few objections to the content of D.L. 18,003, they later ran into opposition from some cabinet members who were distressed by the publicity campaign over the retroactive cancellation of parceling agreements. The Valdez commission was supposed to consider a broad range of opinion but served only to ratify the actions of the Agrarian Reform Agency. Because social security payments were not common in rural areas, evidence could be produced incriminating practically any farm management of unethical behavior. The agency treated even relatively minor labor infractions as sufficient cause for expropriation, which could not be appealed. Encouraged by President Velasco to give Samanez and his allies the benefit of the doubt, the Council of Ministers acquiesced to the canceled partitions. Radicalizing the reform in this way, however, consumed a good part of the agency's legitimacy among both independent farmers and conservative military men. Military support proved to be more difficult to obtain in later disputes with the small and middle-sized farmers.

## The Small and Middle-Sized Property Owners

The most severe test for agrarian policy makers in the first seven years of the reform came not from the large latifundistas but from the small and middle-sized farmers who fought to maintain their rights as individual property owners. Their struggle with the Agrarian Reform Agency revolved around the proper interpretation of Article 22 of D.L. 17,716, which established the maximum property size for Peruvian farms and the conditions for expropriating farms below that ceiling. Conflict was precipitated by energetic land distribution by low-level functionaries, the ability of the so-called middle-sized farmers to form an alliance with the minifundistas, and a political campaign that coincided with the deteriorating situation in neighboring Chile, apparently in the hope that the Peruvian reforms could be slowed under threat of an internal backlash.

### The Interpretation of Article 22

Article 22 of D.L. 17,716 was an outcrop of a similar article in Belaúnde's law which set the largest unexpropriable property size on the coast at 150 hectares (subject to increases along a scale) while the maximum in the sierra varied according to province. The legislation of a similar ceiling under Velasco (without the scale) was due to the fact that no political entity, including the National Agrarian Society and FENCAP, had raised objections to the 150-hectare limit. Samanez and Figallo's motion to reduce the ceiling to 50 hectares was defeated in the COAP drafting committee.

Article 22 of D.L. 17,716 guaranteed to farmers whose property was smaller than 150 hectares that their lands would not be expropriated except for two main reasons: absentee management (*conducción indirecta*) and illegal labor practices. But as the political community polarized and the pace of expropriations increased, these guarantees became either fictitious or insufficient. The slogan of the Peruvian agrarian reform was "La tierra para quien la trabaja" (Land for the person who works it). By maintaining title and administering the land, even if on a part-time basis, many small and middle-sized farmers considered that they actually worked it. At the beginning of the Velasco regime this conception was actually encouraged. With progressively more vehemence, however, such peasant groups as the CCP argued that "working the land" meant full-time physical labor. Gradually ministry officials, especially at the lower levels, believed that the purer definition should prevail. After they saw that the outcome of the parceling controversy threatened them with expropriation too, the small and middle-sized farmers reacted strenuously.

Who were the small and middle-sized farmers? The definition of "small" and "middle" was debatable, but on the coast
the farmers themselves preferred to think of a small owner as
one who possessed a piece of property of less than 15 hectares;
the medium owner, of from 15 to 150 hectares; and a large
owner, of any farm above the expropriable limit. Under this
definition, the small landowners generally were pre-1969
minifundistas who had received their plots under one or
another agrarian law. The middle-sized property owners were
either professional farmers who had been involved in agriculture before June 1969 or persons who had bought or received
parcels before the promulgation of D.L. 18,003. The widespread
belief among professional farmers was that when the large
latifundistas were eliminated, it would be their turn to bask in
the sun as the new rural elite. The remaining middle-sized
"farmers" were members of the middle class who wished to
raise their prestige, income, and enjoyment of life through
landownership. They had neither the technical knowledge nor
the baronial outlook of traditional landowners, and some had
obtained false documents signed by local officials (such as the
police) certifying that they worked the land when they did
not.[26]

Publicly, the government said that it was trying to protect
and strengthen the small and middle-sized farmers who
worked their land and had not obtained it by fraud. Why was it,
then, that many of these farms were nevertheless expropriated

26. In a suggestive article published in the government newspaper *La Nueva
Crónica* in June 1973, commentator Emilio Montes Varela described his impression of the social composition of the small and medium-sized property
owners. First, they were former landowners whose farms were left intact because they were under the 150-hectare limit. Though their holdings were small,
these new latifundistas did not want to lose their privileges. Among them were
drivers, teachers, and policemen who had bought the land either legally or
illegally under Title IX of D.L. 17,716 as a capital investment, who had no
intention of cultivating it directly. According to Montes, even "the small and
middle-sized farmers in the peasant communities are really usurpers of land
titles, or part-time farmers with other professions. Former renters (*yanaconas,
feudatarios, colonos, huacchilleros*) with newly acquired land titles have a
mentality similar to that of the more wealthy rural elite. The new individual
property holders in the countryside are not traditional latifundistas, but an
'agrarian bourgeoisie,' conscious or unconscious heirs to all the defects of the
oligarchic latifundistas now extinct."

and some of them, by almost any objective yardstick, unjustly so? First, the number of expropriation teams was small and their training was poor. Ministry officials felt that the reform could not dally if farm investment and agricultural production were to hold steady. But the faster the reform moved, the more errors were committed. One official pointed out that

> rapid agrarian reform means thousands of files and processed forms. It means that the ministry has to improvise personnel and can't train them as it should. It means that the ministry's self-learning and self-correction go by the wayside. All are sacrificed to speed. The ministry would have made fewer errors if it had taken twenty or thirty years to implement the reform and abide by all the regulations. But rapid action was the only alternative.[27]

Second, upper-level policy makers lacked routines to monitor the actions of lower-level functionaries. The field administrators acted on their interpretation of the clauses of D.L. 17,716, which left much to their discretion. At the upper levels of the ministry, consensus existed that 150 hectares were too many to leave in individual hands. Many lower-level agrarian reform officials, however, believed that *any private ownership whatsoever* was anathama to the Peruvian revolution. In 1971 and 1972, the attacks from the Right against the agrarian reform were counterbalanced by an effective campaign from the Left, which had a radicalizing effect on agrarian reform agents. They tried to outdo the communists and Trotskyites in enthusiasm and proceeded to expropriate farm after farm, from small properties under five hectares all the way up to the maximum limit allowed.

Meanwhile, policy makers added to their own difficulties by subjecting D.L. 17,716 to repeated modifications that gave substance to the impression that when its own legislation got in the way, the Agrarian Reform Agency simply discarded or broadened it. The first alteration of D.L. 17,716 took place two days after the law was passed, and the changes proceeded unabated thereafter. After some twenty modifications had aroused the complaints of landowners, Minister Barandiarán promised

---

27. Interview no. 74.

in August 1970 the publication of a definitive version of the law (*Texto Unico Concordado*, or TUC) so that "*ya no habrá más confusión*" (there won't be any more confusion).[28] The TUC, however, was barely a breathing spell. The law continued to be modified, some fifty times by the end of 1976. In 1972, when expropriations of small and middle-sized holdings began in earnest, farmers' associations rang the alarm, publicized extensively, and used the occasion to question the government's ultimate motives. This publicity overlapped with the last-gasp effort of the large landowners to retain their land parcels, and these persons, with family names that had been prominent in rural society over the last century, were leaders of the small and middle-sized propertyholders' movement.

### Resistance by the Small and Middle-Sized Farmers

*La Prensa* and *El Comercio* ran a long series of advertisements, paid for by wealthy middle-sized farmers in Ica, Cañete, Piura, Arequipa, and Lima, containing such statements as "Some functionaries of the agrarian zone of Piura have said that it would be better to get rid of the small and middle-sized properties and form three to four cooperatives. Is there anything in the law about this?"; "The rumors about an approaching modification in the agrarian reform law *must* be mistaken because the minister has said that the TUC of August 18, 1970, was the final word"; "Isn't it strange that the Agrarian Reform zonal office in La Convención said it needed to expropriate certain properties to form a production cooperative, when these properties already belong to a marketing cooperative? . . . Ex-guerrillas are working in the region"; "We, the small and middle-sized property owners of Cañete, Palpa, and Nazca, question whether we can any longer trust the government"; "We are slated to disappear! Agrarian functionaries in Piura have privately conceded that they want collectivization"; "Ica, Pasto, Palpa, Chincha, Cañete, and Nazca farmers want to know: If there are bad functionaries in the Agrarian Reform

28. See *La Prensa*, August 19, 1970, p. 2; *El Comercio*, March 23, 1971, p. 14. The TUC can be found in S. Martiínez G., ed., *Legislación de reforma agraria* (Lima: Martínez, 1971).

Agency, as President Velasco and the minister of agriculture
have said, why aren't they fired? When the captain is in charge,
the sailor doesn't give orders!"[29]

As the campaign proceeded, the political leadership of the
middle-sized propertyholders succeeded in enlisting the support of the country's minifundistas by convincing them that
eventually they would be forced to join the cooperatives. Leaders could point to actual cases of dispossessed minifundistas to
bolster their case. The ministry's almost blanket expropriation
procedures did little to separate the small coastal farmers,
numbering 250,000, from approximately 2,000 farmers with
much larger holdings. Leagues and federations of small and
middle-sized owners sprouted all over the country, and the
suppression of the National Agrarian Society in 1972 and the
activities of SINAMOS in the countryside gave new vigor to the
opposition. Convinced that the government's intention was to
separate them from their land, owners of all sizes did not want
to sit with their arms crossed until they had to fight the government alone.[30] In retrospect, some policy makers felt that the
regime had proceeded imprudently with the issue. They
should, they felt, have followed the adage

29. For the public declarations of the small and medium-sized farmers and
other aspects of their protest, see *Ultima Hora*, November 28, 1972, pp. 27; July
25, 1973, p. 3; and September 10, 1973, p. 14; *La Pronsa*, June 17, 1973, p. 10;
June 18, 1973, *passim*; June 23, 1973, p. 3; June 24, 1973, pp. 4 and 5; June 25,
1973, p. 2; June 28, 1973, p. 2; June 29, 1973, p. 6; July 11, 1973, p. 7; July 17,
1973, p. 4; July 19, 1973, p. 1; July 25, 1975, pp. 3 and 27; and September 14,
1973, p. 27; *El Comercio*, June 14, 1973, p. 6; *La Nueva Crónica*, June 14, 1973,
p. 6, and July 24, 1973, p. 9; *Unidad*, June 21, 1973; *Expreso*, June 27, 1973, p.
5; June 29, 1973, p. 4; and July 18, 1973, p. 8; and *El Peruano*, August 15, 1973,
p. 1.

30. A leader of the movement explained in interview no. 86:
> The small and middle-sized farmers responded enthusiastically to
> D.L. 17,716 because they knew that income redistribution was a
> necessity if Peru were going to take off economically. But soon we
> saw that the military regime was socialist. There was nothing
> Peruvian about its "noncapitalist, noncommunist" revolution in
> the countryside, because it was heading toward collectiviza-
> tion. . . . Our attitude was "Don't touch us, whether our property is
> four hectares or a hundred hectares, and we won't do anything to
> you." After the government took the large latifundios, we felt it
> would move on the hundred-and-fifty-hectare properties, then the
> fifty-hectare properties, and then take everything. They said,
> "We'll stop at fifty hectares." We said, "You're damn liars!"

"Never touch the small farmers." Convince them to join associative enterprises or, like the Cubans, give them bonuses if they leave. It is not their fault they are small, and treading on them will cause serious problems. [As for the medium owners] from Caesar's time onward, we know that you cannot do everything simultaneously, even if injustices do exist. We should have delayed moving against them when we did.[31]

Besides newspaper advertisements and an alliance with minifundistas, the middle-sized farmers had another important means of influencing policy: their links with the upper levels of government. The landowners shared family, schooling, and friendship ties with military men and the high civil servants who formulated public policy. As the expropriation process gained headway, they gained greater access to the regime's support coalition and their protests became more shrill. One high-level official interpreted this special circumstance.

Previously the agrarian reform was hurting the large property owners, the rural oligarchy, the *gamonales*. People in policy-making circles did not know them. They were somehow distant and hostile. But when the agrarian reform began to affect people like ourselves, it was a different story and cries of anguish seemed more real. The injured parties could gain access to this ministry, either directly or through other levels of government.[32]

A spokesman for the small and middle-sized farmers confirmed this penetration of governing circles: "Our contacts were not necessarily with the government but with members of the armed forces. Government officials did what Velasco ordered. But there were many people like us in the upper levels of the army, air force, and navy who thought that private enterprise must continue in Peru."[33]

### Agrarian Reform on the Defensive

Agriculture authorities suddenly became vulnerable to attack. Adding to their immediate difficulties was their decision to take over such farms as those belonging to the Tomassini, Jaramillo, Sánchez Aste, Ríos, and Luna families. All of these

31. Interview no. 84.
32. Interview no. 74.
33. Interview no. 86.

men had either relatives or close friends in the regime, and for political reasons the Agrarian Reform Agency had placed them at the bottom of the expropriation list. As the last farms in certain areas to be affected, they were on the verge of being invaded by neighboring campesino communities and the ministry felt it had to expropriate at once.

In the first half of July 1973, while Minister Enrique Valdez (who had replaced Jorge Barandiarán in mid-1971) was delayed in London by illness, the Council of Ministers insisted on reviewing the progress of the agrarian reform in special session. Civilian officials were called upon to explain Agriculture's attitude with respect to the national cattle plan, the food-shortage crisis, and, most important, the relationship between agrarian reform and agricultural productivity. Ministry officials feared that the session would turn into an attempt by navy and air force officers to paralyze their activities. They attempted to line up backing from such key numbers of the core and support coalitions as Leonidas Rodríguez, Jorge Fernández Maldonado, Guillermo Marcó del Pont (head of the INP), and Arturo Valdez, but agreed that they would resign their posts if the reform were stopped or significantly stalled.

President Velasco reportedly began the discussion on productivity by saying, "Several ministers have complained that the Agrarian Reform Agency has acted unjustly and done things like taking machinery improperly from the Gotuzo family." After he finished, Luis Vargas Caballero and Rolando Gilardi, ministers of the navy and the air force, respectively, enumerated other complaints. Samanez, who was assigned the task of defending the ministry's policies, argued that many small and so-called middle-sized farmers had backdated deeds and employed other ruses to protect illegal ownership. He challenged his adversaries' contentions and tried not to show lack of resolve. The president's respectful treatment of Samanez in the meeting contrasted markedly with the disdain of Vargas and Gilardi.

Disparaging Samanez's defense, the cabinet followed the recommendation of the navy and air force leaders to appoint a high-level commission to investigate abuses in the countryside. The commission was made up of the heads of the intelligence services of the three branches of the armed forces (Rear Admiral

Jorge Luna, General Hernán Souza of the air force, and General Atilio López Ameri of the army) and representatives from the Guardia Civil and COAP. Starting in Cajamarca and Ferreñafe in northern Peru, the investigation team quickly gathered data. Its members were sympathetic to the denunciations of the small and medium-sized farmers and uncovered numerous examples of injustice and arbitrary behavior. The report submitted to the cabinet was very critical and recommended the firing of persons in SINAMOS and the Agrarian Reform Agency.[34]

Also in July, as a further effort to quiet the agitation, President Velasco received a delegation of small and middle-sized farmers from Nazca, Ica, San Lorenzo, and Cajamarca and listened attentively to their complaints about widespread uncertainty in the countryside. At this point, the president and other ranking members of the core coalition were becoming concerned about the example of the right-wing movement in Chile, Patria y Libertad, which had built a coalition among small and middle-sized property owners and was actively seeking to topple the Allende regime. Velasco's intelligence services told him that leaders of the small and middle-sized farmers saw the Chilean example as a way of paralyzing the agrarian reform, and even doing away with a government it abhorred.[35]

After reviewing the commission's report, the Council of Ministers decided that the government had to clarify, once and for all, the conditions under which small properties could be expropriated, and subsequently award certificates of exemption from expropriation to owners of properties that qualified for them. Because the Agriculture Ministry was being accused

34. President Velasco was aware of the conservative bias of the commission but apparently felt that it was a suitable means of defusing cautious and cantankerous opinions within the government without closing off the possibilities of continuing with the agrarian reform once this impasse was circumvented. Later, he delayed removing the criticized officials as long as possible, and once he accepted their resignations, allowed them to be reappointed to other posts, some higher than the ones they held previously.

35. Said a leader of the farmers' association: "No, we were not linked with Patria y Libertad in Chile, even though we knew what was going on there. Remember that our aims were not political but just to defend our land.... It goes without saying, however, that everyone wanted the government to fall. But we recognized that it would have to fall from within, not because of outside pressure" (interview no. 86).

of malfeasance, this particular law could not be drafted in the Agrarian Reform Agency, and so was entrusted to COAP, with the assistance of some Agriculture officials. López Ameri led the drafting commission, joined by Figallo, Samanez, Lorenzo Tolentini (the chief counsel of Agriculture), and Rodolfo Rivas, a representative of the small- and middle-sized property owners. As it turned out, the farmers' association made a poor choice. Motivated to protect personal interests, Rivas reportedly insisted that a clause in the law permit him to sell land acquired after 1969 at a price not governed by the expropriation price of surrounding plots. After securing this concession, he did not participate actively in the discussion of the other clauses.

For fifteen days the drafting committee examined the complexities of the problem through reports, memoranda, and information gathered from the agrarian zones. The proposed law and supporting materials were submitted to the COAP, which proceeded with "coordination" and presented the recommendations to the Council of Ministers. D.L. 20,120 was approved on August 21, 1973.

Upon its promulgation, however, the small and middle-sized farmers unleashed an outcry, claiming that the law was still insufficiently specific on exemptions from expropriation. Suddenly awake, Rivas said that he had been surprised by the underhanded maneuvers of Samanez and Figallo. Both the farmers' group and the government, each for its own reasons, agreed that the law needed to be rewritten. D.L. 20,136, the next legislative action, laid down more explicit criteria for expropriation, removed much administrative discretion from low-level field teams, and delimited the evidence needed to establish direct management. Samanez and Figallo, however, took advantage of the second round to insert a clause advancing one of their old battle positions, the 50-hectare maximum. Hotly debated in the Council of Ministers but finally accepted, Article 15 prohibited the acquisition or transfer by any means (including inheritance) of more than one-third the unexpropriable limit. In that way the two old hands at agrarian reform legislation succeeded in taking the first step toward reducing the maximum property size to fifty hectares in Peru.

## Breaking the Farmers' Coalition

Government strategists hoped to use D.L. 20,136 for other purposes. They saw that the countryside's new rural elite, with properties near the maximum of 150 hectares, had taken advantage of minifundista insecurity to organize a political movement to preserve their privileges. To break up the coalition, the Agrarian Reform Agency began issuing certificates of exemption (*títulos de inafectabilidad*). Five days after the law was published, a thousand plots in the Chancay Valley were exempted. In mid-September 1973, Eduardo Morán, vice-minister of agriculture, announced that 70,000 farms on the coast would be protected. By early October, all of the Lima newspapers were reporting on the issuance of hundreds and thousands of certificates of nonexpropriation to small farmers in Ica, Arequipa, Pisco, Piura, and Chincha, the main centers of organized dissatisfaction.

These certificates did not go to all properties under 150 hectares, only to properties of about four hectares. The official explanation of this imbalance was that issuing a certificate for a small farm (fifteen hectares or less) required only proof of land possession, which could be obtained quickly from the rural registries. For larger properties, additional requirements prevailed. The owner had to prove that he had abided by all labor legislation covering his workers, that he held no other occupation that could interfere with his working the land directly, and that he had paid his taxes. Because the paperwork was onerous and the disregard for labor and tax laws widespread, few middle-sized owners bothered to apply for certificates. Under the circumstances, they viewed D.L. 20,136 as only a partial solution to their problem.[36]

Some agrarian reform officials believed that indeed the massive distribution of nonexpropriation certificates had broken the farmers' coalition, and cited, as a prime example, the failure of the large gathering of the federations of the small and

---

36. On December 31, 1973, the Lima daily *La Ultima Hora*, p. 38, declared 1973 as the year of victorious struggle for the small and middle-sized farmers. Several days later it published a disclaimer from a middle-sized farmer who stated that the fight was not finished.

middle-sized farmers to reach accord on a common plan of action in Arequipa in September 1973.[37] Others, however, were not quite so sure.

> The government never succeeded in breaking the coalition be-
> tween the small and middle-sized farmers. Law 20,136 nor-
> malized land titles for small plots, but that did not work. As long
> as the individual peasant does not see what he wants to see with
> his own eyes, he does not believe whàt he reads on paper. In
> every area of the country, the minifundista saw that the process
> of expropriation had not been completed. Every time the agrar-
> ian official went into town, he was asked, "Is this expropriation
> the last one?" Obviously the functionary could not say yes, and
> every time he said no, the minifundista got nervous and there
> was new pressure on the government.[38]

Toward the end of the Velasco regime, additional legislation strengthened the hands of the middle-sized property holders. Under D.L. 21,168 (1975), small and middle-sized farmers in Arequipa were permitted to hire outside help, regardless of the size of their units, and could engage in other gainful employment simultaneously with farming. Samanez and Figallo had fought these provisions because they felt that when farmers had other vocational interests, cultivation was just a hobby. Soon after Morales Bermúdez succeeded Velasco, the government passed D.L. 21,333. The regime heralded it as a revolutionary measure because it explicitly reduced the largest permissible landholding size from 150 to 50 hectares, and required the employment of one agricultural worker for every 5 hectares of land above 9 hectares. The articles of the law, however, catered to the interests of middle-sized farmers because at most it would expropriate only 20,000 hectares of land owned by less

---

37. A leader of the farmers' groups conceded, "It is true that large-scale issuance of certificates of exemption weakened our movement. But this was political demagoguery on the part of the government. There was no law in Peru that exempted you from expropriation, and the government gave these certificates and expropriated anyway. The small farmers subsequently did feel more secure about their land but many with certificates continued to work with us" (interview no. 86). Other measures designed to weaken support for the coalition were the increase in the price of milk in Arequipa, the reduction in the cost of vaccinations to small farmers, and passage of D.L. 19,977, which exempted small renters from repaying the government for land received.

38. Interview no. 84.

than 1 percent of the group. Furthermore, the law eliminated absentee ownership and labor-code violations as sufficient causes for expropriation. The middle-sized farmers who had complained for years that expropriation was too severe a punishment for these infractions finally won their point. Subsequently, store owners, teachers, government functionaries, military officers, and truck drivers could own property, administer it on weekends, fail to register their workers with social security or pay them the minimum wage, and not fear expropriation.[39]

## Conclusions

This issue brought more actors into play than the previous two cases discussed, and its outcome reflected accurately the power balance at different points of the Velasco regime. Though the Ministry of Agriculture held the initial advantage, it frittered it away by condoning the rampant expropriation of small units. The middle-class farmers took advantage of a coincidental political situation in neighboring Chile which troubled the Peruvian military coalition. That Samanez and his advisers were obliged to write D.L. 20,120 at the same table with a representative of a political movement desiring their political demise was in sharp contrast to the exclusive atmosphere in which they drafted the original agrarian reform and partition laws. Equally illustrative were their near resignation in July 1973 (saved only by the commitment of President Velasco to continuation of the reform), their submission to judgment by dissatisfied members of the support coalition, and the subsequent legislation catering to the demands of a vociferous minority of Peru's rural population.[40]

39. Another aspect of the law favorable to the landowners was payment for land in cash over ten years at 7 percent interest, instead of in 6 percent bonds over twenty years. On April 5, 1978, via D.L. 22,133, the government even annulled the 50-hectare limit, returning the land ceiling on the coast to 150 hectares.
40. These men ultimately did resign: Figallo in January 1975, to become a Supreme Court justice, and Samanez in August 1976, after Minister Gallegos was replaced under the Morales Bermúdez government. By the time of Samanez's resignation, however, the government had expropriated 7 million hactares, and the original goal was in sight.

## Military Government and Public Policy Making

The military government found it relatively easy to draw up comprehensive land-reform legislation because an outline already existed in the political arena. Men who had dedicated their careers to agriculture allied themselves with military officers, who provided the political power (mainly coercion) to move forward with determination. Policy makers had a clearer idea of what they did not want (latifundios) than what they did want when the process began. The original agrarian reform law encouraged an agricultural sector consisting mainly of middle-sized productive units managed by hard-working individual farmers, complemented by large cooperatives in the midst of subsistence-level minifundios about which little could be done. The mockery made of Title IX parcels encouraged senior policy makers to favor a predominantly cooperative land structure. Carried to its logical conclusion, that goal meant no parcels, middle-sized farms, or minifundios. Failure to measure the farmers' power capabilities accurately, however, led to crisis and partial defeat over the conditions for expropriation under Article 42.

The government's procedures for settling issues in the agrarian sector varied according to the origin and scope of the political agitation these issues raised. Policy making included the three styles described in Chapter 1. The original agrarian reform bill, D.L. 17,716, was drawn up in centralized fashion in a situation of high autonomy from dominant economic actors. The drafting of D.L. 18,003 was also centralized but involved the participation of a military investigative commission. The multiple clarifications of legislation on ceilings were "coordinated" with the direct input of small and middle-sized farmers. Here autonomy was severely attenuated, partly because the armed forces were less unified than in 1969. The policy-making style was considerably more open at the conclusion of the Velasco presidency than at the beginning.

# Chapter 3

# The Chira-Piura
# Irrigation Project

Prosperous farmers dominated the agricultural sector under Belaúnde, and the state itself was greatly influenced by the interests of Peruvian financial and industrial elites, multinational corporations, and international lending institutions. Velasco, after a few months of indecision, proceeded to increase the state's operating capacity, tighten internal controls, weaken the traditional elites, and assert independence from the world financial community. To compensate for the loss of backing from these classes and institutions, the regime tried to build up the power of unmobilized groups, such as the peasants, who were expected to support the goals of the revolution.

One of the most suggestive concepts to emerge from current interpretations of Marxist theory is that of the "autonomy of the state." A discussion of this concept helps to distinguish the behavior of the Belaúnde regime from that of the Velasco regime. Karl Marx, in almost all of his writings, assumed that in a capitalist system the economic substratum had a predominant influence on superstructural phenomena, including the nature of the state. Under capitalism, the bourgeoisie was by definition predominant and the state displayed no autonomy, since it ruled in the bourgeoisie's short-term and long-term interests.

Marx conceded, however, that in atypical periods of social fragmentation, a near equilibrium of forces could occur.[1] In such a situation, the state could have a seemingly independent role by tipping the balance in a way that appeared not to be in the immediate interests of the bourgeoisie.

Nicos Poulantzas attempts to resolve this apparent contradiction by speaking of the *relative autonomy* of the state. He argues that the state often does not appear to be ruling on behalf of the bourgeoisie, or any other faction of the power bloc, but its role is essentially to unify the bloc and make its interests coherent. Thus the state is not an instrument subjected by the dominant classes or subjecting them, but retains relative autonomy vis-à-vis their interests, an attitude that actually permits the bourgeoisie to maintain its hegemony over the long term. He also postulates that this autonomy correlates positively with the internal unity of the state.[2]

One difficulty with the approach used by Poulantzas is that it restricts itself, artificially perhaps, to the state versus the dominant classes, which in capitalist societies are presumed to consist of the bourgeoisie. Poulantzas does not deal with the state's ability to forge alliances with workers or peasants to counterbalance the influence of the bourgeoisie. He does not treat coalitions between the state and international capital, except to the extent that they can perpetuate the hegemony of bourgeois groups. Furthermore, the Marxian legacy is not applicable to societies that are precapitalist or socialist, or to those in which social fragmentation is the rule rather than the exception.[3]

1. Karl Marx, *The Eighteenth Brumaire of Louis Bonaparte* (New York: International Publishers, 1963), pp. 16ff.

2. Nicos Poulantzas, "The Capitalist State: A Reply to Miliband and Laclau," *New Left Review* 95 (January–February 1976), 72–75.

3. Poulantzas is ambiguous about whether his theory, as presented in *Political Power and Social Classes* (London: NLB, 1973), applies to these situations. Analysis of the ambiguity can lead to the conclusion that the theory is tautologous and functionalist. Although the book progresses inductively, it appears that deductive reasoning was the method used to establish the veracity of Marx's emphasis on substructure. Poulantzas asserts that the bourgeoisie is the dominant economic group because the modern capitalist state is a social formation in which the capitalist mode of production prevails. Even when other modes of production coexist, the capitalist mode has a predominant effect on political outcomes. The issue of which classes are dominant is crucial be-

Other scholars working in the Third World have broadened this formalistic conception of the relation between the economic and political spheres by focusing attention on state autonomy with respect to classes other than the bourgeoisie. State autonomy becomes the ability of a state over time to generate interests inconsistent with the objectives of the most powerful economic classes, and sometimes to the direct benefit of no discernible social grouping other than the state itself.[4] In one

---

cause the state has no power of its own. Power is the "capacity of a social class to realize its specific objective interests" (p. 112). And "When we speak ... of state power, ... we can only mean the power of a determinate class to whose interests (rather than to those of other social classes) the state corresponds" (p. 100). "But this does not mean that power centers, the various institutions of an economic, political, military, cultural, etc., character are mere instruments, organs or appendices of social classes" (p. 115). "The capitalist state, characterized by hegemonic class leadership, does not directly represent the dominant classes' economic interests, but their political interests" (p. 191).

The tautology of the analysis lies in the predefinition of the system as capitalist and the other definitions that Poulantzas associates with that concept. Power is understood only in class terms. State power has no meaning unless it is linked to class power. Although the social formation is not a "pure" capitalist mode of production, the capitalist mode of production stamps its impression on social and political relationships. And in the capitalist mode of production, some fraction of the bourgeoisie is, by definition, dominant. Thus, even if the state seems to go against the interests of the bourgeois, it is still acting on their behalf (e.g., a timely concession prolongs their rule). In other words, it is impossible to construct a null hypothesis from this theory, because even contrary evidence confirms the central proposition.

The argument is also functionalist. Poulantzas identifies the functions of the state: it (1) acts as the political organization of the dominant class, (2) keeps the working class disorganized, and (3) ideologizes, in support of the state, those fractions or classes that are ambivalent about their interests. He defines the state as "the organization for maintaining ... both the unity of a mode of production and of a formation" (p. 50). In other words, the proof that the state is doing everything possible to maintain the capitalist mode of production is manifest in the fact that the capitalist mode of production still exists. The only way for the state to support the capitalist mode of production would be for this mode, and all traces of it, to disappear, taking the state with it.

For additional comments on Poulantzas' contribution, see A. B. Bridges, "Nicos Poulantzas and the Marxist Theory of the State," *Politics and Society* 4:2 (Winter 1974), 161–90.

4. In reviewing Fernando Henrique Cardoso's *Autoritarismo e democratização* (Rio de Janeiro: Paz e Terra, 1975), Ross Zucker comments, "It is particularly interesting that even when Cardoso acknowledges the role of the bourgeoisie in the power bloc, he refuses to accept that this implicitly demonstrates that economics conditions politics ... the fact that the bourgeoisie possesses a share of power does not necessarily mean that the military must rule in its interests" ("The Relative Autonomy of the State," seminar discussion paper, Department of Political Science, Yale University, 1975, pp. 41–42).

interpretation, state autonomy means the capacity of a unified state to impose its will on a resistant or passive society, generally to reshape prevailing social and economic relationships.[5] This conception encourages the prospective researcher to treat the state's interaction with a more diversified set of social actors than the bourgeoisie and the workers. It does not, however, clearly distinguish between (1) the state's propensity to formulate policy objectives inconsistent with the interests of specified classes and (2) its ability subsequently to execute; or, worded differently, state autonomy (to define national goals) and state power (to carry them out)

In our discussion, the term "state autonomy" denotes goal formulation independent of class or group pressure, including that which is generated internationally. Absolute autonomy occurs when the state defines goals on the basis of its institutional interests or its conception of national objectives that counter the goals of all identifiable social classes and groups, whether they are dominant or subordinate in the economic sphere. Total dependence occurs when the state simply arbitrates among the preferences of competing classes, and blindly caters to those interests that emerge victorious. This situation describes circumstances under Belaúnde. Some degree of relative autonomy occurs when the state defines goals that counter the interests of some but not all classes and subgroups, and/or favors nondominant social groups in line with the state's interpretation of national interests. Viewed in these terms, the concept of state autonomy is not restricted to capitalism. It is applicable whenever the analyst can identify the goals of various classes, economic actors, and the state, and measure their overlap.[6] Power is a separate but related issue because these goals become ethereal if none of the parties has sufficient force to implement them.

The main actors in this chapter are the bourgeoisie, international capital, the rural lower class, and the state. The

---

5. Alfred Stepan, in *The State and Society* (Princeton: Princeton University Press, 1978), applies the concept in this sense to the Velasco regime in Peru.
6. Naturally, determining what these goals might be is not simple. Administrative theorists have had considerable difficulty ascertaining the goals of discrete organizations, a task that would presumably be less problematical than determining them for a whole class, state, or nation.

bourgeoisie of the Chira-Piura region, however, was severely divided; international capital included representatives from both Western and socialist countries; lower-class elements did not display unity of interests; and the views of state agrarian officials did not coincide. These divisions revolved around questions of water. While the military government did not ignore all class interests in resolving water disputes, it did define goals that countered those of the dominant economic actors in the region. The Chira-Piura irrigation project is a good example of the relatively high autonomy of the Velasco regime during the first years of its mandate.[7]

## Agriculture, Water, and Social Structure

Agriculture in Piura Department, which is bordered in part by Ecuador on the north, has depended historically on the availability of water. Until the twentieth century, agriculture was carried out with traditional techniques on a modest scale by a few small farmers and approximately forty indigenous communities, of which Catacaos was the most populated in the

7. Many archeologists and anthropologists have argued that the construction and management of large-scale irrigation systems require a centralized bureaucratic apparatus to undertake investment, allocation, and maintenance activities. See Robert McC. Adams, *The Evolution of Urban Society* (Chicago: Aldine Press, 1966); Réné Millon, "Variations in Social Responses to the Practices of Irrigation Agriculture," in *Civilizations in Desert Lands*, ed. Richard B. Woodbury (Anthropology Paper no. 62, Department of Anthropology, University of Utah, 1962), pp. 55–58; Barbara Price, "Prehispanic Irrigation Agriculture in Nuclear America," *Latin American Research Review* 6:3 (Fall 1971), 3–60; and Kent V. Flannery, "The Cultural Evolution of Civilizations," *Annual Review of Ecology and Systematics* 3 (1972), 399–426. Classical works are Karl Wittfogel, *Oriental Despotism* (New Haven: Yale University Press, 1957): Edmund Leach, *Pul Eliya* (Cambridge: Cambridge University Press, 1961); Wolfram Eberhard, *Conquerors and Rulers* (Leiden: E. J. Brill, 1965); and William T. Sanders and Barbara Price, *Mesoamerica* (New York: Random House, 1968). These studies refer largely to precapitalist or traditional societies in which agriculture is the predominant or almost exclusive type of economic activity. Other scholars discuss more recent impacts that have little to do with despotism or the rise of civilization. See Eva and Robert Hunt, "Irrigation, Conflict, and Politics: A Mexican Case," in *Irrigation's Impact on Society*, ed. Theodore E. Downing and McGuire Gibson (Tucson: University of Arizona Press, 1974), pp. 129–57; and William P. Mitchell, "The Hydraulic Hypothesis: A Reappraisal," *Current Anthropology* 14:5 (December 1973), 532–34.

country. Despite the generally good quality of the soil and the favorable climatic conditions, the irregularity of the Piura River and the flat terrain, which called for extensive use of pumps for irrigation, limited the expansion of the agricultural frontier. In 1905 only 8,000 hectares were being cultivated in Piura (mainly in cotton), compared with 54,600 hectares in Lambayeque, the country's foremost sugar zone. In 1967, by contrast, with water from the San Lorenzo irrigation project, the area cultivated in Piura had increased to 141,945 hectares, surpassing Lambayeque's 104,808 hectares.[8]

The modernization of cotton growing changed the nature of agriculture in the valley, orienting it toward the international market and favoring larger production units. Cotton had been domesticated and cultivated in pre-Incaic times, and by the 1860s, over 40,000 quintals were being exported, mainly to England.[9] By 1918 the area devoted to cotton cultivation had reached 19,732 hectares. The amount remained fairly steady until after World War II, and increased to 51,000 hectares by 1970. Rice lands rose from 4,252 hectares in 1929 to 19,000 hectares in 1970. Sugar cane never became an important crop, but corn growing increased after 1950. These crops were grown for the market, not for home consumption, and the expansion of the market justified investments in infrastructure, especially new irrigation.

Population growth accompanied agricultural modernization. Immigrants from Europe and from other parts of the Peruvian coast established themselves as small and medium farmers. Migrants from the mountains found work as hired hands, renters, or minifundistas. The local peasants began to lose their land and, more important, their water rights. The new farmers reclaimed land from the desert and invested in pumps, wells, irrigation canals, and "thirstier" seed varieties. The progressive

---

8. Michael Twomey, "Ensayo sobre la agricultura peruana," *Cuadernos del Taller de Investigación Rural* (Pontificia Universidad Católica del Perú) 4 (1972), 8.

9. Federico Moreno, *Las irrigaciones de la costa* (Lima, 1900), p. 66; and Alejandro Garland, *El Perú en 1906* (Lima: La Industria, 1907), p. 120. See also Philip A. Means, "Social Conditions in the Piura-Tumbes Region of Northern Peru," *Scientific Monthly*, November 1918, pp. 385–99.

displacement of the traditional peasantry and concentration of landownership were not checked until the Agrarian Reform Law (D.L. 17,716 of June 24, 1969), the General Water Law (D.L. 17,752 of June 24, 1969), and the declaration in 1971 that Piura Department was a priority agrarian reform zone.

Measurement of the degree of land concentration in Piura Department in 1971 depended on a point of reference. A comparison of the figures in Table 9 with those of Table 1 reveals a similar pattern of minifundia and latifundia but a noticeably greater concentration of landownership in the country as a whole in the 1960s than in Piura. In Peru, 0.2 percent of the agricultural units and 69.9 percent of the cultivated area comprised units larger than 1,000 hectares, whereas in Piura the comparable figures were 0.7 percent and 31 percent for the Chira Valley and 0.5 percent and 37.7 percent for the Piura Valley. Land was more concentrated in Piura, however, than elsewhere on the coast. The Piura Valley had 82.1 percent of its holdings in properties of under 5 hectares and 1.0 percent above 500 hectares, while coastal figures were 78 percent and 0.5 percent respectively.[10] Of eight river valleys on the north coast, Chira and Piura were second only to the Lambayeque sugar zone in land concentration.[11] The peculiar feature of Piura that distinguished it from its sister valleys was the large number of farms in the 100–500-hectare group. These medium-sized farmers were modern professionals whose land was generally handed down from father to son. Absentee ownership was not common, as shown by Table 10, nor had the local economy diversified from agriculture to industry and commerce to a great extent.[12] The zone contained a relatively

10. See Luis F. de la Fuente Uceda, *La reforma agraria peruana* (Lima: Ensayos Sociales, 1966), p. 154.

11. Delbert A. Fitchett, "Defects in the Agrarian Structure as Obstacles to Economic Development: A Study of the North Coast of Peru," Ph.D. dissertation, University of California, Berkeley, 1963, p. 354. Claude Collin-Délavaud discusses the growth of haciendas in Piura and Lambayeque in "Consecuencias de la modernización de la agricultura en las haciendas de la costa norte del Perú," in Henri Favre et al., *La hacienda en el Perú* (Lima: Instituto de Estudios Peruanos, 1964), pp. 259–81.

12. See pertinent statistics in Michael A. Gómez, "The Role of International Technical Cooperation in the Interregional Development of Peru," Ph.D. dissertation, Ohio State University, 1962.

Table 9. Land concentration in the Piura and Chira valleys, c. 1960

| Farm size (hectares) | Number of units | Percent of all units | Number of hectares | Percent of all hectares |
|---|---|---|---|---|
| Piura Valley | | | | |
| 0–2 | 1,136 | 67.6% | 926 | 1.6% |
| 2–5 | 244 | 14.5 | 707 | 1.2 |
| 5–50 | 157 | 9.3 | 2,644 | 4.5 |
| 50–100 | 25 | 1.5 | 1,833 | 3.1 |
| 100–500 | 102 | 6.1 | 24,774 | 42.0 |
| 500–1,000 | 9 | 0.5 | 5,871 | 10.0 |
| 1,000 or more | 9 | 0.5 | 22,207 | 37.7 |
| All Piura Valley farms | 1,685 | 100.0% | 58,962 | 100.1% |
| Chira Valley | | | | |
| 0–2 | 432 | 57.7 | 460 | 1.6 |
| 2–5 | 139 | 18.5 | 434 | 1.5 |
| 5–50 | 106 | 14.1 | 1,490 | 5.2 |
| 50–100 | 20 | 2.7 | 1,521 | 5.3 |
| 100–500 | 38 | 5.1 | 9,605 | 33.7 |
| 500–1,000 | 9 | 1.2 | 6,141 | 21.6 |
| 1,000 or more | 5 | 0.7 | 8,828 | 31.0 |
| All Chira Valley farms | 749 | 100.0% | 28,479 | 99.9% |

SOURCE: Delbert A. Fitchett, "Defects in the Agraria Structure as Obstacles to Economic Development," Ph.D. dissertation, University of California, Berkeley, 1963, p. 282; Comisón para la Reforma Agraria y la Vivienda, La Reforma Agraria en el Perú, document I (Lima: Villanueva, 1960), Table 17.

Table 10. Owner- and nonowner-managed farms in Lower and Middle Piura and in Upper Piura, by size, 1970 (in percent)

| Farm size (hectares) | Lower and Middle Piura | | Upper Piura | |
|---|---|---|---|---|
| | Owner-managed | Nonowner-managed | Owner-managed | Nonowner-managed |
| Less than 4 | 99% | 1% | 98% | 2% |
| 4–15 | 93 | 7 | 95 | 5 |
| 15–45 | 75 | 25 | 90 | 10 |
| 45 or more | 70 | 30 | 68 | 32 |
| All farms | 97 | 3 | 96 | 4 |

SOURCES: Ministerio de Agricultura, Diagnóstico sector Alto Piura ZAI (Piura: Zona Agraria I, 1972), Table 33, and Diagnóstico sectores Medio y Bajo Piura ZAI (Piura: Zona Agraria I, 1972), Table 33.

prosperous middle sector of farmers who managed their own properties side by side with a very poor population of indigenous communities and some large properties.

Water, not land, was the main determinant of prosperity, and competition for water pitted members of the same class against each other. Figure 3 shows that farmers downstream on both the Piura and Chira rivers, the first areas of this arid region to be settled by cultivators, were at a disadvantage in obtaining water for their crops because upstream settlers, especially during droughts, left the water level extremely low. Downstream farmers resolved this issue near the start of the twentieth century by physically attacking their upstream neighbors to prevent them from siphoning off water, and violence was commonplace thereafter. On the Piura River, the level of conflict abated somewhat as Lower and Middle Piura farmers bought tracts of land on the Upper Piura and cultivated them only when there was a water surplus. Eventually, the most powerful farmers on both rivers set up a rationing system administered by the municipality, which they controlled.[13] The expansion of the agricultural frontier and the demographic explosion, however, continuously increased the demand for water.

## The San Lorenzo and Chira-Piura Projects

### San Lorenzo

The San Lorenzo Project was the first attempt to solve the water problem beyond the individual efforts of farmers. Conceived during the government of José Luis Bustamante y Rivero (1945–48) and implemented during the governments of Manuel Odría (1948–56) and Manuel Prado (1956–62), the project consisted in the diversion of water from the Quiroz River, a tributary of the Chira, to the San Lorenzo Dam (see Figure 3).

13. Luís Odar Seminario, "Historia de las instituciones de regadío en los departamentos de Piura y Lambayeque," in Congreso de Irrigación, Anales del primer congreso (Lima: Torres Aguirre, 1929), pp. 1150–56. The Anales are an illustrated four-volume compendium resulting from the 1929 Congreso de Irrigación y Colonización del Norte. They contain technical and impressionistic articles by the local farmers which reveal their belief in free enterprise and aversion to interference by the central government.

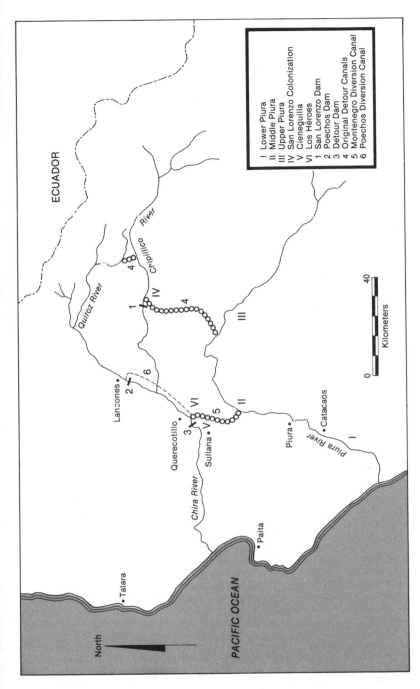

Figure 3. The Chira-Piura irrigation zone

These waters were to open up 50,000 hectares of new lands for cultivation in the San Lorenzo area and regulate the flow of water along the Piura River. The objectives were to expand the agricultural frontier with the colonization of new lands and to diminish the conflicts among the farmers in Lower, Middle, and Upper Piura over access to water.[14]

Unfortunately, the project experienced planning and programming problems. The detour canals were ready two years before the dam; once the dam was finished, the colonization was delayed. Meanwhile, the farmers of Lower and Middle Piura had been using the water detoured from the Quiroz River to expand cultivation. Because they could use the San Lorenzo waters, they lessened their pressure on Upper Piura farmers for strict control of irrigation. Accordingly, agriculture in Upper Piura expanded. Finally, despite calculations in the original studies that showed otherwise, the area available for land settlement in San Lorenzo was overestimated by 30,000 hectares in order to obtain additional credits from the World Bank.[15]

For ten years agriculture flourished along the Piura River. Once San Lorenzo was settled, however, a new conflict arose between the San Lorenzo colonists and the farmers of Lower and Middle Piura. When San Lorenzo colonists irrigated, waters diverted from the Quiroz River no longer reached Middle and Lower Piura. The Piura Agricultural League was incapable of resolving the matter because its membership now included both farmers from San Lorenzo and Middle and Lower Piura, and state agencies during the Belaúnde administration were indecisive. The World Bank, which was funding several development projects in Peru and was committed to colonization at the time, finally insisted that its water go to the San Lorenzo colonists. In the words of one Lower Piura farmer, who was not an admirer of the bank's operations:

> Everyone knew that the original law authorizing financing and construction gave clear preference to increasing the water supply of Lower Piura farmers, and the San Lorenzo colonization

14. Albert Hirschman provides some background to the problems of the San Lorenzo project in *Development Projects Observed* (Washington: Brookings Institution, 1967).

15. Interview no. 68.

would be created only with leftover water up to 20,000 hectares. Everyone also knew that this new area was arbitrarily enlarged to 50,000 hectares without accounting for where the water would come from. Notwithstanding, the bank put its foot down and pushed "its" colonization forward.

[Resentment increased] when the directors of the Colonization Administration were beholden more to the World Bank than to the Peruvian government, and obeyed the bank's orders directly. The Colonization Administration was a country apart. Peruvian laws almost did not apply within its boundaries. The engineers did not depend on the Agriculture Ministry, the schoolteachers on the Education Ministry, or the roads and highways on the Development Ministry. All depended on the World Bank. The Lower Piura farmers remained silent, less because they feared retaliation by the World Bank than because it was clear that even President Belaúnde could not modify the bank's decisions.[16]

## Chira-Piura

Confronted once more with social conflict due to water scarcity, local authorities again looked for a way to increase water availability. The Chira-Piura Project was first conceived during the presidency of José Balta (1868–72) as part of a hydroelectric project. The project's utility for the modernization of agriculture became apparent at the turn of the century, and in the 1920s in Piura Department influential Chira farmers promoted construction of the Poechos Dam as a way to irrigate the left bank of the Chira. But concrete plans were not drawn up until the conflicts over San Lorenzo in the 1960s lent urgency to the project.[17]

The first step was Belaúnde's creation of ORDEN (Development Office for the Northern Region) as part of the national planning system. ORDEN used World Bank funds to conduct a hydrological study of the Department of Piura.[18] The bank did not officially recognize the conflicts created by the San Lorenzo Project, but this financing was an implicit admission that to colonize the San Lorenzo area successfully it would be neces-

16. Interview no. 68.
17. See *El Peruano*, April 17, 1971, p. 1; *El Comercio*, April 17, 1971, p. 1, and May 21, 1971, p. 8; *La Crónica*, October 25, 1971, p. 6; and interviews nos. 55, 63, 65, and 68.
18. *Correo*, October 18, 1971, and interview no. 55.

sary to treat the agricultural zone as an integrated whole. This 1967 study recommended the diversion of water from the Chira to the Piura as the most promising way to increase the amount of water for agriculture in the valley. ORDEN carried on with the project, supervising the prefeasibility and feasibility studies made by the International Engineering Company (IEC), affiliated with Morrison-Knudsen, the U.S.-owned construction company.[19] In Congress APRA deputies Ricardo Temoche and Alejandro Alberdi introduced a proposal for the rational use of the Quiroz, Piura, and Chira waters.[20] The project was still under discussion, however, when the Velasco Alvarado government assumed power in October 1968.

Because the APRA party had no access to the military government, members of the Piura Agricultural League lobbied for the project in Lima, where they met several times with President Velasco.[21] The last meeting was with a delegation from the Chamber of Commerce, the Workers' Confederation, the Bar Association, and CORPIURA, a local economic development board, which urged the president, who was born in Piura, to sponsor the project as something of benefit for his home town.[22] In a more accommodating frame of mind than he was to display a year later, Velasco agreed to the promulgation of Decree Law 17,463. This law declared that the project was in the national interest and of top priority, and that to implement it, the government would seek financing from national and international sources up to the amount of U.S. $109.3 million. The law also gave considerable authority to the Council of the Chira-Piura Project, which had its headquarters in Piura and included, with only one exception, representatives of local Piura interests. Its president, Juan Espinoza Vasi, had helped to

19. International Engineering Company, *Estudio de planificación* (Lima: Instituto Nacional de Planificación and Ministerio de Fomento y Obras Públicas, 1967).

20. *El Tiempo,* July 12, 1967, p. 7.

21. *El Comercio,* September 28, 1969, p. 1. The League was carrying forward an earlier interest in the project. In the early 1960s it had commissioned a study of the feasibility of pumping water from the Chira to the Piura.

22. CORPIURA, or the Corporación de Desarrollo Económico y Social del Departmento de Piura, was later absorbed by SINAMOS.

organize the San Lorenzo Project and was a personal friend and former classmate of President Velasco. Other council members came from CORPIURA, the Piura branch of the Engineers' College of Peru, and the Agricultural League, and one was a local engineer with experience in irrigation works. The only public official on the council was the director of ORDEN. As one council member pointed out, "D.L. 17,463 was exceptional in Peruvian jurisprudence because it delegated public powers to an organization of private-sector interests. The law, however, did not enjoy the sympathy of public functionaries. They were jealous of its prerogatives, which in part explains the council's short life."[23]

Because the World Bank had financed the San Lorenzo Project and the feasibility and prefeasibility studies for the Chira-Piura Project, the council looked first to the bank as a possible source of funds. The bank, however, waited until February 1970 to announce that it would send a technical mission, which arrived in April.[24] Despite favorable technical and financial reports, the bank did not approve the project.[25] Evidence suggests that the bank delayed its decision in order to pressure the Peruvian government to pay compensation for the expropriation of the U.S.-owned International Petroleum Company. According to one council member:

> At first, the bank's representatives avoided answering why the bank refused to finance the final studies and the works themselves. The reason was eventually given by bank staff members who visited Peru. While in Lima at the Country Club Hotel, during a drinking session, they mentioned that the World Bank had its own Hickenlooper. Although the U.S. government might decide to waive its famous amendment, the World Bank would not lend money to a country that had acted so brusquely with a North American company. They had the gall to propose that we speak with President Velasco and suggest that he make an arrangement with the IPC and thus open the way for financing the

23. Interview no. 68.
24. *La Prensa*, March 19, 1970, p. 6, and April 25, 1970, p. 4; *El Peruano*, April 25, 1970, p. 1, and April 29, 1970, p. 3; *El Comercio*, April 28, 1970, p. 15; May 3, 1970, p. 19; and May 8, 1970, p. 10; and *Expreso*, May 8, 1970, p. 3.
25. *El Comercio*, May 3, 1970.

project. They thought this option was possible because President Velasco was from Piura. The revelation was eye-opening for the members of the council.[26]

On top of the withdrawal of the World Bank, the council found that it had to find another company to conduct the final feasibility studies because Morrison-Knudsen and its affiliates were ordered to cease their operations in the country.[27] Loans proffered by Germany and Japan were unattractive because of stringent financial conditions. As a long shot, a member of the council wrote to his brother, a career diplomat assigned to Belgrade, who replied that the Yugoslavian government seemed disposed to invest in a large Peruvian project. Agriculture Minister General Jorge Barandiarán visited Yugoslavia and President Tito made an offer of assistance, which was considered together with a dozen others in a cabinet meeting. By late 1970 the government was displaying a more independent nationalist stance, one that would later catapult Velasco's foreign minister into a position as a spokesman for the Third World. The posibility of snubbing the World Bank by striking an agreement with a socialist country weighed positively on the decision to accept the Yugoslavian offer.

The Chira-Piura Project had three stages: (1) the construction of the Poechos Dam on the Chira River, the Chira-Piura and Montenegro diversion canals, and the rehabilitation of ancillary canals in Lower Piura; (2) new irrigation infrastructure in the Piura and Chira valleys; and (3) the intensive agricultural development of the Chira Valley (see Figure 3). The initial financing and construction contracts covered only the first stage.[28] When the negotiations were concluded and their terms approved by the Council of Ministers, the agreement was

26. Interview no. 68. The Hickenlooper Amendment empowered the U.S. president to cut off aid to any country seizing, expropriating, or nationalizing property of U.S. citizens without full and speedy compensation.

27. *La Prensa*, October 6, 1970, p. 2. The government accused the company of failure to fulfill a contract while the company felt that it had not been compensated adequately for work already completed.

28. Ministerio de Agricultura, Dirección Ejecutiva del Proyecto Especial Chira-Piura, *Proyecto ʼntegral de irrigación Chira-Piura* (Lima: Dirección Ejecutiva del Proyecto Especial Chira-Piura, 1973).

signed in a public ceremony in the presence of a multitude of peasants and citizens in front of the cathedral of Piura.[29]

## State Displacement of Traditional Elites

D.L. 17,463 contemplated a predominant role for the local council in the construction and administration of the works. High officials of the Agriculture Ministry, however, wished to control the project from Lima, and these preferences were consistent with the centralizing trend throughout the government at the time. The regime's special project organization for Chira-Piura, created under Decree Law 17,752, coexisted with the council until the council was officially dissolved in December 1970.[30] This act marked the beginning of a severe displacement of traditional power groups in Piura by the Ministry of Agriculture.

First, the implementation of D.L. 17,752, governing the distribution of water, concentrated considerable influence in the hands of state officials, who could use water allotments to favor specific interests and to encourage certain cropping patterns. Each farmer filled in a form setting out his tentative planting schedule. A zonal committee made up of four state officials and one local producer reviewed the forms and allocated water on the basis of its availability and the producers' willingness to plant in accordance with the national cropping plan. When farmers disagreed with the committee's decision, the director of the Agrarian Zone Office resolved the dispute in line with the votes of the state officials. This procedure virtually eliminated the ability of the large farmers to place their water rights above those of smaller farmers and campesino communities.

Second, the economic survival of the middle-sized and large farmers was severely jeopardized by the expropriations described in Chapter 2. Although Velasco had once promised that the department would not be subject to the agrarian reform, the government initiated an aggressive redistribution drive in

29. *La Prensa*, July 8, 1971, July 16, 1971, pp. 1 and 2; July 18, 1971, p. 4; and July 19, 1971, pp. 1 and 2; *El Peruano*, July 16, 1971, p. 3, and July 19, 1971, p. 1; *Extra*, July 19, 1971, p. 2; and *Siete Días*, July 23, 1971, p. 7.
30. *El Peruano*, December 19, 1970, p. 3.

1971.[31] By the end of 1974, the Agrarian Reform Agency had turned over 42,500 hectares to 69 cooperatives. This transferral of ownership took away the livelihoods of many of the persons represented on the former council, converting them from local elites into déclassés. Although they had initiated the Chira-Piura Project to favor their interests, state intervention transformed groups that were relatively unorganized before 1970 into the prime beneficiaries of water from the Poechos Dam when it was completed in mid-1975.

Third, the government sought means of favoring the least privileged economic groups despite their lack of effective power. But it also followed decision-making norms that responded to its own self-interests. The announcement of agrarian reform in the zone had created expectations among peasants of land, water, and jobs, but the region's production cooperatives had not noticeably increased agricultural employment. The cooperatives distinguished between their members (permanent workers who shared profits) and the temporary workers, many from Catacaos, who performed the hardest tasks, received lower wages, and did not qualify for cooperative benefits.

Faced with these inconsistencies, the director of the agrarian zone modified the construction project by finishing first that part of the diversion canal that went from the Montenegro area of the Chira River to its outlet in the Piura River. Instead of waiting for the termination of the Poechos Dam, he had pumps at Montenegro pass water directly from the Chira River into the diversion canal and thus to the Piura River. He calculated that a considerable amount of water could be delivered to Lower Piura about two years earlier than planned, opening up new lands that could be cultivated by temporary workers.

In another case, the construction of the Poechos Dam implied that a substantial area would be covered by water. Although much of this area was desert or semidesert, it also included the campesino community of Lanacones and its lands. The project administration proposed the relocation of the inhabitants to the area of Cieneguilla, which had the advantage of proximity to

31. See Velasco's statement exempting Piura from the reform in *La Prensa*, October 9, 1969.

the diversion canal, to the highway from Sullana, and to an electric power transmission line. The low-quality, sandy soils of this region absorbed a lot of water, however, and cultivation could cause flooding via seepage to the nearby city of Sullana. Middle-class Sullana residents protested vehemently and demanded that these people be relocated in Los Héroes Valley, near the San Lorenzo colonization. This area had the advantage of high-quality soils but would cost more for infrastructure and drain more water from the San Lorenzo reservoir. The two proposals were submitted to the minister of agriculture, who decided against the solution proposed by the Sullana residents. It is noteworthy that the state followed its own best counsel in deciding these issues and certainly not the advice of former landowners. In the first case the diversion canal went to assist marginalized farmers, and in the second a cost-benefit analysis showed the worth of the Cieneguilla option in spite of middle-class protest.

Fourth, the state used the Chira-Piura Project to demonstrate an independent stance vis-à-vis the lending and executing entities. The Peruvian government bowed to Yugoslavian wishes by hiring the Belgrade constructors Energoprojekt but insisted on reviewing and supervising its designs. Energoprojekt had had some prior experience in irrigation construction but never in an endeavor of the size and complexity of Chira-Piura. The Peruvian government retained CORBIN, an English-Peruvian firm, to supervise technical features.[32] In cases of disagreement between the Yugoslavs and CORBIN, the government reserved the right to invite international experts of its own choosing to break the deadlock, a right that it exercised on two occasions. Finally, Energoprojekt was required to present detailed work plans so that the government could actively control project execution.[33] The degree of state supervision was far in excess of that in any previous project carried out with the World Bank.

32. Interview no. 59 and *La Prensa*, October 6, 1970, p. 2; *El Comercio*, January 25, 1971, p. 4, and April 21, 1971, p. 4; *El Peruano*, December 2, 1970; March 2, 1971, p. 5; March 15, 1971, p. 5; April 20, 1971, p. 14; May 13, 1971, p. 7; and July 17, 1971.

33. See D.L. 21,356. Also *La Prensa*, May 15, 1974, p. 6; September 30, 1974, p. 12; and December 17, 1975, p. 1. The Peruvians and the Yugoslavs signed an agreement for the second stage of the project costing $55 million on July 26, 1979 (*El Comercio*, July 27, 1979).

## Social Class, International Actors, and State Autonomy

The history of the Chira-Piura Project can be analyzed in terms of a series of social conflicts, which the state attempted to resolve by increasing the supply of water by means that eventually concentrated power over this scarce resource in its own hands. The San Lorenzo Project was designed to resolve conflict between Upper Piura and Lower and Middle Piura farmers. Local elites, almost bypassing the Peruvian government, approached the World Bank for the economic resources necessary to obtain an amount of water sufficient to reduce or eliminate these conflicts.

The World Bank cooperated by constructing the San Lorenzo reservoir to regulate the flow of water to Lower and Middle Piura. At the same time it developed a goal of its own: the promotion of San Lorenzo colonization as a demonstration project for agrarian reform in Peru and the rest of Latin America under the guidelines of the Alliance for Progress. Experiments in agrarian reform were not a priority concern of prosperous Piura elites, who were more interested in relieving water scarcity for existing farmers. With the increase in the water flow at the beginning of the project, Lower and Middle Piura farmers tolerated the expansion of agriculture in Upper Piura instead of impeding it, as they had done previously. The fact that this expansion endangered the possibility of colonization in San Lorenzo was immaterial. Consequently, the World Bank became the protector of the San Lorenzo colonists (whose need for irrigation was incompatible with the amount of water available to them and all other users in the region) in their eventual conflict with the Lower and Middle Piura farmers.

The Belaúnde government played a relatively passive role in the affair. It received, on the one hand, economic pressures from the World Bank in favor of the San Lorenzo colonists, and on the other, political pressures from the Lower Piura farmers channeled mainly through the APRA party. ORDEN, Belaúnde's central government appendage, fell immediately under the influence of local elites. With the change of government in 1968 the local authorities still had the momentum in dealing with

150

the state. Through the council they succeeded in capturing the direction and control of the Chira-Piura Project. The council tried to combine its local political legitimacy with the World Bank's financial resources to create more water and reconsolidate its power in the zone.

These ambitions were blocked by two factors. First, the World Bank, which was to have financed the definitive studies and the work's construction, had a falling out with the Velasco regime and refused to make available its financial resources. Second, the political resources of the local authorities were desintegrating: the closing of Congress deprived the APRA party of its most important power arena, and the threat of agrarian reform dissipated the energy of previously dominant elites. Although the council's entrepreneurship paved the way for the agreement with the Yugoslavian government, the council soon lost all influence, which passed to the top officials in the Ministry of Agriculture and other state representatives.

In the final stage, the Yugoslavian government replaced the World Bank as a funding source but did not hold the Peruvian government in a similar dependency relationship. By establishing a powerful project management organization, controlling water through the General Water Law, and taking advantage of the confusion among local landowners resulting from agrarian reform, the state transformed itself from a relatively beleaguered arbiter of local conflicts into the dominant actor. It then pursued its self-defined interests, which included goals that coincided with the pressing needs of marginal peasant groups in the region, even though these groups did not have the objective power to impose their goals on the state.

Figure 4 portrays the relationships that prevailed in the San Lorenzo project under Belaúnde and Chira-Piura project at the midpoint of the Velasco regime. The San Lorenzo Project was executed in a situation of state dependency. The World Bank directed and controlled the project in exchange for the financial resources that made its execution possible, and delivered the finished works to the Piura farmers. In contrast, with the Chira-Piura project, the government bestowed prestige on Yugoslavia and its efforts on behalf of poorer Third World countries in return for economic resources and the direction

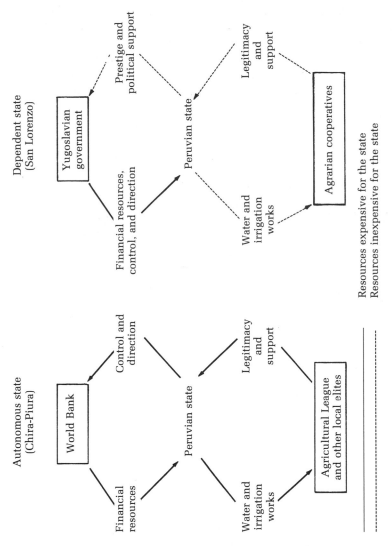

Autonomous state
(Chira-Piura)

Dependent state
(San Lorenzo)

Figure 4. Exchange relations of a dependent and an autonomous state with local and international actors

152

and control of the project. This arrangement represented a trading of less costly resources for more valuable ones, signifying a net profit for the state. Domestically, the agrarian reform seriously weakened the former local power structure. Until the new economic actors could become organized, their political support was a relatively valueless commodity and they had to cede considerable control over their activities to the central government. By obtaining monopoly over the new irrigation project, the state also controlled the distribution of surplus water, which became a relatively inexpensive resource with which to obtain political support.

The net result was the transfer of considerable power to the state. With this power the government was able to favor some of the disadvantaged sectors of the local population whose betterment had become a goal of the Velasco regime.

The Chira-Piura Project was just one example of the Peruvian state's ability to assert a relatively high degree of independence vis-à-vis classes, institutions, and international actors in its environment. The process of resource accumulation, growth, control, and autonomy characterized the centralizing trends that Velasco pursued during the early part of his regime. Centralization also had implications for the internal management of state agencies. Chapter 4 examines the relationship between centralization and personnel practices in the Agrarian Court System.

Chapter **4**

# Personnel Practices in the Agrarian Court System

Rural courts, acting in the name of traditional justice but favoring local elites, obstructed land distribution during the Belaúnde administration. The first institution created under D.L. 17,716 was the Fuero Privativo Agrario, or FPA (Agrarian Court System).[1] Its purpose was to absorb litigation dealing with land matters, including boundaries, water rights, contracts, inheritance, titles, and possession (but not expropriation, which was an administrative procedure during most of the Velasco regime).[2] One of its functions was to achieve justice for poor peas-

1. Little analytical material exists on the Agrarian Court System, whose formal structure is described in Articles 153 to 170 in "D. L. 17,716: Texto único concordado" in S. Martínez, *Legislación de reforma agraria* (Lima: Martínez, 1971). See Alberto Bustamante, *Las alternativas en la ideología jurídica prevaleciente* (Pontificia Universidad Católica del Perú, 1975); José M. Gálvez Vega, *El Fuero Privativo Agrario en el Perú* (Ayacucho: Bolivariana, 1971); and Luis Pásara, *Reforma agraria: Derecho y conflicto* (Lima: Instituto de Estudios Peruanos, 1978).

2. D.L. 17,716 was clear on this matter. In 1971 the FPA Tribunal reaffirmed its unwillingness to become involved by declaring that expropriation is a *sui generis* judicial-administrative procedure to which a judicial opinion does not apply, because the power to expropriate derives from the *jus imperium* of the state, which cannot be questioned. The tribunal's discretion on expropriation increased in March 1974 with the passage of D.L. 20,544, which was a result of

ants, who, individually and in their communities, had rarely been able to redress grievances through normal judicial channels. The land judges were given special "tuitive" powers to help peasants to receive a fair hearing.

The appellate justices of the FPA used certain standards for hiring, transferring, demoting, and separating their members. In most organizations, personnel practices are designed to create a system of inducements and sanctions to reinforce behavior preferred by the organization's dominant coalition.[3] Persons in authority, to abet organizational coherence, compensate subordinates more or less in proportion to their fulfillment of announced or implied performance goals, and the type of behavior rewarded throws light on the leaders' perceptions of the organization's main tasks. Although the FPA justices repeatedly called for high productivity, the land judges were seldom recognized for that quality. Rather, judges who demonstrated technical skills and conformity to directives from above were most likely to succeed. The incidence of negative sanctions to maintain discipline and the physical exigencies of the job made the FPA a coercive organization. The criteria for hiring, firing, promoting, and demoting land judges, especially during the early years of its existence, were symptomatic of centralist managerial practices.

## The Judiciary

In the COAP commission preparing D.L. 17,716, Guillermo Figallo argued that a new judicial system was necessary in the countryside. Delegating land disputes to the traditional Common Court System would be a mistake for several reasons. First, the common courts were riddled with corruption. Low-level officials in the national registries often "lost" or refused to

---

the small and middle-sized property owners' movement discussed in Chapter 2. This decree permitted an embargoed party (*afectado*) to request a temporary injunction (*recurso de amparo*) against expropriation until he could argue the illegality of the measure before the tribunal. In 1974 and 1975, the tribunal issued 584 *recursos de amparo* and adjudicated 501, 20 percent in favor of the propertyholder and 80 percent in favor of the Agrarian Reform Agency.

3. See Paul Pigors and Charles A. Myers, *Personnel Administration* (New York: Praeger, 1967), pp. 455ff.

provide peasants with copies of contracts or deeds that supported their claims, and presiding judges often interpreted the law conveniently to ensure that the litigant providing the most money won.[4] Second, judges administering courts of first petition in rural areas were tainted by their close association with the landowning class. Many judges were the younger sons of hacendados who, after obtaining law degrees, returned to the local area as political appointees to gain practical experience. Or they were from local commercial families, who married into landed interests and socialized with the rural elite. The judicial atmosphere did not improve at the appellate levels. Judges with departmental and national jurisdiction were appointed by the president, less for their judicial wisdom than because of recommendations made by a political clique (*argolla*) of deputies, senators, and, in rural areas, landowners. If the judge imprudently came out on the side of the poor farmer, he would be labeled a troublemaker. If he ignored suggestions from superiors that certain parties be favored, he would be overruled by the higher court. When they earned seniority, "safe" judges would be promoted to superior courts at the departmental level, and eventually might reach the Supreme Court in Lima. Once these persons were acting on appeals, it was unlikely that poor plaintiffs would win against richer adversaries despite the merits of their cases. Since the outcome was seldom in doubt and the appellate process was expensive, few suits between peasants and landowners arrived at higher courts. Indeed, no "Indian" won a case in the Supreme Court during the first 150 years of the republic.[5]

4. The saying goes that when a lawyer offered monetary rewards to soften up (*ablandar*) the common court judge, the judge might respond with three emphatic no's. That was the signal that the offer had to be raised threefold. In a study begun in 1964 and co-directed by William F. Whyte, Lawrence K. Williams, José Matos Mar, and Julio Cotler, 2,715 rural inhabitants were asked: "Are judges' decisions based on law or pull?" The responses were "Pull and money," 70 percent; "Law," 14 percent; undecided, 13 percent; and no answer, 3 percent. When asked, "What chance do you have to get justice?" answers were "Good," 24 percent; "Fair," 38 percent; "Poor to none," 31 percent; and no response, 7 percent. See George H. Westacott, *La confianza interpersonal en el Perú* (Lima: ESAN, 1975). The jury system does not exist in the Peruvian Roman law tradition.

5. Guillermo Figallo, "El marco jurídico de la reforma agraria," *Participación* 2:3 (August 1973), 37.

Third, procedural weaknesses frustrated routine administration of justice and prevented rapid decisions even when goodwill prevailed. The Code of Justice (Ley Orgánica de Justicia) encouraged procrastination. If a litigant disputed the validity of a piece of evidence, he could ask for its nullification and, if rejected, interrupt the proceedings and appeal to higher courts. Often this tactic was a subterfuge to outlast the opposition, and some cases ran on for decades. Table 11 points out that, once it corrected this problem, the FPA was able to dispatch a large number of cases under adjudication for over fifty years.

A fourth reason for dissatisfaction with the Common Court System was its lack of technical specialization in land matters.[6] Law 15,037 required litigants to pass through the National Agrarian Council, a special arm of the Ministry of Agriculture, before bringing land disputes before the common courts. But production-oriented agricultural engineers and biased parliamentary deputies often refused to turn land over to peasants, and the council did not defer to legal considerations in making decisions. Rather than convert the council into a special chamber for agricultural affairs in the Supreme Court, the COAP set up the FPA.

This decision followed upon other steps toward judicial specialization, and left the common courts mainly with criminal and civil cases. The fragmentation of the judicial branch of government began with the creation of the military courts early in republican history and continued in 1919 with the labor courts and in 1975 with the Fuero Privativo de Comunidades Laborales (for disputes under new labor-community legislation). None of these courts was under the authority of the Supreme Court, although defendants in the customs and tax courts could file appeals through the common courts. The labor, agrarian, and labor-community court systems were created because of increasingly complex legislation, a heavy backlog of cases, the emergence of new power groups in the society, and lessening confidence in the ability of the common courts to handle the work load fairly and competently.

In 1971 the government created the National Council of Justice, giving it authority to name and supervise the behavior of

6. See Mario Alegría Campos, *Poder judicial* (Lima: Chiabra, 1972).

Table 11. Cases left over from the Common Court System and resolved by the Agrarian Court System in its first six years

| Year of initiation: | Before 1920 | 1921–30 | 1931–40 | 1941–50 | 1951–60 | 1961–69 |
|---|---|---|---|---|---|---|
| Number: | 745 | 1,333 | 2,119 | 3,331 | 4,912 | 9,893 |

SOURCE: *Memoria del Presidente del Tribunal Agrario* (Lima: Tribunal Agrario, 1976), p. 30.

judges in the common, labor, and agrarian courts. The National Council of Justice, whose members were appointed by the regime from universities, public agencies, and professional associations in the country, was also charged with reforming the Common Court System. In 1976, the Peruvian judicial branch had lines of authority similar to those in Figure 5.[7] Though the National Council of Justice did not have appellate jurisdiction over the activities of the various court systems, its wide-ranging supervisory powers further undermined the traditional hegemony of the Supreme Court. Some jurists hoped that the National Council of Justice would eventually be the core of a unified court system in Peru, but the main effect during the Velasco period was to outflank the Common Court System both laterally and hierarchically, exacerbate institutional rivalries within the judicial system, and allow the regime to influence more easily decisions taken in each of the subbranches.

## Personnel Appointments in the Agrarian Court System

### Higher and Lower Levels

This chapter treats mainly the land judges, but a word on the appointment of other FPA employees helps to complete the picture. The FPA began activities in late 1969 with 3 appellate

7. We are grateful to Jorge Avendaño for assistance in preparing this chart. The president's appellate powers extended only to pardons for penal offenses *(indultos)*, usually announced at Christmas or on July 28, the national anniversary. See F. Bonilla, ed., *Ley Orgánica del Poder Judicial* (Lima: Mercurio, 1972), D.L. 18,831, pp. 112–22, 218–31. The judicial process is described in Thomas W. Weil et al., *Area Handbook for Peru* (Washington, D.C.: Government Printing Office, 1972), pp. 184–86.

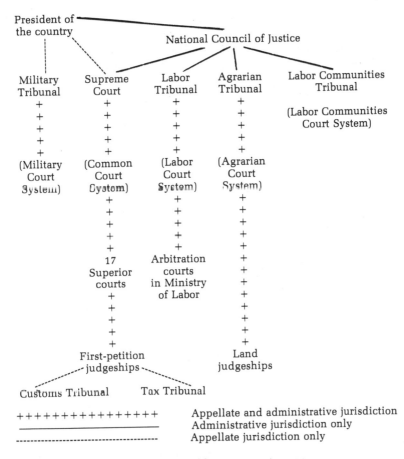

Figure 5. Judicial bureaucracy in 1976

justices *(vocales)*, 10 land judges *(jueces de tierra)*, and 60 auxiliary personnel. By 1976 it included 6 appellate judges, 66 land judges, and 420 service personnel. Guillermo Figallo was the first president of the Agrarian Tribunal, and Carlos Castañeda Lafontaine and Ulíses Quiroga Masías were appointed as comagistrates. Chapter 2 discussed Figallo's role as an agrarian jurist during the drafting of Decree Law 17,716. Later, his public statements on law and agrarian change became part and parcel of the government's ideology for rural areas. Carlos Castañeda received his law degree in 1953. Once an active member of the APRA party, he became disillusioned with its drift to the Right and abandoned it in 1965. He worked for many years in the Labor Tribunal and in the Second Judicial Zone of the Military Tribunal. At the time of his appointment to the Agrarian Tribunal he was state's attorney.[8] Ulíses Quiroga had gained agricultural experience as head lawyer for the Rice Marketing Commission in the National Bank, and also was the legal adviser to the Petroleum Division in the old Ministry of Development and Public Works.[9] His cousin Captain Aurelio Masías was a member of the COAP. In March 1971 the government appointed Guillermo García Montúfar as the fourth appellate judge. His political credentials included public denunciations of the APRA party as a student leader and strong criticism of the International Petroleum Company during the 1960s. These four men represented a mixture of several traits: technical competence, ideological commitment to the goals of the revolution, reputations for honesty, and loyalty to the president of the tribunal or other regime figures.[10]

The FPA's approximately 420 auxiliary personnel (secretaries, clerks, drivers, porters, and guards) were hired predominantly on the basis of recommendations communicated by telephone, on the backs of calling cards, or in person. If the land judge or personnel director had confidence in the integrity of the recommender, was impressed by his importance, or valued his friendship, such support could compensate for a candidate's inadequate education or work experience. The fact that the agrarian courts were new and endowed with an important

8. *La Prensa*, August 23, 1969, p. 3.

9. *La Prensa*, September 1, 1948; January 10, 1969; March 25, 1971. Like Figallo, García Montúfar was a former member of the Social Progressive Movement. In 1972, tribunal justices received salaries of about U.S. $830 per month.

10. Later the National Council of Justice appointed justices to the tribunal, among them Luis Landeo Pineda, who had worked for the Campesino Communities Agency, for SINAMOS, and as alternative prosecutor for the FPA; Alcídes Roca Jiménez, who was director general of the Legal Office in the Ministry of Agriculture; José María Ugarte Benvenuto, who had been a land judge since 1968 in Jaen, Sullana, and Ica; and Hildebrando Castro-Pozo Castro, whose father founded the Peruvian Socialist Party and who had served as land judge in Mayca, Huamachuco, and Huanuco.

mission did not make them immune to clientelism in their personnel practices. In the words of one administrator:

> As for recommendations, the FPA is under the same pressure as the rest of the public sector. In Peru, recommendations are the institutionalized way of hiring people and, despite earnest efforts, the system cannot be abolished. An official in a hiring capacity cannot fight this tradition alone, nor can he ignore his superior's orders and expect to retain his job.[11]

### The Ideal Land Judge

The FPA's responsibilities for reforming justice in the countryside required land judges with special traits: knowledge of D.L. 17,716 and its more than fifty modifications, administrative productivity, sympathy for the plight of the peasant, and capacity to tolerate physical discomfort during on-site inspections. Guillermo Figallo felt that ideological motivation was extremely important.

> The role of rural magistrate requires an ethical commitment. Besides qualities of honesty, austerity, and professional competence, which all judges must have, the land judge shares in the mystique of the agrarian reform. . . . The reform is oriented toward transferring property and political power to the campesino majorities. It also hopes to mold a new man to be the protagonist in historical changes. Imbued with this charisma . . . the land judge is obliged to learn at firsthand the social reality of the countryside so that his decisions faithfully represent the revolutionary will of the law.[12]

To catch up with the case backlog, the land judges had to work considerably faster than the common court judges, and D.L. 17,716 included strict provisions for adjudicating land claims. The process began when a plaintiff registered a complaint (*demanda*) over a territorial infringement, indemnification, or contract violation, or for recovery of property. Within five days, the accused party had to present his defense backed by proof and the judge then had six days to arbitrate the dispute by bringing both parties together, either in his office or at the site of the controversy. If the case was not settled during this

11. Interview no. 120.
12. Figallo, "Marco jurídico," p. 38.

preliminary hearing, the judge then had ten days to conduct an on-site inspection, to talk with third parties, to examine the land under question, and to note the existence and location of physical structures. Within five days after the on-site inspection, the land judge dictated a sentence, which was communicated to the parties and to the Agrarian Tribunal in Lima. The loser in the case could then appeal, with the judge's assent. But the local judge had to complete his work on the case within twenty-six days of its submission, despite his overall work load.[13]

The obligatory on-site inspection was an ordeal, but it promoted justice for the peasant. Previously, rural judges received complaints in their offices and simply sifted through documents to determine the sentence. Reliance on paperwork placed the poorer litigant at a disadvantage because he usually lacked the savoir-faire to gain access to the official registries; each trek to the provincial capital to assemble the required documentation took several days from work; and having a lawyer collect the documents or the judge visit them was expensive. The Agrarian Tribunal felt that on-site inspections were crucial in the majority of land disputes because the agrarian reform law gave more importance to possession than to official ownership. In legal terms, "la tierra para quien la trabaja" meant that possession resided in the person who worked or lived on the land, not necessarily the person who had title to it. The land judge could not determine who showed up for work in the morning without being there.

The judge could display his ideological fervor most skillfully in the "tuitive" function by consciously favoring poor plaintiffs. The tuitive function compensated for the fact that peas-

13. These time periods were lengthened by grace days according to a table of estimated travel time between the site of the dispute and the location of the court. See "Cuadro general de término de distancias," in Ley Orgánica del Poder Judicial, ed. Bonilla, pp. 123–75. The table allowed, for instance, three extra days for each step for suits in the town of Quinuabamba within the jurisdiction of the Pomabamba judgeship. In 1972, 39 land judges resolved 12,033 cases, an average for each judge of more than two every three calendar days. From the filing date of the original complaint to the final appellate decision of the Agrarian Tribunal, the FPA seldom took more than eighteen months to dispose of a case.

ants usually presented their cases clumsily. To improve their chances, the judge could counsel them on their rights and the proper procedures by which to present their cases. *Ultra-petitios* corrected an improper submission of the complaint; for example, if the peasant erroneously requested a recovery of property *(reivindicación)*, the judge could say, "No, you don't want a recovery, you want an injunction *[interdicto]*." If a peasant who had lost his plot asked only for the plot's return, the judge could remind him to sue for damages as well. In the common court, these cases would have been dismissed or the judgments annulled. The ideal land judge was expected to promote the judicial process, and not to let the pace of the proceedings be governed by the initiative of the litigants, especially when the evidence began to weigh against the poorer peasant. It was frequently necessary to go beyond the written law in both meaning and procedure. The tribunal insisted that the judge be not a spectator but a full actor in the courtroom drama in order to arrive at the truth.

In sum, the job of land judge was enormously difficult, requiring dedication at all times, including evenings, weekends, and holidays. Sometimes stationed in places with no electricity, the judges had to start early and work through the day to take advantage of the sunlight hours. The on-site inspections frequently required days of travel, much of it on donkeys over inhospitable terrain, eating unfamiliar foods and sleeping in the open air. Judges in the sierra had to complete most of their travel before the rainy season, from December to April, or suffer additional backlogs. Judges with families had to mollify the complaints of their wives, bored by the isolation, and concerned that in the mountains their children were receiving third-rate education. The justices on the Agrarian Tribunal tried to set examples of abnegation but the land judges in most provinces worked under considerably more onerous conditions.

### Recruitment and Communication

In hiring judges, the tribunal felt that the best candidates had a revolutionary outlook. Although new judicial procedures enacted with D.L. 17,716 facilitated more rapid litigation,

Figallo and his comagistrates did not believe that the habits of traditional judges could be altered simply by the provision of a new law to implement. Judges trapped in the old routine would have sabotaged the law's intent.

> I guess we might have worked with the old judges, just by changing their procedures in dealing with land cases, but it would have been impossible to change their ways. By nature all lawyers are conservative. Imagine the reaction of a magistrate who has sat on a common court for twenty years, trying to adapt himself to the new procedures in the Fuero Agrario!
> The judge has to be committed to the agrarian reform. Obviously persons who have habitually defended the hacendados are not going to render an objective ruling. We needed a judge who was partial to the reform but maintained a clear vision of the law.[14]

Because of the unattractive working conditions, candidates were not numerous, and the tribunal had difficulty in preselecting the ideal judge, one who was simultaneously committed, ascetic, empathetic, and knowledgeable. Nor did the tribunal invest large amounts of time in inculcating the proper attitudes and skills. Its communication with judges was minimal and it relied heavily on negative sanctions to punish deviant behavior.

The tribunal announced the competition for the first group of ten land judges on posters in the Peruvian and Lima bar associations (*colegios de abogados*) and the Ministry of Agriculture. The tribunal justices interviewed candidates on their attitudes toward agrarian reform and their knowledge of the law, preferring lawyers who had written bachelor theses in an agriculture-related field. Five of the first ten judges came from the Agrarian Reform Agency; three had presented cases before the common courts; and two who had worked in the National Agrarian Council under Figallo took up positions in the coveted Lima jurisdictions. The Ministry of Agriculture checked into their moral reputations and verified their curricula vitae. After its creation, the National Council of Justice made the final selection. Initially the land judge's remuneration of U.S. $480 per month plus per diem while on the road was superior to that of

14. Interview no. 34.

the common courts judges. The salary advantage was short-lived, however. Soon afterward, the common court judges pressured successfully for parity and land judges' salaries were frozen during the first six years of the reform, despite inflation and devaluation. Compensation in the state enterprise sector was often 50 percent higher than in the FPA, and mid-career lawyers in private practice earned up to twice the salary of even the tribunal justices. The tribunal became increasingly dissatisfied with the quality of its recruits, and by 1974 the number of vacancies in the FPA exceeded the number of candidates.

After posting the judges, the tribunal made irregular attempts to stay in touch on policy issues. Formal communication was made up of administrative memoranda *(circulares)* and legal briefs *(ejecutorias).* [15] The memoranda contained norms on judicial functions, such as how to organize the office, how to conduct a hearing, and when to insist on receiving the plaintiff's tax papers before sentencing. The legal briefs usually emerged after an appeal over an obscure point. They represented the tribunal's collective interpretation of the law and served as judicial precedents. The briefs were sent to the judges periodically during the year and the most important were appended to the president's annual report. [16]

15. The judges also received the government's official newspaper, *El Peruano*, containing official bulletins and all legislation, but not journals and books covering legal and sociological aspects of the agrarian reform.
16. In the 1970–71 annual report, the tribunal published 45 legal briefs; in 1971–72, 34; in 1972–73, 22; and in 1973–75, 18. The content of the most important reflected the changing nature of agrarian reform legislation and policy disputes, as described in Chapter 2. In 1970, for example, the tribunal declared that land would go to the person who was working it directly; landowners could not evict renters and sharecroppers to work the land themselves, and thus avoid expropriation; and small propertyowners who rented their land lost preferential treatment under the agrarian reform, and the land devolved automatically to the renter. During the 1971–72 period, in cases of labor violations, the burden of proof fell on the employer, and in cases of doubt the plaintiff was considered to be in the right; and stock-issuing agricultural enterprises were legal entities separate from their members, and thus land could not be divided among the stockholders in small plots to avoid expropriation. In 1972–73, once the partition of a farm had been annulled, the farm had to be joined together again as a single economic unit; and campesino communities lacking a suitable amount of land for subsistence could be provided with neighboring hacienda land even if that hacienda were located outside of an agrarian reform zone. In 1973–74, when the tribunal upheld the complaint of a

The tribunal used visits to local areas and biannual seminars as more direct means of reinforcing a spirit of sacrifice and clarifying legal and administrative procedures. On visits, the justices attempted to develop a personal rapport with the local magistrate by complimenting his performance, encouraging him to maintain his dedication, reiterating the importance of high ethical standards, and offering to discuss special requests with other tribunal members. In seminars, the tribunal interpreted recent changes in the law and commented on repeated deficiencies in some judges' procedures. Another objective of seminars was to provide a forum for more progressive judges to let their opinions be heard. Land judges who attended these meetings listened closely to the ideological preferences of the tribunal members for later implementation in their districts.

### Criteria for Promotion and Demotion

How did a land judge know whether he was doing well in his job, and what inducements existed to motivate his performance? The tribunal justices indicated that he would be rewarded for the number of cases resolved, his moral conduct, the consistent ratification of his decisions on appeal, the lack of complaints from his district, and his general office administration. They repeatedly stated that the judges had to identify with the agrarian reform process and understand its true philosophy. The judge's written decisions had to demonstrate dedication, skill, and ideological commitment. The number of cases resolved indicated whether the judge was working hard; a large number of overturned cases suggested that the judge was not empathizing with poorer peasants. A judge whose rulings favored powerful parties, even if based on plausible interpretations of the law, was in trouble. The tribunal was especially disturbed if it discovered that a judge received payment for an on-site inspection, which was free in the FPA.

Designing a personnel policy was somewhat more problematic than establishing merit criteria. The FPA had only two

---

former landowner that the government had paid too little for the property, the decision did not affect the fact that the property had been irrevocably expropriated.

hierarchical levels—the local jurisdiction and the national tribunal—which implied differences in pay, status, or authority, and there was no guarantee that the best land judges would fill positions on the tribunal. The FPA's standard practice was to rotate judges periodically, and the justices found that the best means of inducing high standards was to promise the judge the chance of transferring to a better location. Assignments were ranked according to their desirability, and used as rewards or punishments in response to the judges' past performance. The hierarchy of preferred locations was based on the natural divisions of Peru—coast, sierra (highlands), and jungle. The most desirable assignments were on the coast—Lima, Piura, Arequipa, Ica, Nazca, Chiclayo, Tacna, and Pisco. The coastal city's proximity to Lima and its size helped to determine its relative preference. Size was the determining factor in the sierra.

> Any city on the coast is better than any city in the sierra. There are some places that are considered ideal, like Trujillo and Cañete. Abancay and Ayaviri are undesirable locations in the sierra, especially for men with families or health problems.
>
> If they have to be in the sierra, it's better to be in Cuzco, Puno, or Ayacucho, since all the rest are small towns. But everyone wants to head for the capital or get as close to Lima as possible—places like Arequipa or Trujillo.
>
> The judges try to avoid godforsaken places like Pomabamba, Ayaviri, and Juliaca (which suffers from terrible cold and wind, not to mention the altitude), Huancavelica (where it rains all day long), and Tarapoto, in the jungle (believe me, there's absolutely nothing to do in Tarapoto!).[17]

This hierarchy of preferences gave the tribunal more flexibility in designing a promotion ladder than it would have had if all judgeships had been equally attractive.

Analysis of the career patterns of individual judges helps one to determine whether they were being promoted or demoted each time they were transferred.[18] Promotions involved moving

17. Interviews nos. 34, 35, 36, 37, and 38. A tribunal justice added, "How do we know what is a promotion? Aplao is the end of the world, while Chiclayo is good. You can consider inhospitable those locations in the sierra, like Cuzco and Puno, where the altitude is killing, or like Pomabamba, which has no electricity."

18. For the jurisdictions of the land judgeships, see Angel Eduardo Valdivia Rodríguez, ed., *Guía judicial de Lima* (Lima: AEME, 1972), pp. 39–50. The

to a more desirable location, but a judge who was doing well did not have to accept a better post if he did not wish. When a judge refused to accept a demotion to a less desirable judgeship, he had little choice but to resign. In cases of more serious incompetence, the tribunal asked for the judge's resignation. Resignation in most cases was the ultimate demotion, because the tribunal attempted to avoid firing judges. From 1969 to 1973, 20 judges were promoted, 12 were demoted, and 12 resigned.

Despite the smallness of this universe, the exercise of aggregating performance indications of those judges who were promoted and demoted helps to establish the kind of behavior favored by the tribunal. In its annual report the tribunal published data on the judicial activity in each land district. From these statistics it is possible to determine how many cases each judge resolved (*causas resueltas*), how many local decisions were ratified on appeal (*confirmaciones*), how many were overturned (*revocaciones*), and how many were sent back to the land judge because of procedural errors (*insubsistencias*).[19] These measures are approximate empirical referents for productivity, conformity to directives, and technical skills. (No public records report on other possible criteria, such as moral impropriety, trustworthiness, or office administration.) The number of cases resolved is a straightforward measure of productivity. The percentage of confirmations indicates the judge's ability to abide by the agrarian reform legislation and the tri-

ranking of 42 jurisdictions extrapolated from interviews in the FPA and utilized in the analysis below placed Lima at the top of the list, followed by Trujillo, Chiclayo, Tacna, Chimbote, Arequipa, Ica, Piura, Sullana, Pisco, Huacho, Nazca, Cañete, and San Pedro de Lloc (on the coast); Cuzco, Tarma, Huancayo, Huaraz, Cajamarca, Huánuco, Puno, Juliaca, Sicuani, Chota, Jaen, Ayacucho, Huamachuco, Huancavelica, Abancay, Ayaviri, Puquio, Cangallo, Pomabamba, Huari, Aplao, and La Unión (in the sierra); and Tarapoto (in the jungle). Lima, Trujillo, Arequipa, Cuzco, and Huancayo had two judgeships.

19. In the 1971–72 judicial year, almost a third of the cases at the local level (3,857 of 12,033) came to Lima on appeal, and in the 1973–75 period, about a fifth (7,792 of 34,552). At the thrice-weekly meeting of the tribunal, these appeals were distributed at random among the justices, each of whom prepared briefs on his cases and recommended the action to be taken. In 1971–72, 2,183 decisions (60.0 percent) were ratified on appeal, 666 (18.3 percent) were overturned, 769 (21.1 percent) were challenged for procedural errors, and 19 were withdrawn or abandoned.

bunal's legal briefs. By overturning a case, the tribunal told the judge that he had not favored the deserving party in the proceedings. Persistent *revocaciones* indicated that the judge was failing to interpret properly the tribunal's directives in administering justice in the countryside.

Table 12 shows the correlation between performance and promotion as measured by judges' technical skill. In regard to cases returned because of procedural errors, gamma equals −.478 (that is, the more cases returned for procedural errors, the less tendency to be promoted). The next highest coefficients pertain to cases overturned on appeal (−.273), overall ratifications (.266), and cases resolved (.000).[20] The implication is that technical skill and following orders were more important than productivity for promotion of judges. Ideological commitment is encompassed within these two criteria because the judges were instructed not to wander from the spirit of the agrarian reform law—as interpreted by their superiors. As one justice remarked, "Our judges do not have to be ideologues. They act professionally. Their ideology is in the fundamental texts of the law, and has no other character."[21]

### The Predominance of Negative Sanctions

The tribunal used an elaborate system of negative sanctions to reaffirm the need for technical expertise, discipline, and moral rectitude. These sanctions were more severe and fre-

---

20. We first established whether the 44 relocations represented promotions or demotions (through the scale of city preferences) and whether the judges who resigned had been asked to do so (through interviews with tribunal justices and administrators). We then isolated those judges who had completed a full year of judicial activity in their posts prior to relocation so that information on their performance would be included in the tribunal's annual report. These steps reduced the sample to 34 judges in three of the above categories and 36 in the fourth. The judge's performance in the year of his transfer was then compared with that of his colleagues to ascertain whether he fell in the top, middle, or bottom third of all judges in cases resolved, ratified, overturned, and returned for errors. Contingency tables were constructed and a simple measure of ordinal association (gamma) was calculated between promotion and performance. The judges were ranked in each indicator by thirds to ensure that most cells would be filled. When ranked by fifths, the gamma coefficient for procedural errors was −.419; for overturned cases, −.329; for ratified cases, .143; and for case load resolved, .019.

21. Interview no. 14.

*Table 12.* Number of land judges ranking in bottom, middle, and upper thirds of all judges in four performance criteria, by career outcome

| Performance criterion | Career outcome | | |
|---|---|---|---|
| | Promotion | Demotion | Separation |
| Cases returned because of procedural errors[a] | | | |
| Bottom third | 5 | 3 | 0 |
| Middle third | 6 | 6 | 4 |
| Upper third | 3 | 2 | 5 |
| Total | 14 | 11 | 9 |
| Cases overturned on appeal[b] | | | |
| Bottom third | 7 | 4 | 2 |
| Middle third | 4 | 3 | 4 |
| Upper third | 3 | 4 | 3 |
| Total | 14 | 11 | 9 |
| Cases ratified on appeal[c] | | | |
| Bottom third | 2 | 4 | 5 |
| Middle third | 9 | 2 | 2 |
| Upper third | 3 | 5 | 2 |
| Total | 14 | 11 | 9 |
| Cases resolved[d] | | | |
| Bottom third | 7 | 3 | 4 |
| Middle third | 4 | 3 | 3 |
| Upper third | 5 | 5 | 2 |
| Total | 16 | 11 | 9 |

[a] Gamma = −.478.
[b] Gamma = −.273.
[c] Gamma = .266.
[d] Gamma = .000.

quent than in the Common Court System. Disciplinary actions against land judges proceeded from warnings to fines, suspension, and dismissal, and the tribunal's executive secretary was responsible for keeping a record of the judges' performance and complaints from their districts. The least serious sanction, the warning (*apercibimiento*), simply called the judge's attention to an oversight, such as omitting the number of a plaintiff's official registration card. Next came the fine, levied when the tribunal discovered that the judge had neglected an important step in the judicial process or interpreted the facts incorrectly—had skipped the on-site inspection, for example, or failed to order an equipment inventory in an expropriation dispute, or decided a case on a document that the tribunal justices felt was inconsequential. Fines went from U.S. $7 to $46 and were more frequently employed than simple warnings, because the tribunal found them "more effective."[22]

Complaints lodged against a judge at the local level played an important role in suspension and dismissal. The tribunal did not attribute significance to complaints containing unsavory language coming from peasants or landowners who had recently lost a suit. More important were accusations against a judge's moral character, and the tribunal ordered a full investigation when it received charges that a judge was drunk much of the time, had been involved in a sex scandal, or had accepted money for his services.[23] The first step was to request local agents of the National Intelligence Service to observe the judge's behavior and submit a report. Some magistrates accused of misbehavior were amazed to learn that the tribunal had an accurate account of their day-to-day activities over long periods of time. If the confidential report did not absolve the judge, the tribunal sent him a memorandum requesting an explanation. An unsatisfactory answer provoked a disciplinary trial, after which the tribunal decided whether to acquit, suspend, or dismiss. Suspension, which called for working with-

---

22. Interview no. 39. Tribunal members estimated that 55 percent of its sanctions were fines and 45 percent warnings.

23. In its first six years, however, the FPA earned a reputation for high ethical standards. Litigants learned that favors from land judges could not be bought. Tribunal justices attempted to avoid visits and telephone calls from "friends of friends" by acting quickly on litigation. The tribunal justices also frowned on gift giving, and wished peasants would forget the custom of presenting land judges with a pig or a local cheese when their cases came to court. This caution did not mean that a litigant could not talk privately with a justice before his case was decided, and each judge had about four or five visitors per day. One justice commented, "It is rare that litigants begin by telling about all of their friends in high places or in the justice's inner circle, though some of course do. Most go straight to the point: 'I lost the case in the first instance but I'm right and want to tell you why.' Often they can clear up some complicated but important point" (interview no. 14).

out pay for a length of time, could also be imposed because of repeated procedural errors or falling behind on the case load.

In punishing a deviant judge, the tribunal hoped to avoid dismissal, a severe condemnation that attracted publicity, prevented the accused from holding a judgeship again, and usually ruined his legal career. The tribunal much preferred that such judges resign, and sometimes prompted this choice by threatening not to renew their contracts, an act equivalent to dismissal. One judge who had gone through this experience lamented:

> It is very difficult to do an impeccable job as a land judge because there are just too many pressures and demands. You have to be too careful about your personal behavior. Judges who like to carouse a bit at night have been told in no uncertain terms to toe the line. Each time a decision is overturned, the judge is warned or even fined. Naturally, when you see your paycheck getting smaller, it tends to build up resentment toward the tribunal.[24]

This former judge felt that the Agrarian Tribunal purposefully dispensed fines and warnings so that he would accumulate a fat record of incompetence, which could then be held over his head. But the purpose of this severity appeared to be more forthright. The tribunal felt that it had to dispel an image of judicial corruption in the countryside, and the only way to do so was to maintain a tight rein on judges' behavior. The surveillance system, of which the judges were ignorant until they stepped out of line, was an effective means of checking on their extracurricular activities. While dismissal was distasteful and considered an overly severe sanction, tribunal justices did not shrink from assigning poor judges to the boondocks. Moral laxness and technical incompetence were not consistent with the rectified image of justice that was to prevail in the Agrarian Court System.

These noble purposes, however, were lost on many land judges, who felt that the tribunal's management style engendered little loyalty toward the FPA. Generally, such complaints came from judges who never learned the rules of the FPA. Isolated in scattered locales, they resented working as loners, ac-

24. Interview no. 33.

countable to higher authority but suffering frequent reversals on appeal because of their inability to solicit advice from and explain special circumstances to the tribunal justices. They complained that although the tribunal required on-site inspections, it ignored the judge's factual report and overturned decisions on the basis of submitted documents; that the tribunal said it was interested in speed, but then penalized a judge because he skipped certain steps in arriving at a just resolution of a case; and that the tribunal would use certain rules of thumb in arriving at decisions, but once those rules were known to the defendants, they could easily distort them to thwart justice.[25]

## Conclusions

In the first years of the Velasco regime, the secretive agrarian policy making, the campaign against private property, the assault against the "oligarchy," and the lack of access to judicial recourse placed landowners on the defensive. The heavy emphasis on discipline and conformity to directives inside the FPA was consistent with centralizing trends in the political community. Centralist management principles internally mirrored the FPA's function in rural areas: remove the traditional advantage of local socioeconomic elites in their litigation with the poor. Landowners, critical of Figallo and others on the tribunal, complained that compensatory justice meant that they had no chance of winning any suit before the tribunal. Instead of defending a higher principle, the FPA simply threw up a smoke-screen of legal jargon to legitimize decisions that served the regime's political objectives. Landed interests felt that the FPA was in an unholy alliance with the Agrarian Reform Agency. Calling it a judicial unit was a sham. Its activities meshed perfectly with those of the military regime and they shared the same coercive, totalitarian goals.

To many sympathizers of the Velasco government, these complaints were a source of pride. The fact was, however, that no civilian public-sector organization abided by such strict personnel practices as the FPA. The Velasco regime did not seek

25. Interview no. 35.

the same degree of discipline in other state agencies because its centralizing measures were directed more toward changing the relationship between the state and traditional classes and social institutions than toward administrative reform. Over time, with the large landowners removed from the scene, the FPA's centralist management style was less necessary, and less feasible, given the loose administrative controls elsewhere in the public sector. The FPA's supervisory strictness began to deteriorate, especially after Figallo left the tribunal in early 1975.

The FPA remained sensitive nonetheless to the government's subsequent desire to contain dissatisfaction and generate popular support for the regime. By 1974 only about 5 percent of the judges' time was taken up with litigation involving latifundios. Approximately a third of the cases dealt with the rights of renters, contract fulfillment, damages, boundary disputes, and bankruptcy; the remainder were between small farmers or campesino communities over a few square meters of land, grazing rights, or the ownership of a cow. Litigation over seemingly minor matters filled the FPA dockets, but such disputes could conceivably have led to outbreaks of violence or land invasions if they had not been attended to promptly.[26] Poor peasants appreciated the fact that by appealing to this arm of the state, they could, with the aid of the judge's tuitive powers, obtain a suitable resolution of their grievances. Although the number of new suits declined from 1971 to 1973, they subsequently increased as the FPA interacted with an ever larger portion of the peasantry.[27] The regime found that the FPA was a useful vehicle for channeling discontent and incorporating large numbers of peasants into national institutions at a relatively small cost.

26. See Pásara, *Reforma agraria*, p. 87.
27. The number of cases presented per year was 16,102 in 1969–70, 23,457 in 1970–71, 17,076 in 1971–72, 13,538 in 1972–73, and 37,007 in 1973–75 (*Memorias del Presidente del Tribunal Agrario* [Lima: Fuero Privativo Agrario, 1969–76]).

Chapter 5

# Chartering Interest Groups

The Peruvian military regime passed through centralist, corporatist, and liberal stages from 1968 to 1978. Except in the
Agrarian Court System, these trends were more evident in the
structural and ideological makeup of the government than in
management practices of public organizations. Much of the literature in English on the revolutionary government stresses its
corporatist character.[1] Indeed, these experiments from 1972 to
1974 at integrating the popular sectors into a national system of
rewards were unusual and innovative, although destined to
fail. In part through SINAMOS, the regime created "representative interest groups" under state tutelage for various sectors of
the society: peasants (Confederación Nacional Agraria, CNA),
workers (Central de Trabajadores de la Revolución Peruana,
CTRP), labor communities (Comité Coordinador de la Con

---

1. See David Chaplin, ed., *Peruvian Nationalism* (New Brunswick, N.J.:
Transaction Books, 1976); Alfred C. Stepan, *State and Society* (Princeton:
Princeton University Press, 1978); Julio Cotler, "The New Mode of Political
Domination in Peru," in *The Peruvian Experiment*, ed. Abraham Lowenthal
(Princeton: Princeton University Press, 1975), pp. 44–88; James M. Malloy,
"Authoritarianism, Corporatism, and Mobilization in Peru," *Review of Politics* 36:1 (January 1974), 52–84; and David Scott Palmer, "Revolution from
Above" (Ithaca: Cornell University Dissertation Series, 1973).

175

federación Nacional de Comunidades Industriales, CONACI), youth (Juventud Revolucionaria del Perú, JRP), teachers (Sindicato de Educadores de la Revolución Peruana, SERP), artists (Asociación Nacional de Trabajadores del Arte, ANTA), and professionals (Central de Profesionales de la Revolución Peruana, CPRP). The facts that three of these groups (JRP, ANTA, CPRP) were moribund even during the Velasco regime, that two (CONACI, SERP) atrophied after 1975, and that the remainder (CNA, CTRP) were officially dissolved by Morales Bermúdez or split and affiliated with other independent unions during his administration undermine the thesis that Velasco implemented a state corporatist model in Peru.[2]

Because of the failure of Velasco's corporatist experiments and the wide attention they have received from other authors, our treatment of the CNA need not be extended. The discussion, however, represents a necessary link between the treatments of centralism and liberalism during the military government. By its nature, the CNA did not aggregate the class interests of its supposed constituency, nor could it deliver political support to the government. Early in its history, when it was completely dependent on SINAMOS for funds, it was a dutiful carrier of government policy in the agrarian sector. CNA officials received considerable financial and political support from SINAMOS but suffered from divided loyalties. They acknowledged that the government was the CNA's midwife and showed their gratitude by chanting allegiance to the revolution. They also exulted in their access to military leaders until they recognized that those contacts represented little more than pomp. Increasingly challenged by the Campesino Confederation of Peru (CCP), however, they then saw the need to dissociate themselves from the regime in order to mount an effective defense of campesino interests and avoid being outflanked by competing rural organizations. The CNA developed an independent stance vis-à-vis government, a process that attenuated the government's original ambitions for the CNA but which introduced the possibility for more spontaneous political activity in the countryside.

2. The concept of state corporatism is articulately presented by Philippe C. Schmitter, "Still the Century of Corporatism?" in The New Corporatism, ed. Fredrick B. Pike (South Bend, Ind.: University of Notre Dame Press, 1974), pp. 85–132.

# The Art of Creating Interest Groups

The analysis of government-created mediating organs calls attention to a set of relationships that differs from interest associations formed conventionally by autonomous economic or political actors in a pluralistic setting. In the latter case, one expects that the association's membership accords legitimacy and financial support to its leaders for the purpose of influencing policy to their advantage. Matters of inquiry relate to the leaders' strategies to gain access to, and their effectiveness in extracting benefits from, centers of governmental decision making. In representative bodies spawned by the state, however, the assumptions are reversed. Interest-group leaders, whose appointments are controlled by government, have easy access to top officials in their sector. The main question is: What is the strength of their bonds with their so-called following?

## Agrarian Interest Groups: Conventional and Fabricated

Before 1968 a number of conventional interest associations existed in Peru, among which the sna (National Agrarian Society) was probably the most powerful.[3] Founded in the nineteenth century and officially recognized in 1926 as the voice of private farmers, it interacted with the Executive and Congress on behalf of owners mainly of highly capitalized coastal plantations. In terms of political economy, sna membership accorded legitimacy and some financial backing to sna leadership, which extended political support to the government. The government, in turn, delegated considerable authority to the sna leadership to dictate agrarian policy, which accrued to the economic benefit of its membership. A direct participant commented on these exchanges.

> Before 1968 an important part of the sna's work involved political lobbying. . . . To give you an idea of how this worked, let's take the Agricultural Promotion Law. The original suggestion came from an internal sna committee, which felt it would be

3. These groups are described in Carlos A. Astiz, *Pressure Groups and Power Elites in Peru* (Ithaca: Cornell University Press, 1969), and François Bourricaud, *Poder y sociedad en el Perú contemporáneo* (Buenos Aires: Editorial Sur, 1967).

helpful to give tax breaks to farmers. A basic document was hammered out in this committee, refined by SNA leadership, and then discussed in regional SNA conferences. The resulting proposal was presented to the agriculture minister, who appointed a commission with heavy SNA participation to study it. The minister basically accepted our proposal and presented it with minor changes to Congress. There we got a group of sympathetic congressmen to support the proposal, and helped them draft the law that eventually passed.[4]

In keeping with the elite composition of the SNA and the regimes of the era, its interaction with the state was conducted with the utmost decorum, usually behind closed doors. Groups that did not represent the upper class, such as peasant unions, had to resort to less elegant procedures to press their points, but their relationship with their followers was similar. They maintained the allegiance of their members by producing positive results, but often relied on violence or threats of violence to deal with government.

It is difficult to ascertain the size and strength of rural unions in the 1960s, and no single study follows the ups and downs of organized peasants since the beginning of the twentieth century.[5] Most peasant organization was transitional, such as the peasant movement of La Convención Valley, which involved 11,000 families but dissipated soon after achieving its material objectives in 1963. No reliable documentation confirms the Christian Democratic Party claims of 27,500 rural-based members in 48 unions and 3 community federations (Federación Campesina del Perú), or the membership of 100,000 peasants in the Frente Nacional de Trabajadores y Campesinos in Puno Department. The oldest continuous union is the FTAP (Federación de Trabajadores Azucareros del Perú), which has been affiliated with APRA since 1945 and enrolled approximately 10,000 sugar workers along the north coast. After the sugar

4. Interview no. 89.
5. For information on these rural unions, see Henry Pease and Olga Verme, eds., *Perú, 1968–1973* (Lima: DESCO, 1974), pp. xlviii–1; José M. Mejía and Rosa Díaz, *Sindicalismo y reforma agraria en el Valle de Chancay* (Lima: Instituto de Estudios Peruanos, 1975), pp. 31–71; and Julio Cotler and Felipe Portocarrero, "Organizaciones campesinas en el Perú," mimeo, Instituto de Estudios Peruanos, 1967.

cooperatives were expropriated, the government's attempts to eradicate APRA influence in their management resulted in severe conflict with the entrenched FTAP union leadership. The APRA and Communist parties competed for influence over the FENCAP (Federación Nacional de Campesinos del Perú), which in the 1960s represented 240 indigenous communities, unions of salaried rural workers, and associations of small and middle-sized farmers, numbering altogether probably 200,000 peasants. During the Velasco regime, Agriculture Ministry policy makers received strong backing from Communist Party affiliates of FENCAP along the coast, who protested energetically against the parceling provision of D.L. 17,716.

Aside from the FTAP and FENCAP, the other important independent rural union during the Velasco regime was the CCP, or Peasant Confederation of Peru. It was created in 1956 as the peasant branch of the Communist Party. In 1965 its leadership passed into the hands of the Bandera Roja, which was one of two factions sympathetic to the mainland Chinese. It participated in the 1965 guerrilla uprising and after 1969 organized permanent workers along the coast in strikes and physical occupations of property to force landowners to increase remuneration and job guarantees. Most CCP affiliates left the Bandera Roja in 1973 and recombined under a central committee made up of the Muscovite Communist Party, the Marxist-Leninist Vanguardia Revolucionaria, and Patria Roja (the other pro-Peking faction of the communist movement). By that time the CCP had officially expanded its constituency to include landless peasants and members of campesino communities, who obtained few tangible benefits from the provisions of D.L. 17,716.[6] When it detected that the members of a cooperative were discontented with government or their own cooperative leadership, the CCP also attempted to organize them to demand public services or greater internal democracy. The military paid attention to the CCP because of its proven talent for enjoin-

6. The CCP did not advertize its size but probably numbered over 100,000 permanent members and organized many more in specific encounters with the government or hacendados. See "Especial sobre reforma agraria," *Marka* 2:44 (June 24, 1976), and "La Izquierda peruana," *Marka* 1:21 (January 8, 1976), 26ff.

ing peasants in direct action and the government's concern that failure to resolve local complaints could give rise to a politically disastrous spread effect. Peasants cooperated with the CCP usually after they had exhausted normal channels for resolving their grievances, and sealed their allegiance when CCP methods were successful.[7]

### The Quandaries of the CNA

When police closed the SNA in May 1972, SINAMOS moved in and took possession of the association's facilities and records. SINAMOS' peasant affairs agency had already begun preparations to transform the organization into the National Agrarian Confederation. In its cooperative training program, SINAMOS personnel identified peasants who displayed leadership qualities (many of them with experience in the CCP) and recruited them into various posts of the nascent CNA at the local, regional, and national levels. The enabling legislation of the CNA, D.L. 19,400, was promulgated on May 9, 1972, but two years passed before the national system was assembled.[8]

The CNA was organized in a four-level hierarchy: the production unit (agrarian production cooperatives, SAIS, campesino communities, and associations of individual farmers and landless peasants), the local league (five or more production units), the federation (five or more agrarian leagues), and the National Agrarian Confederation (which came into existence after 50 percent of the departmental federations had been constituted). SINAMOS assisted in the election of delegates from one level to the next, a process that was hurried in order that a national assembly might be held in the vacated Chamber of Deputies in Lima in August 1974. In a relatively short time, the CNA claimed to "represent" 6 million peasants in 2,500 production

---

7. The CCP met success in the Huando controversy, discussed in Chapter 2, in the Naranjal cooperative in Lima, in Querecotillo in Piura, and in the Valley of Huaura along the coast. It suffered a serious defeat in 1974 in Andahuaylas, where the police inflicted casualties on CCP-led peasants who occupied unexpropriated hacienda land. See Mariano Valderrama, *Siete años de reforma agraria* (Lima: Pontificia Universidad Católica del Perú, 1976), pp. 106–16.

8. For the text of D.L. 19,400, see Alberto Bustamante, *Legislación sobre reforma agraria* (Lima: DESCO, 1974), pp. 233–42.

units, 152 agrarian leagues, and 20 departmental federations.[9] According to its by-laws, the CNA was financed by dues paid by member production units and surtaxes on certain commodities, half of which went to the departmental federation and half to the CNA. These sources were insufficient to cover costs, however, and SINAMOS subsidized its operations heavily.

D.L. 19,400 contained clauses in the corporatist tradition that disallowed the existence of any peasant organization that competed with the CNA, such as the CCP.[10] Theoretically, such organizations could not coexist in the same region with a functioning agrarian league, could not register as a corporate body to interact with government, and could not even adopt a name that might be confused with that of the officially sanctioned CNA. It would be a mistake, however, to overemphasize the significance of this proscription or to conclude that it was definitive proof of the existence of a corporatist system in Peru. The exclusion is more accurately interpreted as a political maneuver to generate support for the Velasco regime and to elevate the stature of the CNA over that of the CCP and other rural unions. A clause with similar objectives in Title II of D.L. 19,400 obliged all medium-sized farmers and landless peasants (classes that had no common objectives) to form one agrarian association per locality. The association counted as only one of at least five and possibly more production units in each league. If D.L. 19,400 governed social reality, the political power of middle-sized farmers would have been completely neutralized at the grass-roots level because they would have been outvoted by SINAMOS-guided member cooperatives every time. In point of fact, despite their "nonrecognition" by government, both the CCP and middle-sized farmers dealt directly with the regime

9. SINAMOS considered that campesino communities were a source of tension in the countryside, and they represented a majority of 2,500 production units in the CNA. The CNA also registered almost all of the SAIS and CAPS, although the APRA-influenced sugar enterprises and many coastal units controlled by FENCAP maintained their distance from CNA leadership, believing that they could further their interests by acting autonomously.

10. For a discussion of "organic statism," see Stepan, *State and Society*, chap. 1; also Juan Linz, "Totalitarian and Authoritarian Regimes," in *Handbook of Political Science*, ed. Fred I. Greenstein and Nelson W. Polsby (Reading, Mass.: Addison-Wesley, 1975), 3:175–411.

and won some of their most significant gains after they had formally been written out of existence.[11] These examples are simply reminders that one should not place too much credence in the law as a predictor of social behavior.

The CNA's heavy dependence on government in its early days derived from the source of its financing, the prestige accorded to its leaders by the regime in power, and the fact that most sierra SAIS and agrarian cooperatives were feeble organizations that did not function as constituencies in the normal sense of the word. These production units had difficulty articulating interests that could be translated into political demands, and their internal divisions and lack of economic power meant that they could neither effectively threaten nor support the regime. Statements of CNA representatives in the first year reflected their attitude of being beholden to the government. First, the leaders were understandably proud of their close proximity to the reins of power. As one respondent explained:

> We influence agricultural policy through our participation in government. The CNA has a member of the boards of directors of the Agrarian Bank, CENCIRA [a peasant training unit], and the INP, and of the sectoral planning commission of the Commerce Ministry. In Agriculture, one of the minister's top advisers is assigned as liaison with us. The CNA president can telephone the minister directly on a hot line to his office. All officials of the ministry are at the permanent disposition of peasants from the federation. In this way we can represent the peasants' true interests with government.

Second, with their quick rise in social status, CNA leaders were rather condescending toward their *compadres* still working the fields.

> We peasant leaders want to motivate the peasants to greater productivity, and the most effective way to do so is for them to

11. By means of a 1974 mobilization of landless peasants, the CCP negotiated an agreement with government to speed up the agrarian reform in Piura. The small and medium-sized farmers obtained D.L. 20,136 from the Velasco regime and D.L. 21,333 from Morales Bermúdez, when they were theoretically devoid of official status. SUTEP, too, was never recognized by the government, but its officers met personally with President Velasco in a well-publicized 1974 meeting. The nominal characteristic of recognition or nonrecognition is less than a foolproof predictor of political outcomes.

learn about the revolutionary process and undergo a profound *concientización* [consciousness raising]. You ask, are not material incentives more effective than moral inducements? I ask you, where is the government going to get the material incentives when it has no money? We, the peasants, are not looking for money for our labor because the revolutionary process has changed all that. We need to work in order not to become idle. *Concientización* builds moral responsibility and good work habits. The purpose of the agrarian reform is not to let peasants doze in the trees, but to shake them out of a deep sleep.

Third, they were loyal to the revolution, but were sensitive to the need for developing an identity separate from that of the regime.

I and other *compañeros* fully agree with the revolutionary process. But we need greater autonomy.... Unfortunately, we cannot ask for too much independence from government because the peasant is not yet trained. That is why we have permanent training programs, but I can't tell you how long it will take the CNA to finish its training tasks and loosen its links with the state.[12]

The CCP was the thorn in the side of the CNA, and over time its leaders became increasingly aware of its challenge. They were jealous of CCP's tactics, which organized peasants in successful land invasions and prompted the government to act more quickly than their own tamer approach. In the words of various CNA representatives,

The CCP claims to do more for the landless peasants than we do. Well, we have learned that the CCP is lined up with the APRA party and the Vanguardia Revolucionaria, who want to divide the land into private property. Some cooperatives have been infiltrated by the CCP, and CIA, and conservative priests who are working against the revolution.

As for the CCP, I felt that before 1968 it was an authentic defender of peasant interests. But now, when we are strong and getting stronger every day, the CCP does not join with us. The CCP leaders are not real fighters for peasant interests, but opportunists. They do not recognize the agrarian leagues and are trying to destroy the current agrarian structure.

12. The three preceding quotes are from interviews (nos. 90, 88, and 113) at the Lima-based CNA and at the regional federations of Piura and Cuzco, respectively.

The CNA faces competition from the CCP. The CNA needs to keep getting concessions from the government and to improve its services to peasants in order to undermine the CCP, which keeps saying that we are just stooges of the government.

The CCP sees itself as a revolutionary vanguard but few of its permanent leaders are peasants. The CNA, unlike the CCP, does not blackmail the government. We respect the government and expect that it will respect us. It is probably true, however, that the existence of the CCP as an extremist alternative helps us in our demands. We also have to see to it that we satisfy the member organizations because they can always disaffiliate.[13]

Many middle-level officials in the Agrarian Bank, the Ministry of Food, and the Ministry of Agriculture were not enamored with CNA representatives who pestered them with clientelistic requests. Bureaucrats were hostile in part because they felt the demands neglected the technical, budgetary, and personnel constraints on the agencies' normal servicing of the rural sector. At the upper levels most boards of directors and commissions simply ignored the presence of CNA representatives whose points of view seemed strident, parochial, and uninformed.

The CNA eventually realized its predicament. Without authority over distributive decisions, it could not demonstrate its worth to its constituency. Without the backing of the campesino sector, it could not mount a credible threat to government. With a wary eye on CCP activities, CNA leaders concluded that the CNA's future lay in strengthening its ties with its membership and insisting that the state meet the requirements of the rural economy. Adoption of this stance was not the government's original intention for the CNA. Velasco had invested considerable prestige and financial subsidies in an organization that would faithfully transmit official directives to the rural population and obtain its allegiance, not a class- or interest-based challenger of its policies.

By 1974 conservative military officers had induced Velasco to lessen his support of SINAMOS' activities, and the government declared SINAMOS to be in "reorganization." The ambiguous status of the agency gave freer rein to lower-level

13. Interviews nos. 113, 113, 91, and 93.

functionaries to advise the CNA to assert greater autonomy. Simultaneously, SINAMOS' smaller budget prevented its military leadership from using material rewards to hold the CNA's hand-picked peasant officials in check. The growing independence of the CNA was also precipitated by increased pressure and public ridicule from the CCP, the frustration of CNA leaders over their minimal influence (limited to such services as liberating from jail campesinos who had been charged with misdemeanors), and their disillusionment over the rightist shift by Velasco's successor, Morales Bermúdez. The drive for greater autonomy, which hardly pleased the government, was reflected in several events. The CNA petitioned to have its subsidy from SINAMOS replaced by earmarked taxes. Financial independence would help to rid the CNA of SINAMOS oversight of its finances and policy positions, but the Ministry of Agriculture rejected the suggestion. The CNA then proposed that it market the produce from cooperatives to eliminate the middleman and ensure that profits from food sales would accrue to the benefit of the peasant sector. The idea was later dropped as impractical. Later, in December 1975, the Food Ministry announced a new program for compulsory crop planning for CAPS and SAIS. The CNA publicly denounced the proposal, of which it had not been informed previously. The proposal was later modified, but not without the exchange of harsh words between the CNA and the Food Ministry.

As part of its press reform the government expropriated and promised to distribute several major newspapers to various "sectors" of the population. The campesino sector was to receive *El Comercio*, the prestigious daily formerly owned and managed by the Miró Quesada family. The Velasco and Morales Bermúdez regimes repeatedly delayed transferring *El Comercio* to the CNA, even though the peasant organ was the most consolidated of all those created by the military government. CNA leadership refused to accept the government's excuses and pressed for full control over the newspaper's finances, personnel policy, and editorial room. It was spurned. After the fall of Velasco, the CNA hired Leonidas Rodríguez, a member of Velasco's core coalition whom Morales dismissed as untrustworthy, as an adviser on political affairs. Some members of the Morales government felt that the move to preserve Rodríguez's national stature was a deliberate act of provocation. Confirming this view, in 1976 the head of the CNA's departmental federation in Cuzco, Avelino Mar, founded the Front for the Defense of the Revolution. Ostensibly the Front was to provide permanent backing for the military government, but Avelino Mar's true intention was to try to keep the Morales government on the ideological track laid by Velasco, despite pressures from the Right. As the regime changed course, the Front called attention to undesirable policy shifts and became an embarrassment to the regime. Promising to maintain a similarly outspoken line, Avelino Mar was elected president of the CNA in 1977. The Front later supported the Revolutionary Socialist Party, made up of high officials of the Velasco regime, and Avelino Mar and Leonidas Rodríguez were deported.

Throughout this period both the regime and the CNA faced serious quandaries. In order to accomplish its original goals for the CNA, the regime needed to provide enough concessions to placate CNA leadership, keep it on a loose leash, and allow it to make demands consistent with peasant interests as a means of countering the CCP threat in the countryside. The regime, however, was encountering financial difficulties, which constrained its potential generosity. Furthermore, it resented the CNA's ingratitude for services already rendered. The CNA had to build its legitimacy among agrarian reform cooperatives by adapting an independent stance, all the while calculating whether these cooperatives were sufficiently well integrated for the CNA to survive after severing its umbilical cord with the regime. If so, the CNA could define its clientele in more discriminating terms (the food and wool-producing cooperatives, for example, and campesino communities that were not in conflict with neighboring farms), and join in tactical alliances with the CCP and other rural unions on issues that pitted urban interests against those of the peasants. If the CNA's campaign for autonomy was premature, however, its behavior would lead to the further withdrawal of public subsidies and a weakening of its links with the cooperatives. It would need to voice its demands more aggressively and risk government intervention and disbandment. The last scenario was played out at the midpoint of the Morales Bermúdez regime, and the CNA was suppressed in June 1978.[14]

## Conclusions

To its dismay, the government discovered that it was not an easy task in Peru to set up mediating structures between the state and the masses which could contribute to national harmony and integration along functional lines. The regime promoted organizations to split the opposition (SERP, CONACI) and to fill up representational space (CNA) with the hope that they would generate support for its overall polity. If Velasco's political advisers felt that these organizations would tap a hidden historical imperative in Peruvian public life that evoked a corporatist response, they were disappointed. The Peruvian political scene was extremely heterogenous, containing innumerable organizations and factions, some of them spontaneous, others creatures of political parties, and still others fostered by former governments that coexisted and competed with each other. The characterization "a living cemetery" was appropriate, and the Velasco government opened new plots. Indigenous traditions, complicated rural-urban links as a consequence of migration, pre-Incaic trading practices, revered local ceremonies, the penetration of international consumer values, multiple loyalties, and a host of other factors had economic and political consequences that conjured up an image more pluralistic than corporatist. Furthermore, the policy to create the CNA was flawed by the government's wish to avoid conflict with the rural sector and the CNA leadership's realization that only through conflict with the state over matters of substance could it solidify its reputation among campesinos.

The CNA initiative was symptomatic of the Velasco polity

---

14. The government-created industrial communities commission (CONACI) had already gone through a similar process, including the capture of its leadership by affiliates of communist unions and its subsequent intervention by the government. The main problem in that case was the inability or unwillingness of industrialists and workers to put aside class antagonism and adopt the idealistic precepts of the industrial-communities legislation. For mistrustful attitudes of workers toward their employers, see José Mejía V., "El comportamiento del obrero peruano," *Aportes* 24 (April 1972), 101–15.

from approximately 1972 to 1974. The state catered preferentially to certain groups to attempt to win their favor and ensure their passivity. The clientelism that pervaded much economic and social life in Peru, however, was insufficiently dominant to permit Velasco to reorganize the state on a patrimonial basis. The government's resources were too small and social opposition motivated by other ideological precepts too strong for the attempt to succeed. As the corporatist experiments faltered, diverse power actors reasserted themselves and began to influence government policy. This liberal competition accelerated in the political community at large in events such as the conflict between the regime and the small and middle-sized farmers. It also penetrated and undermined the unity of the state, and reduced the autonomy the regime enjoyed during its early years.

# Chapter 6

# Internal State Conflict

After 1969, the Velasco regime pursued policies that transformed public agencies into the largest employers in the country, made them responsible for generating an important part of the GNP, and gave them a great array of social and economic functions including political mobilization. The Chira-Piura project and Agrarian Court System reflected these growth and centralization trends. The state displaced local agricultural elites, severed dependency ties with the World Bank, and defined policies in the interests of campesino communities, farm workers and minifundistas, which were nondominant groups in Peru at the time. The Agrarian Court System even followed centralist principles in controlling the behavior of land judges. Subsequently, the government pursued such corporatist policies as the creation of the National Agrarian Confederation. Controversies over this approach divided the armed forces, and internal bureaucratic politics and financial setbacks led to greater political competition. Finally, the Morales Bermúdez government placed its formal seal of approval on representative government and limited pluralism, a reversal of the centralism followed by Velasco early in his administration.

An important consideration in this chapter is decay in the

189

unity of the state. Because of division of labor and multiple goals, all complex organizations display some differentiation. The state is no exception. Even bureaucratic structures that submit ultimately to the same hierarchical authority and ideology undergo internal discussions over priorities and experience some maneuvering of cliques. The inverse relationship between state "unity" and "autonomy" is relevant when benign differentiation becomes fragmentation.[1] A state riddled by disputes over doctrine, policy options, or personal loyalties cannot have high autonomy for two reasons. First, these divisions invalidate the idea of *a* state consolidating *its* institutional objectives, because the state becomes an amalgam of factions.[2] Second, a fragmented state increases the number of entry points for private-sector elements, who can exploit its

1. Our approach differs from that of Nicos Poulantzas, who does not seem to account for internal state competition separate from divisions in the class structure. "Various organs and branches of the state (ministries and government offices, executive and parliament, central administration and local and regional authorities, army, judiciary, etc.) reveal major contradictions among themselves, each of them frequently constituting the . . . crystallization . . . of this or that faction of the power bloc, this or that specific and competing interest" ("The Capitalist State: A Reply to Milibrand and Laclau," *New Left Review* 95 [January–February 1976], 75). Also, "If it is not true that the contemporary state is being transformed into a simple instrument of the monopolies, it is still the case that it is less and less able, in this context, to play its role as organizer of hegemony effectively. State policy often amounts to a series of contradictory and temporary measures which, if they express the logic of monopoly capitalism, also reveal the fissures and disarticulations of the state apparatuses, reproducing the contradictions of the power bloc in the face of a decline in the hegemonic capacities of monopoly capital" (*Classes in Contemporary Capitalism* [London: NLB, 1975], p. 171). We claim that state agencies can generate doctrines of their own separate from the interests of classes in civil society. The contention that the capitalist state over the long term always furthers the position of the power bloc, and thus is always representing its implicit interests, is formalistic and deterministic reasoning.

2. Some recent literature attempts to reconcile the behavior of the state with class theory by transforming personnel strata in public organizations into "new classes." Although organizational goals are fixed by an agency's dominant coalition, this view ignores the factors that give organizations independent political power such as their control of resources, skills, division of labor, and ability to interpret authoritative regulations. Class theorists might better predict social behavior by treating classes as variably unified organizational forms with common status identities and access to the productive process, and borrow concepts from organizational theory to understand their goals and power capabilities.

internal disharmony to their own advantage. If these private interests are able to gain allies within the bureaucracy, the state apparatus itself is partitioned according to the correlation of forces and its autonomy is lost in the shuffle.

This chapter discusses two examples of disunity in the agricultural sector, one of moderate severity and the other engulfing the whole government. The first involved conflict over urban growth into cultivated areas between the ministries of Agriculture and Housing. The give-and-take was typical of bureaucratic politics, with each agency sharing and defending common goals with clients in the private sector. The second deals with EPSA, the state food-services agency. Soon after its formation, EPSA obtained a near monopoly over food imports and began to displace commercial middlemen in the national food market. Shortly after the midpoint of the Velasco regime, a well-timed and orchestrated attack on EPSA (in the guise of an embezzlement scandal) camouflaged the increasing lack of control at the heart of the state apparatus. Both cases document the gradual decay of centralism under Velasco and provide insights into the concept of relative state autonomy.

## Urban Growth and Agricultural Land

The descent from the Andes to the Pacific coast is marked by numerous rivers that create narrow, fertile valleys. Both on the coast and in the sierra, human settlements have concentrated in agricultural zones. Table 13 presents historical data on urban growth; legislation to regulate it started in the 1940s.[3] The expansion of residential zones has been more of a problem for the Lima metropolitan area than for Arequipa, Chiclayo, Cuzco, and Puno, but everywhere urban growth has gobbled up rich argicultural lands, a rare commodity in Peru.[4] From 1970 to

3. Among this legislation was Law 10,723 (1946), which created the first National Office of Planning and Urbanism, and D.L. 11,006 (1949), which prohibited subdivision not consistent with the Lima zoning plan.
4. For a discussion of the growth and problems of the Lima metropolitan area, see Henry A. Dietz, "Urban Problems and Government Policy Responses for Metropolitan Lima," in *Metropolitan Problems and Governmental Response in Latin America*, ed. Wayne Cornelius and Robert Von Kemper (Beverly Hills, Calif.: Sage, 1977).

*Table 13.* Population growth in selected Peruvian cities, 1600–1980 (in thousands)

| Year | Lima | Cuzco | Arequipa | Trujillo | Puno | Chiclayo | Chimbote |
|------|------|-------|----------|----------|------|----------|----------|
| 1600 | 14 | 30 | | | | | |
| 1700 | 37 | 35 | | | | | |
| 1750 | 40 | 40 | 26 | | | | |
| 1800 | 54 | 34 | 26 | | | | |
| 1850 | 70 | | 21 | | | | |
| 1900 | 130 | | | 10 | 5 | 14 | |
| 1940 | 618 | 41 | 88 | 37 | 14 | 32 | 5 |
| 1961 | 1,784 | 80 | 166 | 103 | 24 | 96 | 63 |
| 1972 | 3,318 | 122 | 312 | 242 | 31 | 190 | 173 |
| 1980 (projected) | 4,679 | 153 | 413 | 343 | 52 | 274 | 241 |

SOURCES: Robert W. Fox, *Urban Growth in Peru* (Washington, D.C.: Inter-American Development Bank, 1972); Tertius Chandler and Gerald Fox, *Three Thousand Years of Urban Growth* (New York: Academic Press, 1974), pp. 34, 36, 188, 378; John P. Cole, *Geografía urbana del Perú*, publication no. 10 (Lima: Instituto de Etnología y Arqueología, 1955).

1976, Agriculture challenged Housing on the matter because urbanization lowered agricultural employment and production. The conflict permitted nonofficial actors to exercise an indirect influence on policy, and governmental decision makers had to compromise to maintain unity among various sectors of the armed forces. Agriculture gained the advantage under Velasco but the Ministry of Housing recovered influence after the advent of Morales Bermúdez.

### Article 42 of D.L. 17,716

Belaúnde's agrarian reform law did not contain specific norms to control urban growth but simply stated that when it infringed on agricultural land, the Ministry of Development and Public Works had to obtain the permission of the Agrarian Reform Agency before approving construction. The COAP agrarian reform commission considered urbanization to be a low-priority issue, but Article 42 of D.L. 17,716 did mention that urban growth had to take place on arid, nonproductive land. The provision took heed of the fact that developers found it easier to use agricultural land because of its location, topography, and access to water.

Architects in the Housing Ministry had only a few hours to study draft law 17,716 before the Council of Ministers meeting. The lapse was sufficient, however, to convince them that Article 42 would place intolerable curbs on urban growth. The housing minister, Vice-Admiral Luis Vargas Caballero, a less than enthusiastic supporter of the revolution, was a ranking member of the military establishment and influential with other conservative navy officers, whose opposition the army-led government hoped to keep subdued. When Vargas Caballero requested a clarification of Article 42 in the cabinet debate, he recognized that the fears of his housing advisers were well founded, and he expressed dissatisfaction. In order not to hold up the law's passage, General Barandiarán and other representatives of the Agriculture Ministry promised more liberal provisions for urban growth after the by-laws of Article 42 were written.

All subsequent legislation on urbanization involved an attempt to clarify or modify the clauses of Article 42, either in favor of Housing and land developers or of Agriculture and the farm workers. The seemingly endless stream of applicable laws included Supreme Decree 70-109-AG (1970), D.L. 19,462 (1972), D.L. 20,069 (1973), Supreme Decree 008-75-VC (1975), D.L. 21,419 (1976), and D.L. 21,461 (1976). Legislation favorable to Housing responded to the power of Vargas Caballero early in the regime, to the government's continuing efforts to maintain its support coalition intact so as not to jeopardize other aspects of polity, and to the failure of Agriculture to develop a rational land-use policy after the fall of Velasco. Decrees favoring Agriculture were based on the high priority of agrarian reform under Velasco, the active protests of affected peasants, Peru's severe food shortages, and Morales's attempt to keep the revolutionary mystique alive after his takeover in August 1975.

### Bureaucratic Conflict

Agriculture and Housing came into conflict because Agriculture wanted to preserve agricultural zones while Housing wanted construction to keep pace with the demand for family dwellings, public buildings, and industry, even at the expense of cultivated land.

The reasons agricultural officials cited for limiting urban growth were first of all technical, including the maintenance of high farm employment and the avoidance of the spoliation of farmland. Also, the demand for food in Peru was increasing faster than production, the cost of irrigating new farmland was high ($1,500 per hectare), and it was not wise to allow existing agricultural terrain to be eaten up by an unneeded urban sprawl. In order to maintain the previous ratio of 0.2 hectares per capita for a population growing by 500,000 persons annually, the country needed 100,000 hectares of new irrigated land each year, representing an annual investment of $150 million; a sum clearly beyond the country's means. Military advisers to the ministry observed that Lima, for strategic reasons, should be surrounded by a wide horticultural ring. If rains, earthquakes, or hostilities blocked the roads from the sierra, the city had to have access to produce from nearby barns, silos, and agricultural land to last several days. Agriculture also believed that excessive profits made by urban land developers (whom they called speculators) were inconsistent with the government's ideological position. In the words of one defender of agricultural interests,

> Why should we play into the hands of the individual property owner? When the government puts in a road, hospital, or school, the value of the land increases from $1,200 to $20,000 per hectare. The landowner does not lift a finger to earn $25 profit per square meter, a profit generated by the investment of all the Peruvian people. He just waits. This is the business deal of the century![5]

Housing felt it tempered its push for urban growth by giving priority to industrial, educational, and public-service building over private homes, which it discouraged in favor of high-rise apartments. One Housing official characterized his ministry's approach as sedate and reasonable, while that of Agriculture seemed to be half-cocked.

5. Interview no. 83.

> The Agrarian Reform Agency has a very radical position toward protecting agricultural areas. It never says yes first to urban growth on unprogrammed areas. It always resists. Admittedly, some good has resulted from its cautions, but eventually Agriculture comes over to our side when it sees that so-called cultivated land near urban areas loses all value when the urban residents pilfer the harvest. . . . I like to think that we have a rational attitude toward these questions. Agriculture does not give any importance to the technical challenges of urban growth and, unlike us, is not interested in relating population with roads, sewers, schools, and other municipal services. I fear on occasion its valiant defense of cultivated areas is exaggerated.[6]

As in much bureaucratic in-fighting, each side had clients affected by the decisions taken. Urban developers had access to the Ministry of Housing, not necessarily for drafting legislation or city plans, but for gaining a favorable hearing for housing and industrial projects. Their position was bolstered by the lobbying of the Peruvian Construction Bureau (Cámara Peruana de la Construcción, or CPC), which argued that if the entrepreneur were regulated too much, private construction in the country would be paralyzed. Small and middle-sized landowners, living some distance from large urban centers, wanted unrestrained growth because eventually they could reap large capital gains. Many such properties were bought by men or relatives of men in the armed forces, an invisible set of interests that played a role in the policy deliberations. The final group in Housing's constituency consisted of middle- and lower-class city residents living in crowded conditions in old sections of town or in squatter settlements who shared the hope of obtaining a single-family dwelling in a new neighborhood. The Housing Ministry was partially responsible for providing a sufficient number of homes to dissuade them from invading urban land to press their demands.

The most vitally affected people, however, were the peasants, and after 1970 those living in areas of urban growth were under continual threat of losing their land or jobs. Many peasants who at first believed that the agrarian reform would serve their interests later feared that they would remain salaried workers

6. Interview no. 82.

and renters until the owners of the land said, "Get out." The CCP and the CNA competed with each other to raise the shrillest outcry against urban growth. Peasants took their complaints to the Ministry of Agriculture, which was under much greater public pressure on this issue than Housing, which discussed alternatives behind closed doors.[7]

Because Article 42 of D.L. 17,716 and subsequent laws stipulated that Housing had to consult with Agriculture before approving certain types of urban projects, the two ministries were in continual interaction. Under Velasco, the question was always how far Agriculture, with its close links to the core governing coalition, could restrict the interests of Housing and its clients, led by a minister from the navy. The debates between technocrats of the two ministries were spirited. On the matter of despoiling irrigated lands, Housing officials recommended that Agriculture increase the productivity of currently cultivated lands so that total acreage would not be so important. Agriculture officials retorted with studies by international experts showing that even if all land currently under production were harvested at maximum yields, the country would need to increase the supply of land by one-third to meet internal demand for food. Housing claimed that it was too expensive to build private and public facilities on desert or arid land. Agriculture agreed, and pointed to the reluctance of urban capitalists to invest their own money in public works necessary for their projects to function. Housing denied that it was helping urban speculators to increase the value of idle property and obtain windfall projects. It pointed proudly to D.L. 17,803, which allowed the government to expropriate these lands at their approximate rural value. A public agency, for example,

7. Despite appearances, such as the rental of offices in the CPC headquarters by the Ministry of Housing, there was no allegation of wrongdoing in these relationships. The affinity of interests responded to the Housing Ministry's interpretation of national goals and the most appropriate technical means of reaching them. For a similar case, see Peter S. Cleaves, *Bureaucratic Politics and Administration in Chile* (Berkeley: University of California Press, 1974), pp. 235–73. Of the six largest Lima real estate holders, two were nonprofit organizations (Catholic University and the Fundación Canevaro) which were prohibited by law from owning agricultural land and thus obliged to subdivide, rent, or sell their land.

could expropriate land at $5 per square meter for cooperatives, schools, and public buildings, instead of a market price as high as $30. If that were true, queried Agriculture, why did not the Housing Ministry expropriate all of the land on the urban apron and put it to public use, without undue destitution of agricultural workers, and in the interests of all Peruvians? Housing officials shrugged and said they did not have a large enough budget.

When disputes occurred over matters of substance, the officials first attempted to resolve them amicably among themselves. If agreement was not forthcoming, the matter went to the level of vice-ministers of housing and agriculture, respectively, then to the two ministers, and eventually to the COAP. Urban-growth issues went to the Council of Ministers on the average of only once per year because COAP's recommendation usually prevailed. The debates in the council did not harp on ideological concerns (for example, that urban expansion allowed profiteering by rich urban capitalists); technical and practical matters predominated.

*Subsequent Legislation*

The by-laws for Article 42 of D.L. 17,716, contained in D.S. 70-109-AG of May 1970, reflected the compromise reached in the Council of Ministers. This supreme decree defined which lands were in the so-called urban zone (controlled by Housing), the urban-growth zone (under joint administration), and the suburban zone (regulated by Agriculture). It also set out the conditions under which urbanization could proceed in the urban-growth zone and exempted from expropriation under the agrarian reform those lands programmed for urbanization according to Housing's master plan.[8] The regulations stipulated that all property owners in the urban-growth zone had to submit project plans to the Housing Ministry for approval, and these plans had to be completely implemented within five years (that is, by 1975).

Theoretically D.S. 70-109 was in the interests of both Hous-

---

8. Between October 1972 and November 1974, the Council of Ministers passed all of Housing's zoning plans for cities of over 100,000 population.

ing and Agriculture: the former could develop certain areas in the vicinity of large cities, while the latter put a limit on the time urban speculators could leave land vacant in the expectation of windfall profits. Unfortunately, it did not work. The owners of undeveloped properties visited Housing during the first six months after the issuance of the decree to explain their ideas and obtain permission to begin construction. They had little choice. Article 7 of D.S. 70-109 threatened them with expropriation if they failed to lay out roads and subdivide plots almost immediately. Agriculture soon became alarmed by the accelerated preparation for urban expansion. The threat of drastic sanctions was on the verge of converting practically overnight most of the agricultural areas in Lima Province into cement.

D.L. 19,462 represented Housing's attempt to have Lima grow by districts in congruent fashion rather than in isolated areas spreading forth in response to the uncoordinated plans of the developers. Agriculture was concerned about halting the urbanization rush it had inadvertently promoted in the earlier decree. It now insisted that only land with the least productive value should be used for construction, and that all lands outside of these zones had to show signs of being used for food production within ninety days or they would be declared abandoned and liable for expropriation. Agriculture also included in D.L. 19,462 a provision for additional compensation for peasants evicted by the bulldozer. While formerly peasants had received only the barest severance pay, D.L. 19,462 allowed for double indemnification for those who owned or worked land in urban-growth zones, the amount increasing according to the number of years of residence on the farm.

Even though D.L. 19,462 was precisely worded, Agriculture officials encountered new problems in its implementation. A thorny issue involved what constituted "food production." Future developers covered their lands almost exclusively with maize—for consumption by humans, cattle, or chickens—because maize seeds were inexpensive and easy to sow, and the plants required little attention. Corn production around Lima was not the most desirable crop pattern but it did fall within the dictates of the law. Property owners who looked forward to urban development produced food only to mark time.

Vargas Caballero left the Housing Ministry early in 1972 to become minister of the navy, and Agriculture sprang to the offensive with the goal of clamping down permanently on what it considered inefficient agriculture and irresponsible expansion in the urban-growth zone. In 1973 it convinced the Council of Ministers of the need for D.L. 20,069, which required that urban-growth zones be used for intensive agriculture, and obliged owners of barns and stables to move them to the outlying suburban zones if urbanization took their property out of agricultural production. The law's objectives were to maintain rural employmont, protoct tho rightc of rontore, broadon tho terms of indemnification for permanent and temporary workers, and further specify preconditions for expropriation. Later, Supreme Decrcc 008-75-VC actually rollcd back thc outer limit of the urban-growth zone. After a heated debate with the National Credit Bank, Agriculture (now under the leadership of General Enrique Gallegos) was able to exclude 7,000 hectares from urban development in the Lurín, Chillán, and Rimac valleys near Lima. In this particular case, the National Credit Bank, a public-sector dependency, owned a large piece of property that it wished to develop as a housing project. The farm workers on the property resisted, and with the assistance of the Ministry of Agriculture succeeded in overriding the bank's position despite its support in the Ministry of Housing.[9] With this restriction on urban growth near Lima, agricultural officials felt they had made considerable progress since D.S. 70-109-AG, which actually stimulated urban sprawl. Indeed, they were hopeful of further reducing the jurisdiction of the Ministry of Housing in the programming of urban development.

Agriculture did advance once more, and would have checkmated the developers had the measure prevailed. One of the structural changes promised in the Plan Inca was an urban reform whose details never emerged but which contracting firms and property owners feared would freeze rents, prohibit eviction, and limit the number of houses owned by any one

9. See *La Nueva Crónica*, November 10, 1974, p. 1; March 19, 1975, p. 2; *Correo*, March 11, 1975, p. 4; *El Comercio*, April 10, 1975, p. 3; and *Expreso*, September 19, 1975, p. 5.

family. The government postponed the design of a comprehensive urban reform in part because the piecemeal adjustments executed by Housing and Agriculture had proved to be so complex and ineffective. The matter was part of the unfinished business left by the Velasco regime and inherited by Morales Bermúdez, whose Agriculture Ministry hoped to combine urban reform with a resolution of the urban-expansion issue.

The proposal contained in D.L. 21,419, which passed in February 1976, gave Agriculture the right to declare which lands in the urban-growth zone had to remain agriculturally productive, and made them subject to expropriation; annulled all planned urbanization, even if it had already been approved by Housing; ordered a cessation of all privately sponsored urban renewal until building permits could be reviewed; and declared a public enterprise, EMADI, to be the state monopoly for buying and selling all urban land in Peru. With these measures it appeared that the sun had finally set on "urban speculators," and the leftist press, campesino interests, and spokesmen for the Ministry of Agriculture were ecstatic.[10]

The victory was short-lived, however. Eight weeks later, D.L. 21,461 and its by-laws watered or reversed the major provisions of the previous legislation, including the nullification of land sales and EMADI's monopoly over land transfers.[11] The balance of power tilted again in favor of urban interests.

### The Evolution of Policy Responses

In summary, these two ministries adopted their clients' interests as their own and represented their demands before each other and the upper reaches of government. The army core coalition was identified with Agriculture and the peasants, and the navy with Housing and private developers. The developers

10. The Morales Bermúdez regime was attempting to preserve the military's leftist image through this measure and D.L. 21,333 (discussed in Chapter 2) and thus camouflage the rightist measures it was adopting at the time. These laws were later subverted and the government consolidated itself along conservative lines.

11. The newspaper coverage of D.L. 21,419 was enthusiastic, while D.L. 21,469 generated cynicism. For the contrast, see the "Dominical," *El Comercio*, February 15, 1976, and "En terrenos urbanos, también marcha atrás," *Marka*, April 29, 1976, p. 13.

and campesino unions never opposed each other face to face but relied on bureaucratic interaction to mediate their differences. Agriculture and Housing attempted first to settle grievances by communicating at the middle levels. Specific disagreements frequently went up the hierarchy and were resolved in favor of the party manifesting the greater power or threat of reprisals at the particular moment. The government generally followed a middle road in arbitrating conflict.

The reasons for compromise, however, were not only that the technical arguments of Housing and Agriculture and the power of their clients were in approximate equilibrium. Agriculture could have mobilized more support among key regime officials, but opinions were not pressed as hard as they might have been in order to avoid animosities in the ruling group. This wish to preserve the support coalition intact continued even after Vargas Caballero and the navy manifested their overt opposition to Velasco.

In handling urban expansion and fulfilling its commitment to peasants, the regime was faced with a serious constraint that transcended the two sectors and related to economic stability. A point argued forcefully by Housing representatives in the cabinet was that private investment would vanish if the state cracked down on urban development. The housing deficit would increase and the dissatisfaction of those social groups most unhappy with the regime, the upper-middle and upper classes, would simply be exacerbated. Many of the government's policies already had damped private investment, and the government had filled the void with an expansionary fiscal policy, but that cure had its limits. Despite its ideological preference, the core coalition felt that construction had to proceed normally to maintain employment for a fairly large segment of the work force and stimulate the building trades.

The cautious position of Housing could also be laid to the government's awareness that if it permitted a drastic drop in private housing construction, it had to have an alternative. Despite advantageous powers of expropriation, access to credit, and tax exonerations, EMADI's operating costs and the prices of its houses were not very much below those of private enterprise. The Housing Ministry and Velasco himself were sobered by EMADI's poor performance. Agriculture did insist on an urban reform under Morales Bermúdez, and Housing went along reluctantly with D.L. 21,419. As predicted, however, the measure threw the housing industry into chaos, halted construction, and increased urban unemployment, and Morales Bermúdez beat a hasty retreat. A flexible urban-growth policy again became a means by which the regime could deal with a diverse set of interests, and Morales Bermúdez began to soft-pedal the issue, to the benefit of urban more than rural interests.

## The Growth of EPSA

In 1969 the Velasco government merged several food-related agencies under a new organization, the Empresa Pública de Servicios Agropecuarios (EPSA).[12] Over the next few years, EPSA's budget grew rapidly as part of the government's policy of strengthening the agricultural sector (see Table 14).[13] EPSA's job of minimizing price fluctuations and scarcities in basic foodstuffs gave it an important role in the early stages of the agrarian reform, when the government expected food production to drop, and it obtained loans and foreign credits with little supervision.

The director of EPSA was Alfonso Elejalde, a lawyer hired in mid-1972 from the industrial empire of Peruvian fish-meal magnate Luis Banchero (who had been murdered earlier in the year). For much of his tenure Elejalde was on loan from the Banchero ogranization, working without salary and continuing as a consultant to various companies.[14] Elejalde proved to be

12. See D.L. 17,734 (July 4, 1969), containing the Ley Orgánica de la Empresa Pública de Servicios Agropecuarios.

13. In its *Memoria Anual 1972* (Lima: Ministerio de Economía y Finanzas, 1973), for example, the Central Reserve Bank noted that state investment increased by 14.3 percent while private investment increased by only 0.9 percent. E. V. K. Fitzgerald's statistics are that gross fixed capital formation from the private sector fell from 14.6 percent of gross domestic product in 1960–64 to 7.5 percent in 1973–74. See *The State and Economic Development* (Cambridge: Cambridge University Press, 1976), p. 23.

14. Elejalde also cultivated his relations with the press. During his tenure there was not a single editorial in any of six major newspapers critical of EPSA,

Table 14. Government expenditures in the agricultural sector,
1969–74 (in millions of current soles)

| | 1969 | 1970 | 1971 | 1972 | 1973 | 1974 |
|---|---|---|---|---|---|---|
| Ministry of Agriculture budget | S/1,670 | S/3,115 | S/4,058 | S/4,058 | S/5,557 | S/5,557 |
| Central government budget | 28,034 | 42,124 | 49,485 | 56,467 | 67,411 | 82,650 |
| Agricultural index | 100 | 187 | 243 | 243 | 333 | 333 |
| Government index | 100 | 150 | 177 | 201 | 240 | 294 |

SOURCES: Douglas E. Horton, *Land Reform and Reform Enterprises in Peru* (Madison, Wis.: Land Tenure Center, 1974), p. 98; *The Andean Report*, May 1976, p. 56; Ministerio de Economía y Finanzas, *Presupuestos generales de la República* (Lima: Dirección General de Presupuesto Público, 1960–74).

203

adept at generating programs from a small base, and EPSA's period of major expansion occurred under his leadership. He used domestic and international bank loans, government-to-government agreements, and supplier credits to augment the enterprise's working capital, which was inadequate at its birth. He organized EPSA as a holding company with complete or majority shareholdings in a number of subsidiary firms. A decentralized structure allowed flexibility at the lower levels of the institution at the same time that it gave economic clout to EPSA directors that surpassed the real value of its fully owned operations. Until his death in 1974, Elejalde sought control over a wide network of commercial firms to make headway on EPSA's goal of dominating the food industry in Peru.

*Food Price Controls and Internal*
*Dependency*

Basic foodstuffs, such as bread, rice, potatoes, sugar, beans, and meat, had been subject to price controls for years before Velasco assumed office. Since the 1940s, when shantytown settlements began to form on the outskirts of Lima, politicians took into account the potential of the urban masses to provide electoral support or threaten political stability.[15] Wary of the adage "When the price of rice rises, the government falls," successive governments chose to fix the prices and monopolize the marketing of some products. Low food prices were also helpful in keeping wages low and increasing internal savings to assist industrialization. Price regulations, however, were routinely ignored. To demonstrate its concern for the public's pocketbook, the government carried out occasional police raids on retailers whose prices rose above the official levels.

Instead of examining the economics of food marketing, the Velasco regime ascribed to dependency concepts to explain the

---

but eleven favorable ones from October 24, 1972, to August 3, 1973. Elejalde's close associates report that his ambition was to create an organization in Peruvian agriculture rivaling ENI (Ente Nazionale Idrocarburi), the Italian government's petroleum conglomerate, created by Enrico Mattei.

15. David Collier treats political interaction between Peruvian presidential regimes and shantytown dwellers in *Squatters and Oligarchs* (Baltimore: Johns Hopkins University Press, 1976). See also Alfredo Rodríguez et al., *De invasores a invadidos* (Lima: DESCO, 1973).

gap between official and real prices for food.[16] It argued that a relatively developed urban enclave (subject to control by foreign capital) dominated a marginalized rural population.[17] Within the food industry, large operators used their oligopolistic power to wrest low prices from the farmers and force high prices on the retailers and general public.[18] In a speech celebrating the fifth anniversary of the Velasco regime, agriculture minister Enrique Valdez stated that "a revolution like ours [could not] remain impassive in the face of terms of trade between the country and the city, unfavorable to the peasants, at whose expense the middlemen have enriched themselves. . . . Against these powerful minority groups, regulatory actions have been of little or no value."[19]

EPSA's task was to break dependency in the food sector. The government handled the external question by legislating food importers and exporters out of existence. With the exception of

16. Many of the early writings on dependency theory were available in published form when the Velasco regime took power. See, for example, Osvaldo Sunkel, *El marco histórico del proceso de desarrollo y de subdesarrollo* (Santiago: ILPES, 1967); Helio Jaguaribe et al., *La dependencia política-económica de América Latina* (Mexico City: Siglo XXI, 1969); Theotonio Dos Santos et al., *La crisis del desarrollismo y la nueva dependencia* (Lima: Instituto de Estudios Peruanos, 1969). The regime's speechwriters borrowed dependency concepts to justify many public policies.

17. See Julio Cotler, "The Mechanics of Internal Domination and Social Change in Peru," *Studies in Comparative International Development* 3:12 (1967–68), 229–46.

18. Despite its widespread acceptance by government officials and the general public, there is little evidence either supporting or denying this analysis. The University of Iowa mission in the Ministry of Agriculture produced two studies of food marketing in Peru, one on fruit and vegetables and the other on beans, neither of which was conclusive. The bean-marketing study, which is more complete, argues the existence of an oligopolistic situation but does not speculate on whether wholesalers used periodic fluctuations in prices and supplies to make windfall profits or political hay. The authors of the two studies do conclude, however, that the supermarket chains and small wholesalers were sufficiently deconcentrated to check the worst abuses. See Geoffrey Shepherd, "¿Son demasiado amplios los márgenes del mercadeo de frutas y hortalizas?" and Shepherd et al., "Política de comercialización y precios para las menestras en el Perú," both published by the Iowa and North Carolina State Universities Mission to Peru in February 1967 and June 1969, respectively. Also Marcial Rubio Correa, "Problemas de comercialización agraria," in *Estado y política agraria,* ed. Henry Pease et al. (Lima: DESCO, 1977), pp. 257–342.

19. *La Prensa*, October 4, 1973, p. 7.

sugar and fish-meal exports (managed by state agencies called CECOAAP and EPCHAP, respectively), EPSA was legally responsible for financing and administering all of Peru's agricultural imports and exports.[20] Imports were wheat, milk products, fruit, sorghum, corn, soya beans, and meat; and exports, beans, rice, and coffee.[21] At first, imports were made by a public bidding process, but given the volatile state of the world commodity markets and the risk of losses due to delay, a succession of supreme decrees and ministerial resolutions gave EPSA the right to purchase without public bidding. In the cases of meat and milk products, EPSA made government-to-government agreements to ensure regular supplies. One effect of these measures was to free the company from the financial supervision of the Agriculture Ministry.

Internally, a middleman or his agent bought from the farmers on a regular basis over many years. Often the middleman was a rich farmer in the vicinity who owned a truck with which to take the small farmer's crop to market. The middleman usually made loans to the farmers in exchange for rights to their crops, and for many he was the only source of credit. The middleman paid in cash, an important consideration when most small farmers did not have bank accounts, trust checks, keep records, or pay taxes. The middleman also performed minor services for the farmers, such as trucking supplies from Lima or delivering messages. Occasionally he became the godfather of their children. At the same time, he took advantage of the farmer's ignorance of prices in the Lima markets and sometimes used threats and acts of violence to force him to sell at a low price.[22]

20. The placement of foreign agricultural transactions in EPSA's hands was supposed to secure favorable credit conditions for imports and exports, develop national technical expertise in commodity markets, stabilize the prize of staples, and protect the balance of payments and tax receipts from clandestine vouchering. On the last point, a common practice among private dealers had been to understate the true value of goods exported and overstate the true value of goods imported, thereby generating a continuous drain of hard currency from the central treasury, which was deposited in their private accounts abroad.

21. Juan Gargurevich, "La importación de alimentos afecta nuestra independencia," Expreso, April 28, 1973, p. 6.

22. Interview no. 23. Armed bodyguards often accompanied middlemen who carried large sums of money. On occasion they reportedly intimidated stubborn

EPSA had difficulty dislodging the truckers' influence with small farmers because of its ignorance of local practices and lack of reciprocal ties with the producers. Minifundistas and medium-sized farmers were afraid that if they angered their traditional purchaser and EPSA did not return the following year, they would be left without a buyer. EPSA embarked on a decentralization program to improve its local contacts, and some agents advanced cash payments from their own pockets and got drunk with farmers to simulate the customary buyer–seller relationship. To obtain the food it needed, EPSA depended mainly on contracts with agrarian cooperatives and campesino communities, but often these producers did not fulfill their agreements at harvesttime. Their contrariness was due in part of EPSA's purchasing procedures. Rice cooperatives, for example, complained that EPSA discounted excessively for damp rice and paid with too much delay. More important, many middlemen offered higher prices for quality food products that they could resell easily in Lima. Although it succeeded in becoming an important agent in the rural economy, EPSA was able neither to increase the prices paid to farmers nor break to their heavy reliance on traditional middlemen.[23]

### EPSA Retailing

Elejalde took great pride in his dealings with the consumer. In 1973 EPSA took over the assets of a bankrupt supermarket chain and rejuvenated and expanded it as an outlet where the consumer could purchase at official prices food that had been imported, bought from cooperatives, or obtained from regular wholesalers. EPSA also devised an imaginative scheme by which two thousand corner grocery stores throughout the Lima metropolitan area received basic food products at prices that allowed them to sell at official prices and still make a profit.

---

producers into relinquishing their crops at low prices. See also Norman Long, "Commerce and Kinship in the Peruvian Highlands," in *Andean Kinship and Marriage*, ed. Ralph Bolton and Enrique Mayer (Washington, D.C.: American Anthropological Association, 1977).

23. EPSA claimed to be marketing about 25 percent of all food sold in Peru. See *El Comercio*, March 21, 1974, p. 1. For additional statistics, see EPSA, *Memoria 71–72* (Lima: Officina de Relaciones Públicas, 1973), and the enterprise's public relations magazine, *EPSA* 20:1 (January 1974).

EPSA painted the store fronts in a uniform pattern with EPSA's identifying symbol (a stylized version of Tupac Amarú, the legendary Indian rebel), renovated them, and provided some with scales and freezers. EPSA's plan was to recoup sufficient profits from wholesaling nonfood products to offset the losses from the food products, while at the same time forcing traditional wholesalers to curtail their business or to abandon it altogether.[24]

These retailing arrangements made many foodstuffs accessible to the public at official prices, thus fulfilling a basic policy objective. Supplies were limited, however. Those who could afford to pay more or who found EPSA stocks depleted bought better quality products at higher prices in the traditional markets. The government made a show of attempting to close this escape hatch through prosecutions of grocers, butchers, and bakers who charged prices above official levels, whom the press labeled hoarders and speculators. Between January 1973 and April 1974, for example, 235 retailers were arrested, 18,487 received summonses, and $649,800 in fines were levied to attempt to suppress the parallel food market.[25] These figures suggest the magnitude of EPSA's problem and the relative moderation (an average of $35 per offense) with which deviations were punished.

EPSA's difficulty in achieving closure in the industry was due in part to a faulty vision of where surplus was being generated in the food sector, and who was profiting from it. EPSA's mandate was to serve the urban consumer by making available basic foodstuffs at official prices and the farmer by ensuring him a market and satisfactory income. The proposition was that between the price received by the farmer (which should increase) and the price paid by the consumer (which should not change) there was a surplus, stemming from the inefficiency of the marketing system and/or the exploitive profits of the middlemen, which could be used to compensate the farmers. But in practice

24. Interviews nos. 15 and 26. See also Wilfredo Flores Cisnero et al., "Diagnóstico integral y perfil de estrategia de la Empresa Tiendas Afiliadas," 1976 applied research paper, ESAN.

25. Statistics provided by the Department of Information in the Ministry of the Interior.

this surplus was not easy to find. Almost all of EPSA's internal marketing programs ran at a loss, indicating either that EPSA was inefficient, that prices to the consumer were too low, or that prices to the farmers were too high. EPSA officials defended themselves against charges of inefficiency by claiming that official prices were unrealistically low. Privately they admitted that the parallel price structure was due less to the greed of commercial middlemen than to the insufficient spread between costs of production and official prices. Farm income did not rise noticeably during EPSA's first six years, an indication that the official price policy under Velasco had consequences similar to those of earlier periods: it represented a subsidy to the urban consumer or, in terms of income distribution, a regressive transfer from the rural sector to the urban.[26]

Understandably, peasants did not perceive EPSA as an agent for improvement of their lot.[27] The only significant official price increases in basic foodstuffs in Peru until the phasing out of subsidies were those of wheat and rice. Because national wheat production was insignificant, the price increase did less to benefit farmers than to protect the balance of payments by discouraging consumption. Rice farms were medium-sized, the rice was grown as a cash crop on the coast, and the farmers had a well-organized interest group. By contrast, products which did not have their official prices raised were grown mainly in the sierra by farmers who were poorly educated, unorganized, and whose cash sales represented only a marginal (albeit important) part of their incomes. These farmers did not represent a cohesive group that could make demands upon the political system.

*The* EPSA *Scandal*

The first sign of trouble for EPSA was D.L. 20,488 of December 26, 1973, which created the new Ministry of Commerce. Agen-

26. Richard Webb and Adolfo Figueroa interpret the policy in these terms in *Distribución del ingreso en el Perú* (Lima: Instituto de Estudios Peruanos, 1975).
27. According to a written report by María Mayer de Scurrah. See also David L. Bayer, *Descapitalización del minifundio y formación de la burguesía rural* (Lima: Universidad Nacional Agraria, 1975), pp. 44–48.

cies from several jurisdictions dealing in marketing, exporting, and importing (including customs) were transferred to the new ministry in order to centralize control over commercial activities, including international trade. D.L. 20,677 specified that Commerce would be responsible for all EPSA food imports and exports and for distributing nonbasic foodstuffs.[28] The internal marketing of meat, potatoes, beans, corn, sorghum, rice, sugar, and cooking oils, however, remained with EPSA.

During 1973 Elejalde had reorganzied EPSA's retail organization by creating AGEPSA (Asesoría y Gerencia EPSA), a central control group to advise the subsidiary companies, supermarkets, and affiliated stores, modeled after the system used by the Banchero fishing consortium. The fact that his top managers were not subject to the salary restrictions applying to public enterprises caused resentment within EPSA and suspicion elsewhere. These managers were called *pelícanos*, in an allusion to the fact that at certain times of the year when fish are scarce, pelicans leave their normal habitat on Peru's offshore islands and scavenge public markets for food. The implication was that these executives, faced with the collapse of the fish-meal industry, had flown to EPSA in search of more lucrative pickings. Labor unions within EPSA enterprises denounced the reorganization and high salaries earned by these Banchero executives, and went on strike in May 1974.

In August 1974, irregularities in EPSA's rice marketing were exposed. In Ayacucho an EPSA employee was jailed and the enterprise fined for selling underweight.[29] At the same time, smuggling began to assume significant proportions. Interior Minister Pedro Ritcher made well-publicized visits to Tacna, Puno, Tumbes, and Iquitos, where he spoke scornfully of EPSA employees who failed to curb illegal food exports. These were but straws in the wind, however, and few foresaw the impending assault on the organization. Indeed, in April, Minister Val-

---

28. *La Crónica*, November 14, 1974, p. 10.
29. See *La Prensa*, August 15, 1974 and September 1, 1974, and *Expreso*, September 5, 1974. EPSA had had some previous experience with irregular financial dealings and Elejalde was hired in the aftermath of an affair involving illegal credits and contracts issued to private companies.

dez decorated Elejalde with the Order of Merit in Agriculture, praising him as being "rapid, imaginative, and creative."[30]

On September 8 Elejalde died of a heart attack.[31] One month later, in Velasco's message to the nation commemorating the anniversary of the expropriation of the IPC, the president warned:

> Potentially important problems are lurking in the large state enterprises. . . . The concentration of power, the lack of participation, and the privileges of those who earn excessive salaries foster the return of vested interests and the great danger of bureaucratization. . . . We have to be inflexible in our aim to radically change the character of the state enterprises and to punish as an example any outbreak of immorality.[32]

While executives in the state enterprises were puzzling over the meaning of these veiled comments, the government newspaper, *El Peruano*, reported that a commission had been formed to reorganize EPSA. According to an account at the time,

> On the 14th, Minister Valdez entered the offices of EPSA at 6:30 P.M., accompanied by police officers and Lieutenant Colonel Carlos Carrasco Lespes, president of the new Reorganizing Commission. Carrasco informed the 20 executives assembled that he had come to inquire into corruption, but that this should not be taken as a general accusation because he thought it was possible that half of those present were "clean." The executives were summoned again at 9:30 A.M. on the 15th and were read Agreement 01, which, calling upon God, fired them on the spot.[33]

On the same morning banner headlines in the government-controlled press announced "the fraud of the century" and informed readers that funds amounting to S/5,200 million (over U.S. $100 million) had been embezzled. A total of 134 EPSA officials were implicated in the scandal and 93 were detained in the Palace of Justice. The accused were tried in the newspapers, which received much of their information through Ve-

30. *Correo*, April 19, 1974, p. 2.
31. *El Comercio*, September 9, 1974, p. 1, and *Peruvian Times*, September 27, 1974, p. 17. The president's functions were taken over temporarily by the general manager.
32. Quoted in *Caretas*, no. 505 (November 11–22, 1974), p. 74.
33. Ibid., pp. 74–75.

lasco's press secretary, Augusto Zimmerman. Press articles
villified the former functionaries as "starvers of the people"
and recommended the firing squad.[34]

A prosecuting attorney and judge were assigned full-time to
the complicated task of unraveling EPSA's financial dealings.
The case moved forward with painful slowness for the detained, who were interrogated and then either freed or held in
"indefinite custody." In November the Christian Democratic
Party called for General Enrique Valdez to step down because
of his political responsibility in the affair. In the face of this
pressure, including the leaking of the name of the new agriculture minister, Valdez resigned, and after the fall of the Velasco
government, he too was arrested and held prisoner for several
months.[35] In January 1976, when the proscecuting attorney
presented his report, 206 persons had been interrogated and 11
placed behind bars. (Extradition proceedings had been instigated against five "absent prisoners" overseas.) The prosecuting attorney fixed the total fraud at S/2,500 million (an amount
approximately equal to EPSA's 1974 food subsidies up to the
time of the arrests) and charged 52 with criminal negligence.
The judge's report reduced the amount of the fraud to S/522
million, and indicted 59 on criminal charges.[36] In August 1976
a new prosecuting attorney set the fraud at S/500 million, called
for freedom for Valdez and three other military functionaries,
administrative sanctions against six, and sentences of from one
to six years for nine civilians.[37] By this time four judges had
presided over the case, arsonists had struck EPSA facilities
twice, and the house of one of the prosecuting attorneys had
been shot up.[38]

It was difficult to ascertain what crime EPSA officials had
committed, however, other than procedural laxness in managing the enterprise's affairs.[39] In October 1976, the government

34. *La Crónica,* October 17, 1974, p. 2; *El Comercio,* October 19, 1974, p. 5,
and October 23, 1974, p. 3; *La Prensa,* October 24, 1974, p. 16.
35. *El Comercio,* December 13, 1975, p. 7.
36. *La Prensa,* February 13, 1976, p. 6, and February 18, 1976, p. 7.
37. *El Comercio,* August 24, 1976, p. 6, and August 25, 1976, p. 5.
38. *El Comercio Dominical,* November 9, 1975, p. 18.
39. EPSA officials who were interviewed conceded that many decisions were
made without written records and orders were communicated verbally—poor

issued a new decree under which all criminal charges were dropped, those in jail freed, and only civil charges left pending.[40] The EPSA case was virtually closed, but a nervous disorder dubbed *epsitis* spread throughout all public enterprises. The symptoms of this disease were excessive prudence and unwillingness to take risks, inflexibility and demands for legal justification for even the most trivial decisions, and in general a reinforcement of the conservative attitudes associated with the traditional ministries.

## Conflict within the Public Sector

The competition between Agriculture and Housing and the EPSA scandal are best understood in relation to four "curves" that intersected negatively in 1973, and led eventually to governmental reorganization: the momentum of state growth, which made the state preponderant in economic and political affairs; the deteriorating control of the Velasco group over the armed forces and the large bureaucratic apparatus; the declining levels of foreign reserves used for investment, loan repayment, and durable imports; and a deepening internal debt provoked in great part by subsidies to the state enterprises.

### The Intersection of Four Curves

As late as 1960, Peru still farmed out tax collection to private entities, and one of the key elements of Velasco's polity was to strengthen the state apparatus. The government gained control over financial institutions by taking over the Banco Popular, one of Peru's largest banks; buying the Rockefeller-controlled Banco Continental; reorganizing the stock exchange; creating COFIDE as a developmental lending institution; extending the scope of governmental regulations over insurance companies; and centralizing foreign-exchange transactions in the Banco de

---

practices even in the private sector. They also admitted their negligence in making purchases without sufficient funds in EPSA's current account. The Finance Ministry was always late in approving subsidies for EPSA's hemorrhaging finances, and EPSA officials routinely assumed that the appropriate decree would legitimize their actions at some later date (interviews nos. 15–32).

40. *La Prensa*, October 10, 1976, pp. 1 and 3.

la Nación. The General Industries Law facilitated the nationalization of telephone, electricity, railway, fishing, cement, paper, and chemical companies, as well as the Cerro de Pasco and Marcona mineral operations. Most of these firms were owned by foreigners. State agencies also absorbed the international marketing of fish-meal and mineral products.

In 1968 Peru had 12 public enterprises, whose activities accounted for approximately 8 percent of gross national investment; in 1974 the figure had risen to 41 such agencies, with capital budgets approaching 25 percent of GNI. Of these firms, four (PETROPERU, SIDERPERU, MINEROPERU, and EPSA) accounted "for 83 percent of sales by nonfinancial enterprises, while three (PETROPERU, MINEROPERU, and ELECTROPERU) accounted for 77 percent of fixed investment" in the state sector. The state also owned shares in 131 other companies, and was the majority shareholder in almost all.[41]

During the period of rapid growth from 1970 to 1974, the INP, the Ministry of Economy and Finance, and COFIDE (manned mainly by civilians) proposed the adoption of strict controls over the production and investment decisions of these enterprises. The sectoral ministers, however, all of whom were military men, insisted on maintaining formal command over the industries in their portfolios. In 1972 COAP and the Council of Ministers ruled in favor of sectoral jurisdiction, with some central checks on budgeting, foreign currency, and investment. In actual fact, however, the ministers could not control the activities of the most important public enterprises, whose directors could justify their need for independence on the basis of their development projects. PETROPERU and MINEROPERU (under Minister Jorge Fernández Maldonado in Energy and Mines) and EPSA were especially notorious for their free-wheeling styles. According to direct participants consulted in 1974, "in Energy and Mines there is a real lack of coordination. On the surface one gets the impression that Fernández Maldonado has extensive political power, but of all the ministers, he has the most difficulties with state enterprises acting independently. You

41. The quote is taken from Fitzgerald, *State and Economic Development*, p. 48. See also *The Andean Report*, September 1976, pp. 178–80.

will find that it is Fernández Baca, head of PETROPERU, who can be credited with real accomplishments. Until his promotion, Maldonado had a lower rank than Baca, and even now Baca has seniority. This gives Baca influence." "When General Bossio, head of MINEROPERU, was in active service and the first head of the Army Intelligence School, Maldonado was his subordinate. At a birthday party for Bossio, Maldonado conceded in an impromptu speech that he still felt deference to him as an excellent boss." "At one time, Bossio was even Velasco's commanding officer. Thus he had no compunctions about calling him on the phone to say, 'Hey Chino, I want this project implemented this way and that's all there is to it.' Even the threat of invoking presidential authority had a debilitating effect on the minister and his advisers."[42]

The civilian authorities in central agencies found themselves increasingly unable to exert countervailing influence on these public corporations that were behaving like private companies. One official from the INP observed,

> The financial activities of these enterprises are not controlled by the Planning Institute. For example, EPSA is little more than the queen mother of a bunch of satellite industries. Capital formation in each is not guided by planning criteria. As a matter of fact, the INP does not even have the right to make observations on these policies, which are decided autonomously by the enterprise's directorate. EPSA has floated loans with INDUPERU and COFIDE, but tends to act outside the limits of the state.[43]

Velasco's difficulties with Navy Minister Luis Vargas Caballero and the lack of consensus within the military over the corporatist experiments further weakened central control, as did the combative posture of such groups as the small and middle-sized farmers. Moreover, such organizations as EPSA had contributed to Peru's deteriorating economic situation. The Velasco government borrowed heavily to finance its development plan and to pay for its wide range of imports. In 1968 Peru paid out $129 million to finance a foreign debt of $737 million;

---

42. Interviews nos. 41, 44, and 41. See also Aaron Morales Flores, "El problema administrativo de la empresa comercial del Estado," *Proyección* 3 (June 1976), 12–15.
43. Interview no. 42.

in 1974 the figure had risen to $456 million on a debt of over $2 billion. Food imports rose from $60 million in 1960 to $151.4 million in 1972, while agricultural production grew at an annual rate of only 1.8 percent (see Table 15). Finally, the deficits in the state-enterprise sector were growing at an alarming rate, reaching the figure of approximately $725 million in 1974, or half of total central government revenues. Although much of this deficit was due to investments in capital formation, the public enterprises were barely breaking even in their current accounts, and the overall deficit was feeding inflation.[44]

EPSA overruns were conspicuous because food subsidies were almost forty times higher in 1975 than in 1971 (see Table 16) and the bulk of EPSA expenditures seemed to serve no purposeful economic aim. Indeed, by keeping agricultural prices low, the government could not let the market system provide incentives for increased farm production. It was apparent that the government needed to crack down on the public-enterprise sector. The novel feature of the attack against EPSA was the method that was used. Instead of admitting that the past policy had run its course and coldly cutting food subsidies, the government manufactured an embezzlement scandal that distracted public attention from rising family food bills. The message was clear to managers of other state enterprises, however, that the golden years were over and that a period of austerity was at hand.

If the Velasco regime was intent on correcting the errant ways of the public sector, why did it single out EPSA to make its point? EPSA's general directors had been civilian, not military, personnel. In a military regime, it was safer to impugn the integrity of civilians even though it was widely suspected that many revolutionaries who assisted Velasco used their high office for improper financial gain. Also, it was politically inappropriate to question the performance of state enterprises in the Energy and Mines sector because its minister, Jorge Fernández Maldonado, was a member of the core coalition. None of the

44. See Fitzgerald, State and Economic Development, pp. 14, 17, and 71. Also Bernardo Sorj, "The Socio-Economic Structure of the Peruvian Public Enterprise Sector," mimeo, Faculty of Social Sciences, Universidade de Minas Gerais, 1976.

Table 15. Economic factors provoking the EPSA scandal, 1970–78

| Economic indicators | 1970 | 1971 | 1972 | 1973 | 1974 | 1975 | 1976 | 1977 | 1978 |
|---|---|---|---|---|---|---|---|---|---|
| Commercial trade balance (millions of current U.S. dollars) | $334 | $159 | $133 | $78 | –$403 | –$1,022 | –$611 | –$438.4 | $217.1 |
| Foreign-debt service (millions of current U.S. dollars) | 167 | 213 | 219 | 433 | 455 | 474 | 533 | 690 | 890 |
| Foreign debt (public) (millions of current U.S. dollars) | 945 | 997 | 1,121 | 1,491 | 2,182 | 5,066 | 3,641 | 4,077 | 6,900 |
| Public-enterprise combined subsidy and deficit (billions of current soles) | NA | S/0.3 | S/0.5 | S/3.7 | S/9.4 | S/12.9 | NA | NA | NA |
| Agriculture production (percent increase) | 5.8% | 2.2% | 0.8% | 2.4% | 2.3% | 0.6% | 3.2% | 0.1% | –2.9% |
| Inflation (official) | 5.5% | 7.4% | 4.3% | 12.8% | 17.7% | 24.0% | 44.0% | 45.0% | 73.7% |

NOTE: NA = not available.
SOURCES: *The Andean Report*, nos. 4–10 (October 1975–September 1977); E. V. K. Fitzgerald, *The State and Economic Development: Peru since 1968* (Cambridge: Cambridge University Press, 1976), pp. 49, 71; Ministry of Economy and Finance, unpublished statistics; Clark W. Reynolds, "Reforma social y deuda externa: El dilema peruano," *El Trimestre Económico*, 45:3, 643–68; *Andean Report* 4:6 (June 1978), 102; *Oiga*, April 29, 1977, p. 11

Table 16. EPSA sales and subsidies, 1970–75 (in millions of current soles)

|  | 1970 | 1971 | 1972 | 1973 | 1974 | 1975 |
|---|---|---|---|---|---|---|
| Annual sales | NA | S/2,596 | S/8,517 | S/11,626 | S/12,138 | NA |
| Surplus (deficit) | (S/351) | (137) | (492) | NA | 232 | NA |
| Government subsidies | NA | 97 | 231 | 1,602 | 2,913 | S/3,695 |
| Subsidy index | NA | 100 | 238 | 1,652 | 3,003 | 3,809 |

NOTE: NA = not available.
SOURCES: EPSA, *Memoria 71–72; El Peruano,* October 5, 1974, and July 2, 1976; Banco Central de Reserva.

three agriculture ministers had been in Velasco's inner circle. Finally, any savings accrued from EPSA could be channeled to the huge mining and petroleum ventures, which were of higher national priority than food supports.

### The Relative Autonomy of a "Liberal" State

Soon after Velasco took power, the public sector moved into a bureaucratic centralist pattern accompanied by high autonomy. The Chira-Piura irrigation authority, EPSA, the Agrarian Reform Agency, and the FPA intervened in the political arena in a way that challenged and sometimes destroyed traditionally powerful actors. Sinultaneously, these public organizations seemed to advance the interests of nondominant social groups, which in EPSA's case were producers and lower-class consumers, and in Agriculture's, renters and landless peasants. The growth of the public sector, however, was competitive, not organic. Foreign mineral companies, agricultural elites, and even supermarket concerns could not resist the voraciousness of an acquisitive state that *appeared to be unified* as it made headway in each sector. Over time, however, these ministries and state corporations asserted their independence and became subject to few guidelines except those enforced by their working environments and each other. Ironically, the extensive size of the state was a hindrance to central controllers. The impetus of total state activity far outstripped the invention of monitoring devices; the developmental goals of state enterprises nullified calls for restraint; and, with a weakening of the national economy, individual agencies sought financial support outside of the state budget.

Factions within the army and institutional rivalries among the three armed services complicated the panorama. From a situation of bureaucratic centralism, Peru's large public sector became characterized by numerous cross-cutting cleavages: ministry against enterprises, public corporations at odds with central budget and planning officials, civilians versus military, and core-coalition military versus other factions in uniform. The Peruvian state assumed features usually associated with a liberal or pluralistic system—power deconcentration, competing centers of influence, a certain rotation of elites—except that this fluidity occurred almost wholly within the confines of the state, not between the state and civil society. Indeed, many sectors of civil society were under coercive pressures during this period and played a subsidiary role in determining victors and vanquished.

A large state can be so fragmented that it encompasses liberal behavior in its internal operations, a circumstance that affects state autonomy because, once internal competition arises, organizational rationality comes to the fore. The agency attempts to preserve its prerogatives while adjusting to its environment. To survive, it is likely to cease defending the interests of social classes least able to bolster its internal position (usually the weakest) and forms coalitions with private and public actors, even if such alliances require a change in policy consistent with the ally's wishes. The first eventuality signals a decline in autonomy, as when EPSA raised the price of food produced by organized coastal farmers rather than that produced by more disperse sierra peasants. The second may initiate a turn toward a liberal system, with coalitions such as those evidenced in the conflict between Housing and Agriculture. The EPSA scandal was an example of competition over resources that in the end resulted in organizational backlash and bureaucratic timidity.

Chapter 7 demonstrates that the fragmentation of the Peruvian state, which accelerated over time, eventually divided public agencies assigned to implement the agrarian reform. The bureaucracy split into opposing camps on decisions concerning the management of agricultural production units, causing confusion among peasants and placing in relief the complexity of the rural class structure.

Chapter 7

# Managing the
# Agrarian Cooperatives

The most important of the new units that replaced the hacienda was the agrarian production cooperative (Cooperativa Agraria de Producción, or CAP) and the SAIS (Sociedad Agraria de Interés Social). In the CAP the farm workers absorbed ownership and management functions from the landowners. The SAIS was a joint enterprise between a servicing cooperative (formed from the workers on a previous hacienda) and nearby campesino communities. The cooperative was responsible for production and shared its profits with the communities.[1] By the end of

1. Aside from the production cooperative and SAIS, four other types of agrarian cooperatives were described in Supreme Decree 240-69-AP. First, the service cooperative (CAS, which was not the same as a servicing cooperative inside a SAIS) joined minifundistas in common purchasing, credit, marketing, and storage activities. Second, the parcel-integration cooperative encouraged minifundistas to combine their land and farm it collectively. Third, the central cooperative performed accounting, irrigation, credit, and transport services for CAPS on a regional scale. Fourth, the communal cooperative had a campesino community or village as its core, but worked its lands under the cooperative formula, usually as a concession in return for additional lands allotted by the Agrarian Reform Agency. After seven years of agrarian reform, the government had helped to found 29 central cooperatives and 84 communal cooperatives. Only 292 service cooperatives and 5 parcel-integration cooperatives had been created—figures that reflect the minifundistas' hesitancy to join in collective efforts or to relinquish title to their plots, however small.

eight years of agrarian reform, the government had turned 7.2 million hectares of land over to peasants, 28.9 percent to 521 CAPs and 37.1 percent to 58 SAISes.[2]

## The Agrarian Reform Enterprises

Cooperativism as a form of social organization arrived late in Peru. Although the first laws on cooperatives were passed in 1902 and a state agency for cooperative development was formed in 1942, the movement did not gain momentum until December 1964, when the government promulgated the Gen-

2. Statistics compiled from the Agrarian Reform Agency as of May 31, 1977, indicate that the government distributed 7,205,120 hectares among SAISes (2,674,784 hectares), duly constituted CAPs (2,084,890 hectares), CAPs in formation (1,138,142 hectares), peasant communities (712,071 hectares), groups of landless peasants (251,741 hectares) social property enterprises (184,689 hectares), parcel-integration cooperatives (128,565 hectares), CASes (19,694 hectares), and central cooperatives (10,544 hectares). Using a more comprehensive methodology, a contemporary World Bank preliminary report on the Peruvian economy (1978, unpublished) concludes that the total land formally and informally distributed during this period, and the number of peasant beneficiaries, may have been larger. *Before* the reform it estimates that there were 23,284,000 hectares of agricultural land in Peru, of which 15,093,000 were divided into 1,061,800 privately held units (and the remainder by indigenous communities); 14,800 individually owned farms (1.4 percent of all units) larger than 100 hectares occupied 10,490,000 hectares (45.0 percent of all land); 57,000 middle-sized farms (5.3 percent of all units) of between 20 and 100 hectares covered 2,136,000 hectares (9.2 percent of the land); 990,000 minifundios (92.9 percent of all units) accounted for 2,467,000 hectares (10.6 percent of the land); and landless peasants numbered approximately 381,200 families. *After* the agrarian reform, there were 1,325,600 units on 23,909,000 hectares of land, of which 15,093,000 were privately owned or in new cooperatives; 2,300 units (0.2 percent of all units) remained above 100 hectares and covered 350,000 hectares of land (1.5 percent of all land). The reform created 1,800 new collective enterprises employing 414,000 families and covering 10,150,000 hectares. Twenty thousand families obtained small plots totalling 150,000 hectares, or 8.3 percent of the total land. The number of minifundistas increased to 1,242,000 and they cultivated 3,092,000 hectares (12.9 percent of the land, on plots averaging 2.5 hectares). Finally, the number of landless peasant families declined to 224,000.
These estimates support the statement that the reform process from 1969 to 1978 completely eradicated the large landowners, left the indigenous communities much as they were before, reduced somewhat the prevalence of middle-sized farms, and permitted a one-third increase in the number of minifundios. The principal beneficiaries of the reform thus were the permanent members of the new agricultural enterprises carved out of the former haciendas and latifundios, and those peasants who received title to small plots.

eral Law of Cooperatives.[3] This law (no. 15,260) described thirteen types of cooperatives and created the Instituto Nacional de Cooperativas (INCOOP) under the Ministry of Labor. As the cooperative sector grew larger, INCOOP moved to the prime minister's office as ONDECOOP (Oficina Nacional de Desarrollo Cooperativo, or National Office for Cooperative Development), and in 1972 it passed over to SINAMOS under the provisions of D.L. 18, 896. The COAP commission that wrote D.L. 17,716 included agrarian cooperatives in the law for political and technical reasons. According to official sources, the factors influencing the decision were the economic advisability of preserving large-scale production units and forming new units that could use land, water, labor, equipment, and installations rationally; the potential economies of scale in marketing, financing, management, job creation, and the provision of technical assistance; the advantages of improving social conditions (for example, housing, education, medical care) in dense population centers; and collective ownership and labor to overcome the peasants' traditional isolation and to establish more socially oriented attitudes and behavior among them.[4] Although the regime's policy was ambiguous at first, the negative reaction of coastal unions to the Title IX parceling clause helped Agriculture officials to orient policy toward the creation of cooperatives rather than private family farms.[5]

The standard cooperative structure is reproduced in Figure 6.[6] The General Assembly (made up of all cooperative mem-

3. See Pieter Van Ginneken, *El desarrollo del cooperativismo y la educación cooperativa* (Lima: Centro de Estudios de Participación Popular, 1974).
4. Germán Carranza Izaga, "Reforma agraria y cooperativas agrarias de producción," in SINAMOS, *Cooperativismo y participación* (Lima: Centro de Estudios de Participación Popular, 1976), pp. 103–14. Also included in Douglas E. Horton, *Land Reform and Reform Enterprises in Peru* (Madison, Wis.: Land Tenure Center, 1974), p. 61.
5. See Chapter 2.
6. The government followed a standard procedure for transforming an hacienda into a reform enterprise. After embargo (*afectación*) of the hacendado's land, the Agrarian Reform Agency conducted an economic and social study of the property, establishing alternatives for the type of cooperatives that could be instituted. The Agrarian Reform Agency encouraged minifundistas to form a service cooperative (CAS), which it hoped would evolve into a parcel-integration cooperative. If the production unit was an integral economic unit, the agency would form a CAP, unless there were conflicts with campesino com-

bers) elected the administrative and vigilance councils, and the Administrative Council set general guidelines for the cooperative *gerente*, or administrator, who was responsible for managing the cooperative's daily work schedule. Until the agrarian debt was paid, the Ministry of Agriculture had the right to select the administrator from a list of three names presented by the cooperative.[7] At its first meeting the General Assembly approved internal by-laws and the agricultural production plan. With those documents SINAMOS would formally recognize the cooperative and the Agrarian Bank would entertain requests for loans. The Support Agency for Campesino Enterprises (Dirección General de Apoyo a las Empresas Campesinas) collaborated with the cooperative's leadership on personnel questions and accounting. The Ministry of Food provided technical assistance in crop planning, seeds, fertilizers, and agricultural techniques; and CENCIRA (Centro Nacional de Capacitación e Investigación para la Reforma Agraria) was principally responsible for training.

   Most cooperatives functioned poorly. Agricultural produc-

---

munities, in which case the agency would promote the creation of a SAIS. If the neighboring campesino community had well-justified claims against the previous hacendado and its members made up most of the work force, the land might be adjudicated to the community. The National Adjudication Committee made the final decision regarding the size and form of the new agricultural unit, and SINAMOS approved the number and names of new cooperative members. Before 1975 SINAMOS social workers prepared peasants to enter into the reformed enterprises. Either in tandem with Agriculture or ahead of it, SINAMOS propagandized on the political significance of turning land over to the peasants. Occasionally SINAMOS-generated pressure forced the ministry to expropriate farmland more quickly than planned. Once a farm was officially expropriated, the state appointed a Central Administration Committee (with a minority of peasant representation) to handle all aspects of cooperative management for one year, after which the unit was actually adjudicated to the peasants. Many of these formalities are explained in D.S. 240-69-AP and in Horton, *Land Reform*, pp. 62–77.

   7. The ministry's manual on cooperative norms states: "The general manager is named by the Agrarian Reform Agency from a list of three names proposed by the cooperative. Currently the manager will be named by the cooperative on the basis of the opinion reached by the Agrarian Zone director, for which effect the cooperative must present to the zonal director of the Ministry of Agriculture a list of three candidates." These nominees could not be members of the same cooperative, and often the one selected was a former functionary of the ministry.

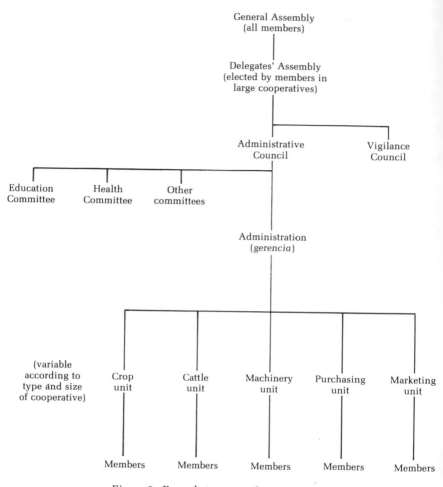

Figure 6. Formal structure of a cooperative

tion was down, internal conflict was pervasive, financial irregularities were common, and it was difficult to determine who was managing cooperative affairs, if anyone. State officials, private-sector intellectuals, and agrarian specialists clashed over the relative merits of the proposals advanced to bring order to the cooperative enterprises. Each had connotations for cooperative management, the distribution of income, lines of authority, and the interrelation of agricultural enterprises throughout the country. The management conceptions were linked to prevailing theories of ideal organizational forms in the contemporary literature on public administration. One was reminiscent of Taylorism (and bureaucratic centralism), another of the human relations school (and corporatism), and still another was a variation on the public-choice model (and liberalism).[8]

### Coastal CAPS

On the coast before the reform, permanent workers in cotton, rice, and sugar represented the rural labor aristocracy, and their situation improved after 1969. Because of the surprisingly rapid expropriation of sugar haciendas, the former owners could not mine their capital and the farms were able to continue to produce with their technology intact. Some decapitalization occurred on other coastal properties, but not to the degree of that in the middle sierra.[9] Even after subtracting obligatory contributions to several reserve funds, the permanent workers had profits to divide among themselves, and they defended this newly won prerogative jealously. The coastal renters improved their lot either by obtaining title to the land they worked or by turning their plots over to the cooperative and sharing in any year-end profits. The family farmers benefited from the reform in terms of social position. When the hacendado was removed, they graduated to the status of being the largest private property owners in the country. The classes not directly assisted by the reform were the landless peasants and the minifundistas, who had to sell their labor to cooperatives or private farmers to enable their families to survive.

Despite this generally favorable picture, the implementation of the agrarian reform on the coast proved to be disruptive, especially in the north, where large sugar plantations were the first units to be expropriated. There the government tried to reduce allegiance to APRA at the same time that it eliminated

---

8. See Chapter 1.
9. See David L. Bayer, *Descapitalización del minifundio y formación de la burguesía rural* (Lima: Universidad Nacional Agraria, 1975).

landowners. ONDECOOP disqualified former plantation unionists from positions of cooperative leadership, which was an unsubtle way of proscribing local APRA officials. The sugar workers opposed these heavy-handed methods and forced the government to compromise, which it eventually did by allowing union leaders to fill cooperative posts and deferring to them on some matters of policy.[10]

Elsewhere on the coast, conflicts with their roots in the prereform tenure system persisted.[11] Often mayordomos and caporales were able to enter into the top posts because of their specialized knowledge and contacts with governmental agents. Many of these laborers became worker-executives, using their administrative privileges to raise their status and income. Another postreform phenomenon that proved to be a major disappointment to the Agriculture Ministry was the tendency of cooperative members to work fewer hours and with less energy and punctuality than they had displayed as permanent workers. This outcome was attributable in part to the workers' image of the hacendado, who allegedly valued leisure more than manual labor. Soon after land transfer, high international prices for sugar, cotton, and rice boosted the income of coastal cooperatives considerably. While working less, cooperative members earned more money and found that they could even dedicate part of their working day to other remunerative pursuits, such as trucking, selling, and usury. The appointed administrators were unable to prevent this time-rationing system because their position was dependent on support from the Administrative Council, and the council members were beholden to the cooperative membership for their posts. Laxity in work-

10. Several studies have dealt with the conversion of the sugar plantations to cooperatives. See Alfred C. Stepan, *The State and Society* (Princeton: Princeton University Press, 1977); Santiago Roca, *Las cooperativas azucareras del Perú* (Lima: ESAN and Campodónico, 1975); and José Mejía, *La reforma agraria en el sector azucarero del Perú* (Lima: Instituto de Estudios Peruanos, forthcoming). The history of APRA in the region is studied by Peter Klarén, *Formación de las haciendas azucareras y orígenes del APRA* (Lima: Instituto de Estudios Peruanos, 1976).

11. An excellent treatment of these antagonisms is contained in Fernando Eguren López, *Reforma agraria, cooperativización y lucha campesina* (Lima: DESCO, 1975).

ers' dedication to the cooperative became tolerated and even encouraged.[12]

A reason that the coastal cooperatives' production did not fall dramatically after the reform, even though members worked less diligently, was that the cooperative, like the hacienda before it, hired temporary workers (*eventuales*) to perform many tasks.[13] The main distinction between the pre-reform and postreform periods, however, was that the CAPS tended to hire temporaries even for noncritical periods of the agricultural year to perform jobs that its own membership failed to carry out.[14] Since the temporary workers were on short-term contracts, their job insecurity and willingness to work were high. Members could stop work at 3 P.M. or even at noon, but temporaries, to be rehired, had to toil until sundown. Finally, because every additional new member meant that the total surplus pot had to be split one more way, the membership joined ranks to resist the incorporation of additional workers. Government social promotors urged cooperatives to accept year-long temporary workers as full members, but met with little success beyond obliging the cooperatives to pay them a minimal portion of the annual profits. In summary, cooperative leaders took advantage of their position, members worked less than they had before the reform, and the CAP as a whole resisted the incorporation of new members.

## Middle-Sierra CAPS

The middle-sierra CAPS produced food crops (potatoes, barley, beans, sweet potatoes, wheat, corn, milk, garlic, rye, and meat) generally for regional markets. They used more primitive technology than the coastal CAPS (and some high-sierra CAPS),

12. See SINAMOS, *Investigación sobre la integración de las CAPs azucareras al desarrollo regional* (Lima: Centro de Estudios de Participación Popular, 1975).

13. See Christopher D. Scott, "Peasants, Proletarianization, and the Articulation of Modes of Production: The Case of Sugar Cane Cutters in Northern Peru, 1940–69," *Journal of Peasant Studies* 3:3 (April 1977), 321–41.

14. Giorgio Alberti and José Mejía, "El funcionamiento del modelo corporativista y las nuevas contradicciones," in Alberti, Julio Cotler, and Mejía, *El estado y las cooperativas agrarias de producción en el sector agrícola* (Lima: Instituto de Estudios Peruanos, forthcoming).

had a greater labor surplus and a higher unemployment rate, and experienced tension with the campesino communities.

Unlike the CAPS on the coast, the sierra CAPS were heavily *enfeudadas*, meaning that much of their land was cultivated individually by the former renters and their families, and only a small part was actually worked in common. Because the cooperative was unable to use its full labor force year round, the members refused to abandon the plots allotted to them by the former hacendado, in direct violation of the laws establishing the agrarian cooperatives. The upshot of this land-distribution pattern was that labor shortages plagued the cooperative when it most needed helping hands, and under-employment prevailed the rest of the year. The cooperative members worked their own parcels first and the cooperative lands last. This decision, rational from the point of view of the cooperative member and his family, placed the cooperative perpetually behind schedule in cultivating, sowing, weeding, harvesting, and marketing, and it rarely met its production plan. Compared to the individual member's produce, the cooperative's was smaller, more vulnerable to disease, and sold at a lower price. Thus the cooperative had difficulty paying back its debts to the Agrarian Bank.

The members with the larger plots tended to dominate the CAP's leadership posts, because they were more affluent and better educated, and could employ excess labor on their own plots several times during the year. Hence, while a typical member might be fortunate to be employed 90 days per year by the CAP, the prosperous former renter, converted into a peasant leader, could often put himself on the cooperative payroll as a permanent employee and receive 280 days of paid wages per year, aside from the income derived from his large individual plot. By hiring temporaries from the same cooperative to work his land during peak periods, he could use his control over wage labor to assure himself of repeated election or appointment in the cooperative.

Even the most modest peasant detected an inconsistency between this pattern and the original promises of the agrarian reform. He often complained that the hullabaloo had not altered his situation very much. Although he no longer feared arbitrary brutality or eviction, he had difficulty comprehending the advantages of collective ownership. In most cases, he received few or no profits at the end of the year, could not put cattle on cooperative land as he did before under the hacendado, had to pay high fees to recover strays, and could not take wood and other fuel from the common cooperative stock. In light of the large number of peasant leaders in his midst, his attitude was: "How can this be my cooperative? Instead of one hacendado, now I am faced with fifteen or twenty."[15] Peasant leaders, however, denied that gaps of privilege separated them from their followers:

> There is no problem of distance between the leaders and the members. We cannot yell at them and treat them badly or they will remove us from office. There is a great deal of mutual understanding. The leaders have a number of sanctions that they can use against the workers who do not perform, among them warnings and suspensions of up to three days. We should apply these sanctions when the member does not show up for work or fulfill his work schedule. But these sanctions are rarely employed. We relax the rules in order to maintain good relations with the members.

Another cooperative leader remarked: "Those workers who say they are unhappy here are just lazy and don't want to work. The fact is that everything's going great on our cooperative."[16]

A characteristic that the middle-sierra cooperatives shared to a large extent with CAPs on the coast and in the altiplano was the predicament of the cooperative manager, when one had been appointed. Although the cooperative law provided for the hiring of an administrator, fewer than a third of the cooperatives had an administrator after six years of the agrarian reform. Many cooperatives that did hire one at some point fired him and did not repeat the experience. Often the peasant leaders grew accustomed to their authority role during the first year after expropriation, and saw little reason to relinquish it. Those administrators who were hired could not operate in traditional

---

15. Interview no. 112.
16. Interviews nos. 116 and 108. The peasants who interrupted this conversation to consult with the cooperative leader on business addressed him as *papa*, which is the traditional Quechua term for a person of high authority.

ways. Their deferential attitude toward the worker was in stark contrast to the typical treatment of the renter in the prereform period. The administrator's authority was seldom clear-cut, and he often found his instructions countermanded by the Administrative Council. In the words of one, "The existence of the Administrative Council divides authority in the cooperative, and this has been repeated in my case. The administrator is reduced to little more than an adviser, and I cannot even sign a check on my own.... The administrator must learn to adjust his ways, because if he cannot settle issues in a friendly manner, he will not last more than twenty-four hours."[17] The wise administrator who wanted to keep his job threw his lot in with the peasant leaders, thus perpetuating the idea among many cooperative members that the cooperative administrative structure, backed by the state and the newly arrived peasant leaders, had locked him into a system that was quite similar to the pattern under the hacendado.

### High-Sierra CAPs and SAISes

Above 3,500 meters, where food production was difficult, pastureland was the basis of the peasants' livelihood, and cattle, sheep, and alpaca represented the largest capital investment. A few modern units rivaled the coastal CAPs in advanced technology, but most of the region shared the problems of the middle sierra: excess labor, low educational levels, and extreme isolation. Herding required little manpower, making the altiplano the most impoverished area of underemployment in the country and a source of high out-migration. Social stratification continued to be sharp within the peasantry itself. The *huacchillero*, or independent herder, refused to merge his herds with those of the cooperatives, just as the former renter in the middle sierra was reluctant to abandon his plot. Their attachment to their own property superseded their loyalty to the collectivity.

A hold-over problem from prereform days affecting high-sierra SAISes was the long-standing desire of campesino communities to regain their lands. The *comuneros* (community

17. Interview no. 115.

members) believed that the permanent workers and huacchilleros were illegitimate heirs to usurped land, just like the
hacendado before them. Sensitive to the issue, the government
promoted the creation of SAISes as a means of reducing conflict.
Under this system, the servicing cooperative (made up of the
former hacienda workers) and each of the surrounding campesino communities were legal entities and shared equally in
the SAIS' profits. The share going to the servicing cooperative
(which actually did the work) could be distributed among the
workers, but the portion going to the communities had to be
used for social or economic investment in the community itself.
Unfortunately, in the first years after the reform the SAIS did not
generate sufficient income to satisfy the financial demands
made upon it. Even though some SAISes produced small profits,
they were used for immediate consumption. The servicing
cooperative did not reinvest, and the community projects were
of little economic consequence—construction of a chapel in
honor of a favorite saint, a green area in the plaza, a new school
building, a dance festival. The lack of investment undermined
productivity, thus lowering earnings and feeding a vicious circle. The members of the servicing cooperative disliked the SAIS
arrangement because they saw the communities absorbing the
few profits of their work. If permitted, they would have annulled the relationship and kept the profits for themselves.
Neither were the communities satisfied with the marriage because the pittance they actually received was insufficient compensation for their ancient land claims. Hence the communities
continued to invade land supposedly reserved for the servicing
cooperative.

After the promulgation of D.L. 17,716, decapitalization was
severe in the high sierra. The hacendado's herds, which were to
have provided the mainstay of the new cooperatives, were sold
off, and machinery was not maintained. The new production
units started on a poor economic footing and the relative power
and income of the wealthy huacchilleros increased.[18] Better

18. Horton (*Land Reform*, p. 145) believes that puna livestock cooperatives
could better respond to decapitalization because cattle and sheep reproduce
naturally and cropping operations need physical investment in tractors and

educated and more politically aware, prosperous huacchilleros assumed positions of leadership and established smooth working relations with state officials. Many of these same peasants maintained their ties to the communities, a practice that resulted in a curious mixing of roles. While speaking in a CAP assembly meeting, the huacchillero could call for putting a stop to the poaching on the cooperative's land; when attending the campesino community meeting, he could support invasion of the cooperative's land to redress past claims against the hacienda. While dealing with government officials, he could ratify a plan to set up fences around the best pastureland and the purchase of purebred stock; while tending his own herd, he could graze it on the cooperative's finer pastures, thus undermining the effectiveness of the investment. Most of his behavior, however, was consistent with protecting and furthering his possibilities as an individual herder in a resource-poor environment.

### Objective Measures of Cooperative Performance

After seven years of agrarian reform, the Peruvian government was not releasing statistics on cooperative performance, such as productivity per region, farm earnings, employment, loan recuperation by farm, turnover of cooperative managers, and land invasions. In many cases, the Ministry of Agriculture simply did not have the data, but in others they were considered "reserved," as part of a standard policy of restricting information to the public. But indicative data on these youthful cooperative enterprises can be culled from three sources. The first, representing the conclusions of an impressive field survey

---

equipment. Cynthia McClintock spent a total of nine months studying the highland SAIS Cahuide and two coastal cooperatives, and reports her findings in "Socio-economic Status and Political Participation in Peru: The Impact of Agrarian Cooperatives, 1969–1975" (Beverly Hills, Calif.: Sage, 1978) and the later "Self-Management and Political Participation in Peru, 1969–1975: The Corporatist Illusion," paper presented to the November 1976 meeting of the Latin American Studies Association. The SAIS Cahuide was so poorly managed that in 1976 the government appointed a supervisor (*interventor*) to oversee its operations.

of Peruvian agriculture by Douglas Horton, is positive and optimistic. The second was compiled from individual monographs by Peruvian students who lived on widely scattered
cooperatives for approximately three months, and is negative
and pessimistic. The third is a sampling of opinion of interviewees knowledgeable about the state of the Peruvian countryside after 1969. Their assessment of the success and future of
the cooperative movement was mixed.

Horton visited twenty-three collective production units four
years after the start of the agrarian reform. Staying on each
approximately one day, he gathered as much information as
possible on output, profitability, production, investment, employment, and member support. These findings were translated
onto an ordinal scale giving each cooperative a score between
+14 (increased profits and high participation) to −14 (increased losses and member opposition to cooperative model),
with ±0 meaning member ambivalence toward the cooperative
and no economic change in the units after the reform. Horton
concluded that wage-labor enterprises on the coast and renter-
livestock enterprises in the high sierra performed considerably
better than their renter–crop-production counterparts in the
middle sierra (see Table 17). It is worth noting, however, that
the scale is weighted toward productivity and capitalization.
Only one of the seven criteria dealt with employment and income distribution (critical on the coast) and only one touched
on member equality (usually lacking in the livestock cooperatives in the altiplano).

In 1973 and 1974, SINAMOS provided a special training program in accounting, organizational methods, and participation
for future administrators of cooperatives and other reform enterprises. One course requirement was three months' residence
as an intern on one or another type of cooperative. The intern
provided technical assistance when requested and drafted a
monograph dealing with the social, economic, and organizational aspects of the unit visited. Thirty-three of the fifty
studies that eventually emerged dealt with CAPs. Fifteen were
on the coast, fourteen in the middle sierra, and four in the
altiplano. Although the methodology used by these authors

*Table 17.* Relative performance of three types of reform enterprises

| Type of enterprise | Area | Average score |
|---|---|---|
| Wage labor | Coast | 7.4 |
| Renter, crop production | Middle sierra | −3.0 |
| Renter, livestock production | High sierra | 7.9 |

SOURCE: Derived from Douglas E. Horton, *Land Reform and Reform Enterprises in Peru*, 2 vols. (Madison, Wis.: Land Tenure Center, 1974), p. 116.

was impressionistic, there was considerable overlap in the types of problems detected (see Table 18).[19] These data were biased by the reporters' excessive sensitivity to administrative failures and lack of participation, the main reasons for their presence at the cooperatives.

In 1976 we interviewed twenty public- and private-sector professionals with extensive experience with the postreform agrarian production cooperatives. These persons reported on some successes, but disillusionment with the performance of cooperatives was widespread because of low profits, low productivity, little income redistribution, unwise investment, and weak management. Characteristic remarks were as follows:[20]

LOW PROFITS

I would say that of 550 operating cooperatives, maybe 200 are earning money. [Sociologist]

19. These students were graduates in business administration, agronomy, economics, and teaching. The SINAMOS course included relatively equal portions of material on political ideas and technical administration, to help "transfer real power to the peasant majority." See SINAMOS, *Primer curso de entrenamiento en servicios para gestión empresarial* (Lima: Centro de Estudios de Participación Popular, 1973). Because no standard survey format was used in gathering data for the monographs, the students simply recorded the main problems as they saw them. There was no attempt to quantify their severity or to ensure that the monograph mentioned all of the problems that might have prevailed.

20. Cited are nos. 87, 99, 100–3; and 106, 109, 111, 118, 119, which overlapped with the celebration of the seventh anniversary of the promulgation of the agrarian reform law. The law was signed on June 24, the day peasants in the sierra traditionally pay homage to the Inca sun god, Inti. Formerly "El Día del Indio," after 1969 this date became a national holiday as "El Día del Campesino."

*Table 18.* Endemic problems affecting three types of CAPs

| Type of enterprise | Number of enterprises studied | Problems | Number of enterprises with problems |
|---|---|---|---|
| Wage labor (coast) | 15 | Poor accounting and cost systems | 10 |
| | | Low investment | 9 |
| | | Low participation | 8 |
| | | Individualistic behavior | 7 |
| | | Social inequality | 7 |
| | | Educational, health, housing, nutritional deficiencies | 6 |
| | | Poor technical assistance | 6 |
| Renter, crop production (middle sierra) | 14 | Social inequality | 10 |
| | | Poor accounting and cost systems | 10 |
| | | Cultivation of private plots | 8 |
| | | Educational, health, housing, nutritional deficiencies | 6 |
| | | Individualistic behavior | 5 |
| | | Participation limited by power group at top | 4 |
| | | Poor technical assistance | 4 |
| Renter, livestock production (high sierra) | 4 | Social inequality | 4 |
| | | Participation limited by power group at top | 4 |
| | | Tending of private herds by huacchilleros | 4 |
| | | Educational, health, housing, nutritional deficiencies | 4 |
| | | Poor technical assistance | 3 |
| | | Poor accounting and cost systems | 3 |

SOURCE: Derived from mimeographed reports by 33 administrative trainees at SINAMOS's Centro para la Participación Popular, 1974, 1975, 1976.

This region has 60 cooperatives, and only 10 turned a profit last year. [Provincial official of the Ministry of Food]

During the 1974 and 1975 fiscal years, the Agrarian Bank achieved a good rate of loan repayment. But this does not mean that these cooperatives are generating the surplus that they could and distributing dividends to the members. When they have a profit, it is minimal. [Agrarian Bank official]

LOW PRODUCTIVITY

Production has not risen since the initiation of the agrarian reform. The best farms are recovering but production is still down. [Academic researcher]

Production on 55 percent of the coastal cooperatives is disappointing, while 45 percent are meeting with more success. [Rural sociologist]

Eighty-five of the CAPS in the middle sierra are in serious difficulty. Production levels at 15 percent are more or less satisfactory. [Food extension agent]

### NO INCOME DISTRIBUTION

Rarely does a CAP accept new full members, and when it does, the new member is usually a blood relative of a current member. [Anthropologist]

The first SAISes were founded in 1970, when the campesinos' mentality was different. The members of rich CAPS did not realize that they would lose by joining a SAIS. We still try to persuade rich CAPS to form a SAIS with neighboring campesino communities, but only in Cajamarca has one CAP voluntarily become a SAIS. All other such attempts have been rejected by the cooperative members. [Agriculture official]

### UNWISE INVESTMENT

Many sections of cooperative land are not being exploited rationally. The cooperative works the same land that has always been worked and does not improve technology. The pressure of the cooperative members to increase their consumption reduces investment. They split up all profits among themselves. [SINAMOS official]

The J.Z.L. CAP may produce a slight surplus, but it used much of it last year to subsidize a movie about its creation. This may serve political ends, but probably does not represent an advisable use of investment funds. [Agrarian Bank officer]

### WEAK MANAGEMENT

The Administrative Council does not delegate authority to the administrator because the campesino leaders feel that they can direct and manage the cooperative themselves. [Agriculture official]

There is a continual changing of administrators in the cooperatives, and some 45 percent of the cooperatives in my region do not even have administrators. [Agriculture official]

The CAPS resist hiring an administrator because they believe that he will be the new boss. The campesino leaders make all the decisions and they do not communicate with the members. Thus the members remain ignorant of their cooperative's activities. [Agriculture official]

## Three Solutions for the Cooperative System

The government officials' negative conclusions regarding the cooperative sector did not make them passive or apathetic. While they were sincerely concerned about the state of affairs, they also disagreed fundamentally in their interpretations of the cause of the difficulties, and on the most appropriate ways to improve the situation. Three currents of thought prevailed, which were linked to traditional philosophical positions on the nature of man, to different strains of management theory, and to the three conceptions of political system discussed in Chapter 1—centralist, corporatist, and liberal. The descriptive sections that follow characterize these approaches as they emerged in long conversations with government officials who occupied middle- and upper-middle-level posts. Although no single individual defended his point of view so systematically as we present it here, our descriptions of the three approaches represent an idealized picture of the thoughts on cooperative management that permeated the agrarian bureaucracy at the time.

### The Centralist Approach

For public officials ascribing to a centralist solution, the campesino was ignorant and lazy, and needed firm guidance. The peasants' abysmally low cultural level meant that a generation or more of education was necessary before they could fulfill responsible roles in the cooperative. Lax work discipline could be blamed on the Velasco regime's mistake of telling campesinos that they were landowners and their own bosses. The peasants' limited mental capacity interpreted this slogan to mean "Why should I do more work than the next guy?" Another Velasco error was to make campesinos leaders in the cooperatives. Instead of setting an example by working, they spent their time at the bank, the local office of the Front for the Defense of the Revolution, or the Agriculture Ministry, hobnobbing with bureaucrats and glorying in their new status.[21]

---

21. The Frente de Defensa de la Revolución Peruana was supposed to be the forerunner to an official political party in support of the government. Founded in 1975 and led by a campesino leader from the Cuzco area, Avelino Mar Arias, it contained several interest groups allegedly rooted in the popular sectors of

To compensate for the poor human quality of the rural inhabitants, the centralist solution was to manage the cooperative with a high degree of expertise and authority, preferably in a national command network. Adherents to this approach emphasized that the best functioning cooperatives were those that maintained the prereform mayordomo and caporales in leadership positions. Afraid, the peasants obeyed them. In other cooperatives where the government had taken a strong stand, the results were positive because no-nonsense talk and threats made the leaders more responsible and the peasants more hard-working. The inescapable conclusion was that the state had to stop political demagoguery, intervene in the cooperatives, establish production plans, and dictate orders. More specifically, the state had to take immediate action when cooperative general assemblies voted themselves unwarranted pay hikes or reduced work loads; when Agrarian Bank loans were not repaid; when campesino leaders fired administrators and told state agents to keep off their "self-managed" land; and when donated fertilizer was sold for cash or "traded for liquor."[22]

To improve the current situation, the state needed to strengthen administrative authority, play an active part in cooperative management, insist on adherence to a centrally determined production schedule, and distribute profits only after allowances had been made for investment. If a cooperative asked the Agrarian Bank for a loan, the state would refuse until the campesinos had hired an administrator and an accountant and agreed to strict supervisory procedures. The state had generously given land, credit, and technical assistance, and the

Peruvian society but, at least during the early stages, dependent on the government and beholden to its interests. These groups and their 1976 presidents were the Confederación Nacional Agraria (CNA), headed by Eustaquio Maylle Ortega; the Central de Trabajadores de la Revolución Peruana, headed by Sergio Aparicio Rodríguez; the Comité Coordinador de la Confederación Nacional de Comunidades Industriales (CONACI), headed by Roberto Mejía Alarcón; Juventud Revolucionaria del Perú, headed by Wenceslao Quispe Segovia; the Sindicato de Educadores de la Revolución Peruana (SERP), headed by Julio Gutiérrez Rodríguez; the Asociación Nacional de Trabajadores del Arte (ANTA), headed by Gabriel Figueroa Montoro; and the Central de Profesionales de la Revolución Peruana, headed by Teófilo Laos Rodríguez.

22. As one partisan of the centralist position claimed (interview no. 103).

peasants had to reciprocate by producing, even if the state needed to force them to do so. In the words of one exponent of these views: "The government imposed the cooperative system, and now it can impose something else. If the Peruvian peasant has suffered for four hundred years, why shouldn't he suffer a few more? Unfortunately, that is the only way we can achieve a large increase in productivity."

### The Corporatist Approach

The corporatist approach differed from the centralist by arguing that rigid bureaucracy was the real problem, rather than the solution. Strict authority and economic exploitation were demeaning to the innate character of the peasant, who was intrinsically generous, alert, and motivated to attain the greatest common good. Unfortunately, the cooperative model brought out the worst in the peasant because of its hierarchical structure and capitalistic objectives. The cooperative assembly nominated an administrative council that controlled the activities of the farm manager, who in turn sought similar authority over field hands. Division of labor deepened the gap between the leaders and the led. Power groups evolved within the cooperative, and the manager supported them by siding with the Administrative Council. The cooperative members were neither managers nor owners, just wage earners.[23]

Spokesmen for this interpretation considered that the sharing of profits on the basis of membership rather than work performed prevented the peasant from understanding his functions vis-à-vis the national community. The cooperative members had an exaggerated group identity and refused to distribute profits equitably with temporary workers. This un-

---

23. One adherent to this approach speculated on why members were relegated to a subordinate position: "Many of the administrators are trained in the United States, where the curricula are based on the assumption of much capital and few workers. In the cooperatives the situation is one of many workers and little capital, and the same principles of administration do not apply. It is necessary to train personnel with a different orientation, one that is respectful of man, his personal and social value, and his collective creativeness. University programs must be designed to emphasize the training of administrators of self-managed enterprises who appreciate the human side of the productive process" (interview no. 106).

natural selfishness could be corrected through a form of social property, which would reduce distinctions among members of the cooperative, and between them and those outside the cooperative, through comanagement, profit sharing, joint investment decisions, and global ownership.[24] The administrator would be as responsible to the membership as the workers were to the interests of the collectivity. At the field level, committees would discuss work plans and advise the administrator, and the administrator would consult with the field before executing any decision. Learning by doing, trial and error, and on-the-job training, though costly in the short run, would eventually narrow the educational and cultural gaps between administrators and peasants.

A national social-property system, structured on a corporatist basis, would include representatives elected from CAPs and SAISes at the local and regional levels. Compensatory mechanisms would link the cooperatives to the community and facilitate a fluid transfer of resources and knowledge guided by the national interest. The system would not only subsidize production units with large deficits but also create a fund to transfer technology and investments to help inefficient CAPs to start producing a surplus. To the degree that the social-property system was implemented, more peasants would understand their role in society. Their participation in work would also represent their participation in the nation and their service to their fellow countrymen. The system would be humanistic, harmonious, and organically integrated.

24. In April 1974 the government actually passed a social-property law, D.L. 20,598. The best summary of this measure is by Peter T. Knight, "New Forms of Economic Organization in Peru: Toward Workers' Self-Management," in *The Peruvian Experiment*, ed. Abraham F. Lowenthal (Princeton: Princeton University Press, 1975), pp. 351–401. See also Roberto Abusada-Salah, "Propiedad social: Algunas consideraciones económicas," and Luis Pásara, "Propiedad social: La utopía y el proyecto," both in the series Documentos de Trabajo CISEPA, issued by the Pontificia Universidad Católica del Perú (October 1973); Fernando Lecaros, *Propiedad social: Teoría y realidad* (Lima: Rikchay Perú, 1975); Lucrecia Maisch von Humboldt, *Comentarios a la ley de propiedad social* (Lima: Justo Valenzuela, 1975); Carlos Torres y Torres Llosa, *La empresa de propiedad social: El modelo empresarial peruano* (Lima: Asesor Andino, 1975).

## The Liberal Approach

The liberal approach contrasted with the centralist and corporatist by assuming that the cooperatives did not need to be discarded in favor of state intervention or social property. If given time, they would work. The liberal attitude toward the campesino was benign and pragmatic, based on the idea that he had been mistreated in the past, reduced to a subhuman condition, but could achieve self-sufficiency given the proper incentives. For the liberals, the peasants' apparent infantilism and affinity for paternalism were due to centuries of exploitation and deception. As predicted, the peasant had made rapid progress after the agrarian reform. No longer did he drink chicha and chew coca to forget his woes. These habits had lessened, and consumption was restricted to religious and social occasions.

The liberals felt that the cooperative model had been badly implemented, but for understandable reasons. Traditional peasant leaders, who had suffered persecution and incarceration under the hacienda system, concluded that they had earned rights to privilege and status, and adopted attitudes that denatured the ideals of the cooperative. Daily wages for work on commonly owned land were insufficient to persuade renters and huacchilleros to give up their land and herds. The pace with which land was expropriated and adjudicated left many cooperatives with a poor person/land ratio. Naturally, those cooperatives with more land resisted any reduction of their holdings. Finally, the cooperatives suffered from poor technical, economic, and financial management, shortcomings that were the fault more of the state than of the peasants.

The liberals did not consider that these difficulties stemmed from the shortcomings of the cooperative model, which they considered to be the best means of gradually solving them. But the government had to enforce a new type of interaction between the administrator and the CAP's administrative council, and ensure that a manager was not removed until a replacement was available. If productivity were improved, the profit at the end of the year would be higher, and this income could be divided up among the members, who would increasingly realize that working hard in the cooperative (rather than attending to their own plots or herds, or hiring temporary workers) would result in more economic benefit for them and their families. According to this view, the cooperatives' capitalist base and "group egoism" were strengths, not weaknesses. The system, however, needed fine-tuning, taking into account the CAP's technology, size, access to labor, proximity to markets, and altitude. Occasional negative sanctions would be necessary; cooperative leaders needed to make use of the penalties included in the CAP's internal regulations, such as temporary suspensions and even removal from the cooperative. When leadership proved lax in enforcing these rules, the state could back it up more strenuously. More effective coordination of public agencies would assist in consolidating the cooperatives.

Liberals stressed that the country should not be discouraged about the performance of the agrarian cooperatives. Although production had declined, the number of hours worked was reduced, conflicts existed between the leaders and the led, and individualism persisted, the situation was improving. Better marketing had translated higher productivity into more profit. The peasant leaders and CAP members were identifying more closely with the cooperative, communication and participation were increasing, and the peasants no longer yearned to divide the land up among themselves. These significant steps forward did not negate the need for investment and technical assistance, or constant and sympathetic support from designated public agencies. In the words of a liberal advocate in 1975: "Given the complexities of the problem, it is not surprising that it will take ten years for the cooperatives to be functioning properly. The excellent potential of Peruvian agricultural and human resources, however, should encourage patience and confidence."[25]

### Additional Comments on the Three Approaches

The internal logics of the centralist, corporatist, and liberal approaches permitted empirical data to be interpreted in diverse ways. They also resulted in systematically differing defi-

25. Interview no. 110.

nitions of agrarian reform goals and vocabulary. For the centralists, production was both the purpose and the solution. If the peasant could be forced to work harder and increase his productivity, the agrarian issue in Peru would be virtually solved. The hierarchical structure of the reformed enterprise would justify its existence, and through increased rural income, equality between rural and urban workers and the integration of Peru's different regions would eventually occur. The corporatists, on the other hand, saw equality and integration as the necessary *first step* toward other goals. For them, greater access to decision making by peasants at all levels would require the cooperative to take a more humanistic form. Once the peasant was integrated into a national economic system, his self-motivation would increase and productivity would rise. Increased production, however, was a middle- or long-term goal, not an immediate one. The liberals were committed to making the cooperative work. A smoothly running cooperative, representing the balance of interests among the field workers, the technicians, the administrator, the peasant leaders, and the state, would contribute to production because enlightened self-interest would convince peasants of the wisdom of accepting technical advice and respecting lines of authority. Once the cooperatives started earning money, their membership would benefit from material rewards and identify both instrumentally and symbolically with the nation.

The different approaches also had implications for the ideal size of the agricultural unit. The centralists preferred large farms because they could achieve economies of scale under a vertical authority pattern. The corporatists needed smaller, face-to-face groups to make their theories feasible. The liberals were not sure of the ideal size under various ecological and technological conditions, and were willing to experiment with alternative possibilities. Spokesmen for the three positions placed heavy emphasis on the need for peasant *training*. Their definitions of training were consistent with their more general philosophies or policy ideals. Technocratic centralists felt that training was to remind the campesino of his duties as a producer. The position was summed up by a provincial official of the Food Ministry:

The campesino must be trained. You should tell him why he is working, that is, to feed Cuzco, Arequipa, and Lima. He has to know where he is situated in the national scene. Instead the politicians fill him with abstract ideas, such as "The hacendado will no longer feast on your poverty," or "You will elect your own leaders." These slogans may be O.K., but they should come only after the peasant understands his obligations.[26]

The corporatist felt that training should inform the peasant of his rights within the collectivity. The effort involved teaching him the magnitude of his exploitation under the previous system and the need to be continually alert to prevent a recurrence, especially vis-à-vis the state. Training also should show the peasant that he could not hope to further his interests as an individual in isolation from the community around him. He had to interact with his co-workers, his production unit, his sector, and his nation in mutually beneficial ways, and not ignore the plight of compatriots less advantaged than he. Finally, liberals filled early training sessions with discussions of political rights and obligations associated with the agrarian reform. The emphasis later was on skills to make the cooperatives resemble modern organizations in their accounting, personnel practices, cultivation plans, and use of credit.

Believers in one or another approach were not above usurping the catchwords of opposing philosophies and imbuing them with different meanings. Such was the case with *participation* and *social property*. For the advocate of social property, participation meant the peasant's ability to control decisions affecting his daily work schedule and to influence decisions weighing on national policy, especially in the agrarian sector. For the liberal, participation involved the peasant's successful fulfillment of the membership functions of a cooperative. When he conscientiously took an interest in increasing profits, the peasant was participating. Finally, the centralist also valued participation, but his notion was different: "We want the peasant to increase his participation, that is, work more hours per day."[27]

Both the centralists and the corporatists found value in the

26. Interview no. 118.
27. Interview no. 103.

concept of social property, but again for different reasons. For the corporatists, social property would restructure most of the national economy under a new system of self-management, peasants and managers would develop more harmonious working relations, and the contradictions between labor and capital would disappear. Human beings would not exploit each other, nor would the state dictate to them. Although each productive unit would benefit from the surplus it generated, some of that surplus would be invested in poorer areas and all members of the social-property sector would take part in investment decisions. The outcome would be the elimination of economic classes and group conflict, and a heightening of national consciousness. Technocratic centralists, however, considered social property to be a useful shortcut to capital investment, depoliticization of the countryside, and restoration of authority in the productive units. In the words of a government-appointed cooperative manager,

> The first advantage of switching to social property would be to solve the campesino community problem once and for all. Inside a social-property firm, they would renounce their traditional land rights and stop invading our land. Second, we could diversify our production beyond agriculture to include small industries, processing plants, and marketing facilities. Now we meet innumerable obstacles when we request bank credits. They say, "Why do you want this money? You're a farm, not a factory." Third, and most important, the administrator of the social-property firm would have more power. According to the law he cannot be removed unilaterally by the workers but only with the approval of representatives of the social-property sector as a whole.[28]

The liberals saw little reason to make the enormous adjustments to implant social property when the cooperative system needed only slight adjustments and fuller appreciation to function properly. They would have the government officially proclaim cooperatives as a fifth sector of the economy. It would

28. Interview no. 115. This agronomist was trying to persuade nearby campesino communities to join in a social property firm, arguing that it was similar to the CAP, only better. His slogan to the male-dominated assembly was "Propiedad social es la misma cholita con calzón nuevo" (Social property is the same gal with new undies.)

then share equal status with state ownership, private reformed (such as the industrial communities), social property, and small enterprises).[29]

These orientations were reflected in the outlooks of educated elites in the private sector, and were debated hotly in forums and in the press. They were also deeply embedded in the activities of public agencies dealing directly with agriculture. Although the fit is not perfect, the Ministry of Food and the Agrarian Bank espoused the centralist approach; SINAMOS and the National Social Property Commission (CONAPS), the corporatist; and the Support Agency for Campesino Enterprises and CENCIRA, the liberal. Table 19 summarizes these tendencies.

The organizational goals of public agencies, their staff skills, and their reference groups in the larger political community affected the way they approached the cooperative issue. The Ministry of Food was formed from the Ministry of Agriculture in 1974 (after the EPSA scandal, discussed in Chapter 6) to in-

---

29. The various economic reforms instituted by the Velasco Alvarado government directed public attention to the types of legally constituted property that would receive priority in the country. Jorge Avendaño describes the four types of officially recognized forms of property and compares them as to formal ownership, type of service or product, participation in management, distribution of profits, and beneficiary in the case of liquidation. *Private firms*, with a capital base of under U.S. $500,000 and in nonpriority sectors of the economy, were owned completely by stockholders, had no workers on their boards, but had to distribute a share of their profits to workers. *Reformed private enterprise*, under the original laws governing industrial and labor communities, had to turn over a share of their profits to workers until the labor community, which sent a representative to board meetings, owned 50 percent of the company. (In 1977 the Morales Bermúdez regime, responding to the industrialists' displeasure, passed measures undermining the workers' ability to purchase firms.) *State enterprises*, operating in areas of national economic priority, were wholly owned by the state, allowed only token worker participation on their governing boards, and issued public national development bonds to their employees when the enterprise earned a profit. *Social-property enterprises* were owned by the social-property sector, made up of all the workers of its component firms, and emphasized self-management in their operations. See Avendaño, *La propiedad en el Perú* (Lima: Pontificia Universidad Católica del Perú, forthcoming).

The CAPS did not correspond neatly to any of these forms, a fact that caused anxiety in the rich sugar cooperatives, which did not want to be converted into social-property firms. One of the differences between the cooperative and the social-property firm was that the cooperative kept its profits for distribution among its members while the social-property firm transferred a portion of them to other similarly constituted units through a compensatory mechanism.

Table 19. Three approaches to postexpropriation agrarian
reform issues

| Issues | Centralist[a] | Corporatist[b] | Liberal[c] |
|---|---|---|---|
| Agrarian reform goals | Increase production | Equality, integration | Make the cooperatives viable organizations |
| Size of agricultural unit | Large | Small | Variable |
| Content of training | Peasant obligations | Peasant rights | Peasant rights, obligations, and operating skills |
| Meaning of participation | Increase number of hours worked | Control distribution decisions | Fulfill functions as cooperative member |
| Value of social property | Reduce politicization, increase investment | Restructure national economy on humanistic principles | Social property not really necessary; cooperatives are sufficient |
| National political system | Hierarchical, command network | Functional groups, corporatist segmentation | Autonomous groups, supply-and-demand market |

[a] Representative of the Ministry of Food and the Agrarian Bank.
[b] Representative of SINAMOS and CONAPS.
[c] Representative of the Support Agency for Campesino Enterprises and CENCIRA.

crease agricultural production in Peru. It brought with it most of Agriculture's agronomists, veterinarians, plant geneticists, and marketing experts. It had few ways to evaluate the contribution of its extension and distribution services except through increased production and decreased consumer prices. As a contribution to the reform, the Agrarian Bank reluctantly liberalized its credit policies in favor of campesino enterprises, but it by no means considered that it should subsidize an unproductive agrarian sector. Its own difficulty in obtaining funding from a recalcitrant Ministry of Finance dictated a restrictive stance. The Agrarian Bank joined with the Ministry of Food in calling for more state intervention in the cooperatives as a means of guaranteeing efficient use of its loans.

One original SINAMOS function was to promote the development of cooperatives. Its direct intervention in supervising cooperative activities passed to the Ministry of Agriculture early in 1975, at a time when SINAMOS was reorganized in the face of civilian opposition to its methods and military suspicion of its popular mobilization mission. Many of its more ideologically committed personnel had already decided that the cooperative system was insufficient to achieve social justice in the countryside, and were attracted to social property. Through its ongoing responsibility for strengthening the CNA, SINAMOS continued to proselytize in favor of social property in its leadership training seminars.[30] The unit directly responsible for implementing social property was CONAPS, or the National Commission for Social Property. Created in 1974, CONAPS focused first on the industrial sector and later developed plans to convert CAPS and SAIS to social-property firms.[31] Since SINAMOS had a more active local presence than CONAPS, it acted as CONAPS' political representative in preparing the conditions for the conversion to social property, and both organizations projected participatory ideals.

In Agriculture, the Support Agency for Campesino Enterprises was created in 1975 with technical personnel mainly from SINAMOS.[32] Comprised of accountants, sociologists, organizational specialists, and social workers, the agency provided cooperatives with technical assistance, assisted peasant leaders, and advised the Food Ministry and the Agrarian Bank of crop problems and credit needs. The agency also worked

---

30. Thus while some government agencies promoted the strengthening of the cooperative, others criticized the cooperative and praised social property. Mixed signals confused many peasant leaders.

31. CONAPS was a national-level body composed of twelve representatives of state agencies and three workers from social-property firms. One of its functions was to approve the creation of new social-property firms, the projects for which it submitted to COFIDE, the state development bank, or FONAPS, the National Social Property Fund, for financing. The first president of CONAPS was Angel de Las Casas Grieve, whose objective was to create as many social-property firms as quickly as possible, despite the fact that the number of quality project plans was relatively small. He was eased out of this job after the advent of Morales Bermúdez.

32. The Agrarian Reform Agency was active in the embargo, expropriation, and adjudication stages of the reform. Once the cooperatives were legally recognized, the Support Agency for Campesino Enterprises became the ministry's main link with the production units. The Agrarian Reform Agency transferred its attention to minifundistas, colonizations, and the rationalization of tenure structures.

closely with CENCIRA, whose main responsibility was to train peasants in all aspects of cooperative development and management. Subjects of instruction included finances, crop selection, billings, procedures for obtaining credit, and cooperative ideals.

These organizations fell along as a continuum from the centralist to the corporatist: Food, Agrarian Bank, CENCIRA, Support Agency for Campesino Enterprises, CONAPS, and SINAMOS.[33] This spread was another example of diversity and competition within the Peruvian state. These agencies differed in philosophy, interpretation of national priorities, and opinions on how to reach them. As in the case of Agriculture versus Housing, agency representatives articulated resentments against sister organizations.

> The technocrats have a fear of the power of the people that borders on panic. They say the peasant does not know the best agronomic techniques, and that if it were not for technical expertise, Peru would sink into chaos. They want to train great accountants, appoint eminent administrators, and mold the peasants to their wishes. [SINAMOS official]

> Everything was going well in this zone until SINAMOS came. It fomented dissention in the cooperatives. SINAMOS told the peasants not to work so hard and to take Saturdays off. The agronomists would say, "Here is the cultivation plan." SINAMOS would get the membership to respond, "Why should that be the cultivation plan? We will decide ourselves what to produce." People in SINAMOS have no scruples. They promote whatever happens to be in vogue. They cannot even describe the new social-property firms they are advocating. [Ministry of Food extension agent]

> I personally think that, if given a chance, the peasant can produce of his own free will. That does not seem to be the prevailing attitude in the Ministry of Food. [SINAMOS promoter]

> SINAMOS went so far as to tell the peasant leaders not even to appoint administrators. How can you turn over an enterprise worth millions of soles to complete self-management? How is a peasant without any training going to administer that? [Agrarian Bank official]

---

33. This general statement is drawn from our survey; naturally, not all agency activities were perfectly consistent with these lines, nor did all employees necessarily subscribe to them.

The officials in the Support Agency for Campesino Enterprises were the go-betweens, as evidenced by the comments of one of them: "Our relations with the Agrarian Bank, the Ministry of Food, and the Agrarian Reform Agency are very close. In collaboration with CENCIRA we are preparing a course for new administrators. In 1975 the auditing functions belonging to SINAMOS passed smoothly to us. SINAMOS still engages in useful leadership training."[34]

## Conclusions

Prereform stratification, labor, production, and marketing patterns persisted into the postreform period with only slight variations. The removal of the hacendado, the principal political goal of the agrarian reform, left much of the rest of rural life intact. The campesino communities did not renounce their ancient land claims, and were unlikely to do so voluntarily in the future. Economic interchange in many places defied the money market system. Ironically, the ayllu, which was a historical vestige that agrarian policy makers hoped would make the cooperative ideal work, was a myth. That collectivist notion went bankrupt when the typical campesino community could not sustain its members at above a subsistence level. The individualism that displaced the collective norm became dominant, and even after the agrarian reform the desire for individual ownership was pervasive. Both on the coast and in the sierra, high status was still defined in great part by the employment of the labor of other peasants. Although distrust of technicians and administrators ran deep, peasants still sought protection by establishing *compadrazgo* and kinship relations with them, as well as with peasant leaders. After the reform, somewhat more than a third of the rural population moved up a notch in social status and economic opportunity; the rest remained virtually where they were.[35] Few cooperatives were

34. Interview no. 101.
35. The economist José María Caballero calculates that 38 percent of the economically active rural population obtained ownership rights to a collective enterprise. This figure rises to 45.3 percent when farmers who received individual parcels are included. Some 25 percent of ownership beneficiaries ob-

integrated units; most lacked consensus concerning common purposes. Pressures for family-sized plots were strong, and even during the military government some cooperatives subdivided the commonly worked land among their members. Various economic and social forces of considerable tenacity were denying the validity of an artificially constructed organizational unit. If management means the orientation of behavior in mutually reinforcing ways, then it was the heavy hand of the past that was "managing" the agrarian cooperatives.

The centralist, corporatist, and liberal approaches were formulas for the sweeping away of these contradictions. These solutions, however, were lodged in contemporary ideological debate in the modern state sector, and there was no reason to believe that any was congruent with the complex and diversified rural reality of the time. Each minimized at least one significant aspect of the cooperative environment. The liberal approach did not take into sufficient account the latent strength of the campesino communities and temporary workers, neglected by the cooperative solution, who did not rule out the use of force to achieve their aims. The corporatists were overly optimistic concerning the speed with which entrenched individualism could be eradicated from peasant attitudes, even if the whole nation switched to social property. The centralists underestimated the state power required to overcome peasant resistance to an effective command production system. These comprehensive solutions, on the one hand, and rural reality, on the other, were passing each other like ships in the night.

The three positions nonetheless are reminiscent of the ideal types introduced in Chapter 1; indeed, they could be part of

tained steady employment from the land distribution, but that figure would improve as the cooperatives become more productive. Nonetheless, Caballero concludes that "impoverished campesinos who are condemned to remain on the land in Peru will increasingly become the most politically explosive sector of Peruvian society because of their desperation" at their failure to earn a subsistence income. See "Reforma agraria y capitalismo del Estado: Discusión de algunas tesis sobre reforma agraria militar en el Perú," Department of Economics, Pontificia Universidad Católica, June 1976. Using a different approach, Adolfo Figueroa estimates that only about 15 percent of the rural population was materially benefited from the reform. See Richard Webb and Adolfo Figueroa, *Distribución del ingreso en el Perú* (Lima: Instituto de Estudios Peruanos, 1975), p. 133.

their implementing ideologies. The technocrats would feel comfortable with a national command system, highly rigid and predictable, that could transform the cooperatives over the short term into a machine for agrarian production. This approach would find suitable expression in a bureaucratic centralist system. The advocates of self-management would eradicate customary patterns of social, economic, and political inter-action (possibly through a "leveling effect") and attain a purer state of national integration. This option is congruent with the functions and style of a corporatist system, especially in its implications for reducing class conflict, spurring national harmony and segmenting the community into production and government units with standardized norms for interaction. The liberals maintained faith in the long-term viability of the cooperatives. If given proper encouragement, credit, advice, and time, the CAPs could develop into a feasible mechanism for production and participation. The tactics used to strengthen the cooperative—balancing off opposing forces, entering into alliances with like-minded public agencies, persuasion, sanc-tions, control over important resources (such as credit)—were characteristic of mutual partisan adjustment, albeit purpose-fully induced.[36] Also relevant is the underlying assumption that individual cooperatives would be relatively autonomous actors in a decentralized system, free to seek profit in the mar-ket without coercive directives from the state.

In any political system, forces are present that push toward various ideological goals. Depending on the power and influence of the groups, classes, and movements adhering to a particular view of society, one or another may emerge preponderant. The question is seldom whether a country is heading toward corporatism, liberalism, or centralism. Rather, how closely do various elements of society identify with these objectives, and what are their chances of success within the social struc-ture that constrains them? In Peru these positions were con-tested over policy, and in the bureaucracy; one of their man-ifestations was bureaucratic behavior. During the Velasco

36. See Charles E. Lindblom, *The Intelligence of Democracy* (New York: Free Press, 1965).

Alvarado government, the cooperatives future was being debated in the public sector between centralist and corporatist options, and the forcefulness of the latter's arguments, in tandem with the creation of SINAMOS and the CNA, convinced some people that Peru was becoming a corporatist state. The Morales Bermúdez regime swung closer to liberalism; the positions of SINAMOS and CONAPS weakened and CENCIRA gained stature as the cooperative model was reaffirmed. This jockeying for position in Peru emphasized the diversity of national political life and the lack of an indigenous ideological and instrumental model to bring it to order. Until such a congruence between governing philosophy, social structure, and bureaucratic behavior were achieved, public policy and organizational forms were likely to continue to shift irregularly as successive governments sought to achieve stability and directed change.

# Chapter 8

# Agrarian Reform, Military Rule, and Administration

In the 1970s Peru underwent a historical experience characterized by a nontraditional military government that ruled for six years. This book has drawn lessons from three aspects of this experience. The first concerns political structure, ideology, and bureaucracy. Our objective has been to ascertain whether the Peruvian government was able to implement one or another model of state–society relations that penetrated to the level of administrative behavior. The second is agrarian reform, its implementation, successes, and failures. The third is the art of making revolution. How did a group of military officers who were products of a normally conservative institution maintain a revolutionary momentum over such a long period of time?

## State–Society Relations and Bureaucratic Behavior

The Velasco intervention had a strong effect on state–society relations in Peru, shifting loci of power and changing norms of behavior. All major social institutions except perhaps the Catholic church were shaken from their previous molds and forced to redefine their values and typical operations. The state grew rapidly and took on important functions in investment, production, and distribution. The agricultural elite, private bankers, importers, exporters, transnational corporations, and traditional political parties suffered corresponding losses in influence. The result was a military-induced structural break in the political system which provided an apparent opportunity for the regime to construct a new society that corresponded to its image of justice and progress. The regime, however, did not ascribe to an original philosophy to guide its actions. The slogan "Neither capitalist nor communist" revealed its inability to formulate an appropriate ideology for the Peruvian situation. Many of its centralist policies were justified with imported dependency concepts. Its corporatist approach seemed to be inspired by the Mexican case.

Each of the three governing styles that have prevailed in Latin America since the independence era—liberalism, centralism, and corporatism—has connotations for the organization of society and administrative principles; some administrative doctrines and political structures are more consistent with certain governing ideologies than others. An empirical question has been the degree of cohesion among the three factors. In Peru and elsewhere it has been simple for national leaders desirous of change to broadcast their preferred ideology. They have had difficulty altering the activities of powerful institutions to fit the ideology, and an even greater task to conform bureaucratic behavior to a model that is out of phase with the system of incentives affecting individual bureaucrats. Each step of the process requires greater resources, control, and time for maturation, which is one reason why revolutionary rhetoric is more prevalent in Latin America than wholesale administrative reforms.

The period of military government in Peru demonstrated that changing state–society relations is easier than changing administration. At the end of the Belaúnde period, bureaucratic behavior suggested liberal features with a heavy dose of personalism. Outside economic actors had a predominant influence on policy making, competition among bureaucratic units was rampant, and public agencies hired low-level personnel on the basis of clientelism, which, because those jobs were coveted, lent stability to the system. The Velasco government soon expressed dissatisfaction with these tendencies and experimented sequentially with centralism and corporatism to rationalize Peruvian society. In the end, limited pluralism reemerged, partially because of the wide diversity of interests that survived from pre-Velasco days and those that were formed by Velasco himself. Throughout this period, however, few of the gains achieved at the political level were reflected in any permanent way in administrative procedures. Stated differently, bureaucratic behavior never consistently reinforced the types of state–society relations that the military government was trying to establish.

The government's centralist doctrine proved effective in legislating a radical agrarian reform law and stripping power from landed elites in the Chira-Piura region, but the government had to create a new organization, the Agrarian Court System, to implement strict, hierarchical personnel practices. The FPA's imposition of a disciplined, coercive behavioral code on land judges was unique in the public sector at the time (whereas the decreased status of traditional elites affected all sectors), and even these standards for promotion and demotion eroded over time as the FPA found it increasingly difficult to recruit qualified professional staff. Later, the regime created by fiat "representative" interest groups in agriculture, industry, education, and fishing, but the corporatist initiatives withered. Despite the military's own corporate structure and Peru's embedded clientelism, this political innovation did not ally a sufficient number of groups that believed that corporatism suited their interests. Quite the contrary, the military bristled at SINAMOS' architectonic pretensions, and such organizations as the National Agrarian Confederation were disbanded. Competition within the bureaucracy among such important agencies as Housing and Agriculture and within state enterprises such as EPSA suggested that liberalism might ultimately provide the basic ingredients for a national consensus. The inappropriateness of cooperatives for new agrarian production enterprises discredited this notion, but perhaps less so than corporatist or centralist organizational forms preferred by some state agencies. To the degree that liberalism tolerates autonomous social units and encourages diversity in political goals, the system bequeathed by the military government was more characteristic of liberalism than either of the other two orientations, although again the congruence of bureaucratic behavior with this political philosophy was incomplete.

Such inconsistencies are hardly unique to Peru. In almost all Third World situations, the fit between normative principles of administration and social reality is poor. Schizophrenic bureaucrats verbally espouse one set of school-learned principles while disobeying them routinely in their daily jobs. It is hypocritical of public administration scholars to accuse these bureaucrats of betraying their mission. On the contrary, the bureaucrats should criticize academics for failing to construct a normative framework that is realistically attainable. These sets of norms would take into account the relative power of various private actors, the coherence of the bureaucracy, such motivational factors as personal career certainty, and such general phenomena as authority patterns and economic cycles. Norms would also differ from society to society because of variable intellectual or ideological traditions that legitimize standards of correct behavior. Students of administration and advocates of administrative reform must become increasingly relativistic and systematic in their promotion of guidelines for bureaucratic behavior.

Construction of these models requires sophisticated research that begins with indigenously derived assumptions rather than organizational technologies borrowed from other world areas. More specifically, research leading to appropriate theories of bureaucracy should deal with several sets of concerns. First would be research, mainly in the fields of political economy and political science, that helps to situate the public sector in a broader societal context. Some of these studies would be historical, tracing the growth and activity of public agencies through time. They would analyze the relationship between the public sector and class movements, international economic actors, and various leadership styles. They might also study state functions at various stages of development. Historical bureaucratic processes, for example, evolved quite differently in Peru than in Europe, the United States, or even Mexico. In Britain industrialization triggered urbanization, but the size of the bureaucracy increased only gradually after urban workers had sufficient political power to demand increased welfare benefits and agitate for nationalization. In Peru, urbanization preceded industrialization, requiring the state to expand in order to absorb large numbers of unemployed. In Mexico, the state remained small, and the official party (PRI) had the task of maintaining potentially unruly segments of the lower class under firm control in order to avoid a repetition of the 1910 revolution. Historical research would add to general understanding of the long-term evolution of society and the way it affects bureaucracy as a whole, and vice versa.

A second type of analysis would clarify social and institutional relations in discrete sectors of state and social activity. Too many approaches treat the state as a monolith and ignore internal conflicts over goals and resources, which often involve the participation of outside actors. Discussion of Peruvian bureaucracy in the Marxist-Leninist tradition, for example, has been nonexistent or simplistic because it views the state bureaucracy as so firmly controlled by dominant social classes that it has no autonomy; considers that capitalist bureaucracy is corrupt, exploitive, and worthy of total destruction; and expects the "withering away" of the state (and thus of much of the bureaucratic apparatus) soon after the phase of the dictatorship of the proletariat. Writings in the liberal tradition have analyzed pervasive competition among state agencies and their alliances with important segments of social and economic classes. Several Latin American scholars, departing from the concept of the relative autonomy of the state, have also viewed bureaucracy dynamically. It is at this intermediate level that broader historical trends and individual behavior patterns will suggest the parameters of bureaucratic action.

Third, there is great value in focusing attention on the individual bureaucrats, on the layout of administrative departments, on the efficacy of organizational procedures, on limited studies of interest-group activities in the public sphere, and on variable client relations (ranging from the abusive to the deferential) in an attempt to understand bureaucracy in a specific setting. The objective would be to observe the fate of current administrative principles and their mutations under various social circumstances. Such empirical data would feed into broader generalizations and offer immediate clues on "what will work" given the enormous social burdens on administration in many Third World countries. One key for opening up the administrative sciences and organizational theory in general is the realization that none of these intellectual preoccupations, if treated competently, is intrinsically more valid or requires a less rigorous methodology than any other. Each implies a distinct perspective, but each also depends on the others to fill out and test more useful theories of bureaucracy. Propositions generated at each level should be so structured as to be conversant with those generated at another. Research should be broad enough to be capable of answering questions posed by theorists working with a larger or more limited number of variables.

An important conclusion of our studies is that neither the centralist, the liberal, nor the corporatist model of state–society relations and bureaucratic behavior is fully appropriate for Peru. On the basis of the above guidelines and the material in this book, what ingredients might we expect to find in a casuistic model of Peruvian bureaucracy? While answering this question is venturesome, several tentative observations can be recorded. A model of Peruvian bureaucracy would consider that the individual tempers his self-interest with loyalty to close reference groups, such as the family, within a less than completely integrated concept of nation. The bureaucracy shares with the society a tolerance for ambiguity in interpersonal relations and a relatively great appreciation of symbolic meanings rather than purely instrumental interpretations of social acts. At the macro level, the model would probably recognize the merits of a segmented society. It would seek to preserve cultural and regional identity, and devise political structures for nominal political representation of geographic and ethnic groups, despite joint constituencies. In the bureaucracy, clientelistic hiring for some posts would be accepted as healthy for the system, and procedures would regulate the process rather than disallow it. Policy suggestions would emerge from the interaction of regional, ethnic, and class spokesmen, filtered through powerful institutional actors such as the state bureaucracy and military (especially state enterprises and the army). Coordination of policies would occur by mutual adjustment and authoritative decisions by intersectoral commissions designated to resolve conflict. In such a bureaucracy, personalism, deference, clientelism, organizational layering, multiplicity of functions, and authoritarianism (under certain circumstances) would have their place. Although this behavior might be considered inefficient and unacceptable by many outside observers, it would be congruent with prevalent values, loyalties, ideological currents, and class power. Such an indigenous approach would probably be more effective in achieving national consensus and policy goals than Peru's past habit of skipping periodically from one foreign-inspired model to another.

Students of state bureaucracy have a role to play in preparing the foundations of new paradigms for administration. Their analyses, however, must be relativistic, rooted in the orientations and expectations of the societies themselves, and sufficiently flexible to presume the evolution of national circumstances and bureaucratic functions over time.

## The Peruvian Agrarian Reform in Comparative Perspective

The government's vacillation on a model of state–society relations and the objectives of national development also affected the agrarian sector, but did not totally stymie change. On the contrary, the centralist principles adopted initially proved helpful during the expropriation stage of the agrarian reform. It was later that indecision and conflict revealed the incongruences between public policy and the power and orientations of rural people.

The space available here is not sufficient to permit comparison of the Peruvian land reform with all such similar attempts around the world. Instead, we shall indicate a few features of the Peruvian reform that have parallels with agrarian reform elsewhere. The 1969 agrarian reform, according to objectives included in Title I of D.L. 17,716, was to achieve comprehensive change in the countryside. It would replace the latifundio and minifundio by a just system of property, landholding, and farming, and contribute to the social and economic development of the country. It would create a new agrarian order, guarantee social justice, increase productivity, redistribute income, and provide job security to the campesino, while protecting his dignity and liberty. Furthermore, it would limit property size, consolidate family farms, preserve the autonomy of campesino communities, promote agrarian cooperatives, conserve natural resources, eliminate onerous contractual arrangements, rationalize farm credit, and even insure the campesino against crop damage. The most important objective was land expropriation and transfer, and in these goals the reform met almost all original targets.

The first reason for this success was the correlation of forces during the Velasco period. The president took special interest in agrarian reform, more than in many of his government's other initiatives, reputedly because of his resentment over the status of local farming elites in Piura, where he was raised in a lower-middle-class family. As soon as he consolidated his hold on the presidency early in 1969, his abiding concern was to break the rural-based strength of the Peruvian oligarchy. This ambition was realized first with the expropriation of the sugar plantations in the Trujillo area, and was practically guaranteed after 1972, when the state converted hundreds of large haciendas belonging to some of the country's wealthiest families into cooperatives and SAISes. Despite this displacement of elites, a unique feature of the reform was the negligible amount of violence is engendered. Not one landlord or agrarian reform official lost his life in the execution of the reform (although some casualties occurred in battles between police and peasants who invaded hacienda or cooperative land). The easy surrender by the landed aristocracy of its rural inheritance was due in large measure to the commanding superiority of the Velasco forces, which were backed by a unified military during the early stages of the process. The government's 1972 closing of the National Agrarian Society, the former retreat of large agricultural interests, was simply a postscript to this relentless suppression of the landowners' privileges.

Earlier chapters pointed out that the interests of peasants

diverged according to their labor systems, membership in a cooperative, ownership of land, integration into a campesino community, participation in traditional agricultural or trading practices, relations with government officials, position in the cooperative hierarchy, geographical location, agricultural product, and type of technologies used for farming. Such diversity makes it difficult to generalize about the "orientation" of the peasantry, and many members of the poorer CAPs and SAISes showed little interest in collaborative labor on common lands.[1] The response of the peasants to the idea of expropriation, however, was unequivocal. Peasant unions on the coast threw in their lot with senior policy makers in the Agriculture Ministry who were committed to irreversible changes in the rural power structure, and often helped to tilt the balance in their favor. Although small and middle-sized holders later suffered sleepless nights over the government's ultimate intentions, in 1970 and 1971 they took heart at the fact that they rose a bit in status with the elimination of each hacendado, and expropriation clearly favored their desires for social mobility. In the middle and high sierra, the reform's momentum slowed in the face of severe divisions over the proper management of CAPs and SAISes, but actual expropriation and adjudication evoked positive reactions from peasants, who felt that some such action was long overdue. In short, the expropriation stage of the agrarian reform was clearly in the class interests of the majority of the rural population.

Ministry officials always considered implementation of all aspects of the reform to be a long-term process, and even the act

1. In a little-known but well-focused article, Jacques Malengreau systematically analyzes the reasons for lack of class unity among sierra peasants. See "Solidarité et antagonismes dans un district rural des Andes péruviennes: Conditions d'organization collective," *Culture et Développement* 4:4 (1972), 755–84. A discussion of official misconceptions about the applicability of the cooperative model is Andrea Gaitzsch's "Hemmende Faktoren bei der Modernisierung der peruvanischen Agrarstruktur: Ergebnisse einer Fallstudie in der Pampa de Anta, Cuzco," *Dritte Welt* 2:2 (1973), 235–50. See also Antoinette Fioravanti-Molinié, "Tendences actuelles de la communauté rurale péruvienne," *Sociologie du Travail* 16:2 (April–June 1974), 174–92; William W. Stein, *Countrymen and Townsmen in the Callejón de Huaylas* (Buffalo: SUNY, 1974); and Pierre L. van den Berghe, ed., *Class and Ethnicity in Peru* (Leiden: E. J. Brill, 1974).

of expropriation continued into 1977. Quite sensitive instruments would be necessary to measure the extent of the reform's implementation according to the objectives set out in Title I of D.L. 17,716. On the negative side, agricultural production had not risen noticeably, seasonal workers (with a few exceptions) had not benefited from the reform, agricultural credit flowed mostly to the larger, more firmly established cooperatives, the food deficit represented a serious drain on the country's foreign reserves, migration to the cities remained high, and labor-legislation violations still existed on middle-sized properties and on the cooperatives themselves. But the creation of these units had altered the community of beneficiaries of agricultural income enormously, from 3,782 families owning properties of more than 500 hectares (with an average size of about 4,000 hectares) in 1969 to over 400,000 families spread among 1,800 new agricultural units (averaging more than 5,000 hectares each) in 1979.

The slogan "The hacendado will no longer feast on your poverty" was pregnant with parallel meanings. It implied that gross status differences extending virtually from the princely to the subhuman were no longer legitimate; that national political and judicial structures isolating and oppressing individual peasants had been all but eradicated; that peasants had augmented their feelings of self-worth and begun to demand their rights; and that expectations of social justice among many peasant groups had increased. Once the old order had been questioned and discarded, peasants could more easily challenge the persistence of inequalities between cooperative members and seasonal workers, of the passive attitude of campesino communities and landless peasants toward wealthy neighbors, and of the long-standing pattern of rural subsidization of urban life. These changes represented a significant breakthrough in a previously stagnant situation and helped to justify the Agrarian Reform Agency's claim that the reform was, from its point of view, on the verge of completion. The basic issue pertained to the ability of peasants to translate their newly won economic rights into firmer political power to influence the national scene.

While the Peruvian reform was not perfectly executed and

did not achieve all of its objectives, in terms of redistribution, participation, and production it surpassed all other such efforts in Latin America (except the Mexican under Cárdenas and perhaps the Cuban). It was much more effective than the Indian reform, and many aspects of its implementation simulated the Japanese and Chinese experiences. The questions to pose are: What contributed to the Peruvian agrarian reform's accomplishments and shortcomings? Are there practical and theoretical implications to be drawn from the Peruvian case for past, present, and future agrarian reforms in other Third World countries?

Agrarian reform cycles typically include five stages. Each of these stages either contains the seeds of its continuation or signals the premature termination of the cycle. Table 20 explains this proposition. As long as the agrarian reform proceeds down column 2, the policy has a good chance of continuing forward and eventually stabilizing in new agrarian economic structures. When the reform gets "off track," however, and enters column 3 (which it can do at any stage), the effort will slow down or cease altogether. If it does falter, at some later date the process can be renewed under different contextual circumstances.

Figure 7, illustrating agrarian reform cycles in a single coun-

*Table 20.* Characteristics of factors favorable and counter to agrarian reform, by stage

| Stage of reform | Characteristics favorable to reform | Characteristics counter to reform |
| --- | --- | --- |
| A Preconditions | Backward, exploitive, or inefficient agriculture | Modern, integrated, efficient agriculture |
| B Precipitating factors | Very strong | Medium to weak |
| C Power relations | Favorable to reformers | Favorable to landowners |
| D Momentum during implementation | With reformers | With landowners |
| E New economic organization | Consistent with peasant interests | Contrary to peasant interests |

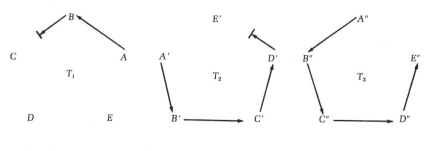

a. First abortion of reform    b. Second abortion of reform    c. Successful completion
                                                                       of reform

*Figure 7.* Three agrarian reform cycles

try at three periods, provides an example of the process. In $T_1$, or the first time period (Fig. 7a), agrarian legislation is promulgated in a situation of exploitive production relations in the countryside. The precipitating factors, however, are little more than an ethical concern by weak leadership over the plight of the peasant and a prod from international development lenders to make a show of reform. The power relations favor the landowners and the reform soon comes to a halt. At a later date, $T_2$ (Fig. 7b), the process begins anew, this time with more success. The reform does not get off track until the stage of instituting new forms of economic organization in the countryside. These structures are not in peasant interests because they do not allow for participation in political activity and do not result in increased production or earnings. The peasant mobilization occurring during $T_2$, however, represents one of the precipitating factors in $T_3$ (Fig. 7c), when the full cycle is completed.

The prime letters ($A'$, $A''$) signify that the situation continually evolves. While the preconditions in $A''$ may be considered intolerably oppressive and inefficient by the principal actors of $T_3$, they are likely to be less onerous for peasants than those prevailing at the early stages of $T_1$, because of the significant changes that occurred in $T_2$. Finally, it is conceivable that stages can be collapsed, or passed so quickly as to appear skipped, especially between $B$ and $D$.

The utility of this construct is manifest in a summary comparison of the Peruvian agrarian reform and other reforms around the world. Peru in the 1960s, like many other Latin American and Asian countries before significant structural change, was characterized by extremely unequal land distribution, oppressive rural labor relations, and agricultural stagnation. Over 80 percent of the peasants owned less than 6 percent of the land, and a minute number of large hacendados held title to over 75 percent.[2] Although statistics are not available from previous periods, it is probable that land concentration was actually increasing at the upper end of the scale at the same time that *minifundismo* was on the rise, as large farmers abided by legislation and turned over plots to renters. Some unionization of farm workers had occurred on the coast, but except for the peasant mobilization in La Convención Valley and occasional spontaneous uprisings, the sierra was virtually unpenetrated by political organization. Traditional labor relations, which we have euphemistically called "renting" only for lack of a precise equivalent for *colonato* or *peonaje* in English, were not consistent with prevailing moral standards for human behavior. Finally, agricultural production had increased at an average yearly rate of only 1.8 percent, while the population grew at an annual rate of 3.1 percent.[3]

These general factors established the necessary preconditions for an agrarian reform effort in Peru, as did similar ones in Mexico, China, Japan, Cuba, India, and Chile.[4] In all of these

2. See Table 1.

3. See Table 15. Also *Demographic Yearbook* (New York: Department of Economic and Social Affairs, United Nations, 1974), p. 129. Peru's average annual population growth from 1965 to 1974 was 3.12 percent. During the Velasco period, the military government and leftist elites were suspicious of family-planning programs.

4. Excellent analyses of these attempts at agrarian reform are Michel Gutelman, *Réforme et mystification agraires en Amérique Latine: Le cas du Mexique* (Paris: François Maspero, 1974) and *L'agriculture socialisée a Cuba* (Paris: François Maspero, 1967); Doreen Warriner, *Land Reform in Principle and Practice* (New York: Oxford University Press, 1969), pp. 136–218; George Rosen, *Democracy and Economic Change in India* (Berkeley: University of California Press, 1966); William Hinton, *Fanshen* (New York: Monthly Review Press, 1966); and Ronald P. Dore, *Land Reform in Japan* (London: Oxford University Press, 1959). Mariano Valderrama has produced a well-written chronology of the Peruvian reform, *Siete años de reforma agraria peruana, 1969–1976* (Lima: Pontificia Universidad Católica, 1976). For a comprehensive treatment of several reforms, see Hung-chao Tai, *Land Reform and Politics* (Berkeley: University of California Press, 1974).

cases, precipitating factors were present that made agrarian reform a policy imperative. In Mexico it was the 1910 revolution; in China, the war with Japan and the Civil War; in Japan, the presence of United States occupation forces with agrarian reform on their agenda; in Cuba, the victory of the 26th of July movement and the U.S.-imposed economic blockade; in India, national independence and resentment against the zamindar landholding class, which had profited extensively from colonial rule.[5] In Chile, precipitating factors were less decisive for the 1963 and 1966 reforms than for Allende's, whose coalition contained many elements wishing to change the prevailing political system and to abolish the landowning class.[6] In Peru, the precipitating factors included the deep crisis of the constitutional form of government, the disaffection of almost all political elites with the Belaúnde reform, the coming to power of unconventionally radical military men, and the army's concern over the implications of the 1965 guerrilla uprising.

Those agrarian reforms that moved farthest along in the cycle, such as the Chinese, Japanese, and Cuban, changed the correlation of forces in the countryside by expropriating the largest landowners and eliminating them as a class. They also gave higher priority to land distribution than to production in the initial years of the reform, although they did not permit output to collapse altogether. In Peru, policy makers knew that the immediate expropriation by force of arms of eight large, efficiently managed sugar plantations might lead to lowered production. Their transformation into cooperatives also made it more difficult for the reformers, at a later date, to institute social property in rural areas financed in part with their wealth. The measure, however, was a dramatic message to three thousand other large landowners that they would not participate in determining the direction of the agrarian reform, and that resistance would be costly. The Velasco government also

5. See Gutelman, *Le cas du Mexique*, pp. 53–64; Hinton, *Fashen*, pp. 3–106; Dore, *Land Reform in Japan*, pp. 129–48; Gutelman, *L'agriculture socialisée à Cuba*, pp. 51–72; Warriner, *Land Reform*, pp. 156–65.
6. Compare Robert R. Kaufman, *The Politics and Land Reform in Chile, 1950–1970* (Cambridge: Harvard University Press, 1972), with Brian Loveman's treatment of the later period in *Struggle in the Countryside* (Bloomington: Indiana University Press, 1975, pp. 279–301).

moved quickly to prohibit parceling, permitted in India and Chile, which would have allowed large owners to reconstitute their property and influence under new titles.[7] The stripping of power from the Peruvian landed oligarchy did not restructure all other class relations in rural areas, but the action did tip the balance of power in favor of the government during the first years of the reform.

Several factors distinguished the efforts of the Agrarian Reform Agency to maintain the momentum of the expropriation drive. First, as in China, agrarian reform decrees adapted flexibly to rural conditions and political changes, but the reformers maintained a clear image of their final goal: massive expropriation and collective production units.[8] Second, unlike the case in India, agrarian policy makers did not wash their hands of the reform after writing the law, but occupied key positions of authority to see it through to the end.[9] Third, when Peruvian policy makers encountered resistance to the reform, even in military circles, they depended in part on the agitation of existing rural unions on the coast to support their cause. The Chilean reformers, for example, were obliged to create peasant unions simultaneously with the implementation of the reform, and these groups were unable to pressure effectively in favor of

7. Warriner points out (*Land Reform*, pp. 171–73) that many Indian states permitted zamindars to parcel their land, often among relatives. Under Eduardo Frei's reform in Chile, landowners were permitted to retain the equivalent of eighty irrigated hectares, usually their best land, containing most of the farm's physical infrastructure. The presence of former latifundistas in the countryside, even if on reduced holdings, was a factor preventing realignment of class relations in rural Chile. See David Lehmann, "Agrarian Reform in Chile, 1965–1972," in *Peasants, Landlords, and Government*, ed. Lehman (New York: Holmes & Meier, 1974), pp. 84–86.

8. For China, see Robert Ash, "Economic Aspects of Land Reform in Kiangsu, 1949–52 (Part 1)," *China Quarterly* 66 (June 1976), 289–91.

9. The Indian reform suffered two breaches from the stage of national legislation to local implementation. First, individual state parliaments had to write by-laws for the national agrarian reform law, and these by-laws contained many loopholes. See Warriner, *Land Reform*, pp. 165–67. Second, state administrators who did not participate in drafting the legislation were required to execute it. They were vulnerable to the local political machinery, which opposed comprehensive agrarian reform. See Paul R. Brass, *Factional Politics in an Indian State: The Congress Party in Uttar Pradesh* (Berkeley: University of California Press, 1965), pp. 62–111, 212–45.

the reform.[10] Finally, although Peru's Agrarian Court System did not adjudicate expropriation disputes, its existence did help to preclude the channeling of cases to the more corruptible Common Court System, where landowners would have vitiated the reform.

During the Velasco period, two phenomena did attenuate its momentum, and the agrarian reform entered difficult straits toward the end of his regime. One was the backlash of small and middle-sized farmers. The Agrarian Reform Agency could neither break their coalition nor neutralize their access to governing circles. These farmers eventually succeeded in obtaining a moratorium on expropriation of middle-sized and small holdings. Also, the deliberate pace of the reform permitted many sierra hacendados to sell their animals and equipment and to neglect maintenance, and thus to leave new cooperatives with a low financial base from which to begin operations. The situation contrasted with rapid reforms in Asian communist countries. Fortunately for their intentions, Velasco's government lasted over six years and the reformers were able to achieve most of their expropriation targets before he fell from power.

Table 21 applies data from the Peruvian case directly to the categories of Table 20. Pertinent characteristics cluster in column 2 until the last stage, that of the institutionalization of new economic structures. Chapter 7 argued that none of the three "solutions" proposed by government agencies corresponded fully to peasant interests. The condescending attitudes of many government functionaries, together with the implicit national development strategy of extracting surplus from the countryside to feed industry, compounded dissatisfaction with this aspect of the reform. Finally, a large percentage of rural inhabi-

10. See David Lehmann, "Political Incorporation versus Political Stability: The Case of the Chilean Agrarian Reform, 1965–1970," *Journal of Development Studies* 7:4 (July 1971), 365–95. This statement does not mean that peasants were passive until the advent of Frei's Christian Democratic government. Loveman provides rich analysis of rural labor complaints submitted to the Ministry of Work in *Struggle in the Countryside*. Although peasant organizations sprouted for brief periods in the first half of the twentieth century, they were repeatedly repressed by landowning interests, and until Frei assumed the presidency, forming a peasant union was an illegal act.

*Table 21.* Characteristics of factors favorable and counter to agrarian reform under Velasco, by stage

| Stage of reform | Characteristics favorable to reform | Characteristics counter to reform |
|---|---|---|
| Preconditions | Unequal land distribution<br>Oppressive labor relations<br>Stagnant agriculture | |
| Precipitating factors | Crisis of civilian rule<br>Recent rural guerrilla experience<br>Progressive military government in power | |
| Power relations | Large landowners eliminated as a class<br>Priority of redistribution over production<br>Reform legislation drafted independent of landed interests<br>Parceling forbidden | |
| Momentum during implementation | Reformers firm about goals but keep legislation flexible<br>Land courts controlled by reform advocates<br>Reform implementers same persons as drafters of legislation<br>Existence of rural unions abets advocates<br><br> | <br><br><br><br><br><br><br><br>Backlash of small and medium farmers not neutralized<br>Pace of execution too slow to prevent decapitalization |
| New economic organization | | Top-down reform fails to integrate peasants into collective enterprises<br>Agriculture perceived to boost urban economy<br>Many campesinos not benefited by reform |

tants were not better off after the reform than they had been before. Many peasants in indigenous communities, and those working minifundios or no land at all, represented a source of continued social tension and instability. The cycle of the Velasco agrarian reform thus apparently stalled before the last stage was reached. In Chapter 5 we pointed out that class-based rural organization seemed to be achieving sufficient cohesion to represent a force for redefinition of the reform in the future.

The reader will now recognize that Figure 7 conforms to our understanding of the Peruvian case. Figure 7a is the Belaúnde reform, which was mitigated by weak precipitating factors and power relations unfavorable to the reformers. Figure 7b is the Velasco reform, which progressed considerably further. If some of the pressures for change described in Chapter 5 materialize, the Peruvian case will enter $T_3$ (Fig. 7c), although it is of course impossible to speculate whether that cycle will successfully terminate in a situation of relatively long-term stability.

Tables 20 and 21 restate some of the conditions necessary if agrarian reform is to be successful. They do not represent a theory of agrarian reform, which would need to establish relationships among economic, technological, and demographic change, and their effect on the agrarian sector. Two such general theories are those of Jeffrey Paige and Michel Gutelman, both of whom refer to Peru to support their analyses. Paige argues that class conflict leads to various changes in the agrarian structure, depending on whether the principal actors own their own land or work it for others, and whether they obtain their income from land, capital investment, or wages.[11] Applying his construct to the Peruvian case, Paige predicts strikes for better working conditions and higher pay in the coastal plantations and revolt in favor of land distribution (most likely for individual holdings) in the sierra. The types of unrest in the Peruvian countryside before 1968 were consistent with Paige's propositions. Unfortunately, because he does not adequately treat the role of the state, he fails to explain why collective

11. Jeffrey M. Paige, *Agrarian Revolution* (New York: Free Press, 1975), pp. 1–71.

enterprises were created both on the coast and in the sierra under the Velasco government.[12]

Michel Gutelman argues that agrarian reforms are the result of a correlation of forces involving a whole society. They are a social product whose nature, scope, and history are functions of a sudden breaking of a social equilibrium. This type of agrarian transformation comes about after some classes conclude that the previous pattern of appropriating surplus labor in the countryside is not conducive to their interests. These classes use the power of the state to dispossess the landowners and establish a new equilibrium of forces in rural areas. Gutelman's explicit application of his theory to the Peruvian case touches on a few of the events recorded in earlier chapters.

> For all classes, therefore, the political power of the landowners, at the heart of the bloc of dominant classes, constitutes an obstacle to their own development. Thus, the coup d'état occurs: the "progressive" and nationalist faction of the army takes over power and proclaims the "peaceful revolution." It decides particularly to undertake an agrarian reform. In fact, the landed aristocracy has already been eliminated from the bloc of governing classes—inasmuch as it is called landed aristocracy. Its displacement from a position of influencing the state permits the execution of an effective agrarian reform. The peasants are to be organized in unions—controlled by the government—and . . . the

---

12. Paige uses Peruvian data in one of his empirical chapters, but does not deal exhaustively with post-1968 developments. His general theory postulates four kinds of outcomes: revolution, commodity reform, labor reform, and revolt. The last two are of most interest to us because they would correspond to the coast and the sierra, respectively. Concerning revolt, Paige states that an "agrarian revolt is directed at the redistribution of landed property and typically lacks broader political objectives. The typical tactic of such movements is the land invasion. An agrarian revolt is most likely when a socialist or reform party has weakened landed-upper-class control of the state and provided the organizational framework lacking among cultivators dependent on land." Belaúnde might have been considered such a reform leader, but the result under Velasco was the formation of cooperatives, not land invasions and division. In fairness to Paige's thesis, however, it is necessary to recall that Chapter 7 argues that the cooperatives did not correspond neatly to many sierra peasant desires for direct ownership, and invasion was a recurrent phenomenon even after cooperativization. Concerning export agriculture, Paige says, "The reform labor movement . . . demands neither the redistribution of property nor the seizure of state power. The typical tactic of such movements is the strike." Again the theory does not account for the transformation of Peruvian coastal plantations into cooperatives. See *Agrarian Revolution*, pp. 70–71.

latifundios are seized and given to the peasants, whether in individual titles, cooperatives, etc. In this case, too, the scope of
the agrarian reform in the field will depend especially on the
power relations the landowners succeeded in establishing with
the peasants and the state. But, since the latter controls the
means of repression, the landowners cannot prevent an agrarian
reform.[13]

While Gutelman argues that an agrarian reform was in the
interests of the emergent industrial bourgeoisie, he minimizes
the autonomy of the state. His approach does not account for
the government's preference for cooperatives over individual
titles, or for the Velasco regime's ostracizing of industrial
classes from governing circles, neither of which was in the
interests of that fraction of the power bloc.

One difficulty with many explanations of structural interrela-
tionships, and this observation relates to both Paige's and
Gutelman's analyses, is that they do not give enough credit to
the prescience and determination of individuals and groups
who transform into reality what others with the aid of
hindsight label a historical truth. Economic and political
change in the agrarian sector does not occur without persons
who take calculated risks in order to push the process in one
direction or another. While structure is a powerful constraint,
room does exist for maneuver. For example, if Peruvian agrarian policy makers had limited their objectives to what seemed
feasible given the correlation of forces in 1970, and later re-
treated in the face of opposition, a much weaker reform would
have emerged. Family farms parceled out of larger latifundia,
not cooperatives, would have predominated on the coast and in
the sierra, and the peasants would have made less headway in
gaining control over their own labor. Agrarian reform bonds
would have been used to consolidate the power of industrial
entrepreneurs. No efforts would have been made to halt the
spread of urbanizers into scarce agricultural land. The agrarian
reform would have been directed first and foremost toward
increasing agrarian production, and redistribution would have
been relegated to a secondary importance. While it would be

13. Michel Gutelman, *Structure et réformes agraires* (Paris: François Maspero, 1971), pp. 148–49.

misleading to declare that "will" and "commitment" explain most of the variance between successful and unsuccessful reforms, often their presence is decisive. This point should not be dismissed even in the most advanced structuralist theory because if historical outcomes were inevitable, no one would lift a finger to help them along.

In summary, the Peruvian agrarian reform over eight years transferred 7 million hectares of land to 1,500 collective units of various types and provided land security for thousands of former tenants and minifundistas. Agrarian policy makers had to make difficult decisions at key points to keep the reform on track and mitigate the pressures of small and middle-sized farmers, developers, and some segments of the military. The ultimate outcome of the reform, however, is still unknown. One of the persistent issues facing the governments that followed Velasco was whether to consolidate the agrarian reform enterprises as cooperatives, state farms, or social-property enterprises. Another was the political organization and autonomy of the peasantry. Finally, the fact that a large portion of the peasants were not among the direct beneficiaries of the agrarian reform meant that there was good reason to predict continuing migration to the cities, lower- and middle-class agitation for redistribution, and the eventual transformation of the current ownership and management structure of agricultural units. Thus, while the elimination, once and for all, of the *gamonal* did not immediately favor the peasantry as a whole, the agrarian reform process offered good prospects of eventually involving almost all peasants in politics. The arbitrariness of the original distribution of benefits perpetuated conflict in the countryside and made it clear that peasants had to struggle to preserve what they possessed or to obtain what they felt was legitimately theirs.

## Peru under Military Rule

The reversal or abandonment of many of Velasco's revolutionary measures by his successor is a clue to the exceptional nature of the Velasco interlude. Héctor Béjar, a leader of the 1965 guerrilla movement who left prison to join forces with the military government, often told radical student audiences that they would be well advised to support the government. To paraphrase: "You may talk of revolution in the abstract or romantic sense. But this is about the best revolution you are likely to get in your lifetime, so make the most of it." The essence of his message was that Peru offered very few of the objective conditions for drastic social upheaval in 1969. Its large, unmobilized peasantry was distrustful of white or mestizo leadership, and was not a prospective vanguard element. The urban proletariat was small and fragile, although the Communist Party was influential in the mining regions. Large United States consorcia owned and managed much of the mineral and agricultural wealth, and the nation was in a weak competitive position with respect to its main commodity exports (copper, cotton, sugar) except for fish meal. The national bourgeoisie contained articulate and progressive elements, including the leadership of the Christian Democratic, Social Christian, and Social Progressive political movements. The middle sector, however, represented only a tiny percentage of the national population, and much of it was tied to foreign companies via licensing, import, export, or service agreements. Another portion, affiliated with APRA, was unlikely to recommend far-reaching change, given that party's conservative stance during the Belaúnde government. Finally, although the Peruvian military had been dissatisfied in the 1960s with United States congressional limitations on arms sales, North American service personnel had maintained influence in the ranks by means of cordial collaborative agreements through the years.

Under these circumstances, Velasco's policy positions were unexpected. He seemed to be immune to the multiple pressures that undid the Belaúnde government. His entourage took forceful command of the situation and began to identify goals that would achieve economic development, increase national sovereignty, redistribute economic power in the upper income quartile of society, and extend some benefits of nationhood to the campesino masses. In studying his overall polity, one must ask: In whose interests was Velasco ruling? The answer is difficult to pinpoint because, as Table 22 suggests, almost all of

*Table 22.* Policies and activities favorable and unfavorable to powerful and weak groups during regimes of Velasco and Morales Bermúdez

| Policy or activity | Importers-exporters | Industrialists | Military | Church | Foreign capitalists | Bureaucracy | Medium-sized farmers | Peasants | Workers | Shantytown dwellers | Number of groups favored and disfavored |
|---|---|---|---|---|---|---|---|---|---|---|---|
| Velasco period | | | | | | | | | | | |
| Industrial policy | – | N | – | – | N | Y | – | – | Y | – | 4 |
| Foreign policy | N | N | – | – | N | – | – | – | – | – | 3 |
| Agrarian policies | N | Y | Y | – | N | – | N | Y | Y | Y | 8 |
| Education policy | – | N | – | N | – | – | – | – | Y | Y | 4 |
| SINAMOS activities | N | N | N | – | N | – | N | – | N | Y | 7 |
| State growth | N | N | Y | – | N | Y | – | – | – | – | 5 |
| Press reform | N | N | – | – | N | Y | N | Y | Y | – | 7 |
| Social property | N | N | – | – | N | Y | – | – | Y | Y | 6 |
| Urban land | – | N | – | – | – | – | N | Y | – | Y | 4 |
| Morales Bermúdez period | | | | | | | | | | | |
| Devaluations | – | N | – | – | Y | – | N | N | N | N | 6 |
| Foreign policy | Y | Y | – | – | Y | – | – | – | – | – | 3 |
| Social property | – | Y | – | – | Y | N | Y | – | N | N | 6 |
| Industrial policy | Y | Y | – | – | Y | N | – | – | N | – | 5 |
| Labor policies | Y | Y | – | – | – | – | Y | N | N | N | 6 |
| Withdrawal of food subsidies | – | N | – | N | – | – | Y | Y | N | N | 6 |
| Military hardware | N | N | Y | – | – | – | – | – | – | – | 3 |

NOTE: Y = group interests generally consistent with policy goals. N = group interests generally inconsistent with policy goals. – = policy goals are irrelevant to group interests or ambiguous.

his policies that were not neutral were contrary to the interests of the most powerful groups in society: the upper class, the industrial bourgeoisie, and foreign capitalists. Only two of the structural reforms (land distribution and state growth) could be construed as being in the interests of the military. Indeed, the polity corresponded more to the long-term interests of the nonhegemonic groups in the society.

The contradiction is that Velasco ruled for six years against the opposition or apathy of major forces in the society, and attempted to implement policies in favor of groups that could offer no immediate support. In this he can be contrasted with Chile's Salvador Allende, who, despite the additional initial advantage of constitutional legitimacy, ruled only half as long; and his own successor, Morales Bermúdez, whose policies inclined toward the powerful rather than the poor. In Marxist terms, many of Velasco's programs were characteristic of relatively high state autonomy, which, when it occurs, is hypothesized to be of short duration and to be to the ultimate benefit of the hegemonic classes. It is debatable whether Velasco's tenure can be considered short or whether his programs, if carried to completion, would have been advantageous to the privileged groups in Peru. (It is more likely that he will be reviled by most historians for his actions, except perhaps for the agrarian reform.) International observers praised Velasco's successor as a pragmatist. If "pragmatism" meant the quality of recognizing the rules of the game and objective limits to independent action, the question remains: How did the Velasco regime maintain its exceptional quality for such a long period? And was there any way that the political movement he began could have continued?

The answer lies in six interrelated factors that propelled the Velasco regime along its course but had dissipated by the time Morales Bermúdez took command. First was the presence of the core coalition, to which we have referred repeatedly and whose role was paramount. This group of trusted military officers, unified during most of this period, shared a common mind set leaning in a leftist or populist direction, interacted continuously in designing the polity, and was well positioned during most of the Velasco regime to execute and defend various policies. Leonidas Rodríguez led SINAMOS; Jorge Fernández Maldonado, Energy and Mines; Enrique Gallegos, military intelligence and Agriculture; and Rafael Hoyos, Food and the army's Special Forces. Over time Velasco widened the core group's membership to include José Graham, who headed the COAP; Pedro Richter, Interior; and Javier Tantaleán, Fishing. The main clue to these men's power under Velasco was that, when programs with which they had been entrusted faltered, they were not held personally responsible. Indeed, they might go on to more important posts. Such was the case with Rodríguez, who, when SINAMOS stumbled badly, became head of Lima's military garrison. Fernández Maldonado was not sacrificed after it was apparent that no cost-benefit analysis had preceded the construction of a pipeline from the jungle to the sea. Though his poor judgment threatened to burden the country with an $800 million white elephant, Maldonado's position in the power structure was unimpaired. Graham weathered accusations of corruption, and Tantaleán, allegations that he was leading the "fascist" wing of government. Richter remained minister of the interior even after torture was proved to have occurred under his jurisdiction. Members of the support coalition were dismissed for errors or deviations of much less import. The difference was that the former group's support of Velasco was reciprocated by his protection, and the latter group was expendible for short-term political advantage. Velasco realized that the core coalition had to survive if such a small group was to achieve its ambitious objectives.

By contrast, although Morales Bermúdez was highly respected in military and civilian circles, he did not assume the presidency with "his men": persons who could be positioned strategically in the bureaucracy and the army to secure support and loyalty. The fact that Velasco had systematically retired or delayed the promotion of many military men who would have been capable cabinet ministers under Morales meant that his governing group, at least in the first few months, was disparate, possibly less qualified, and certainly less in agreement on policy matters.

Second, Velasco entered power at the head of a unified army, which was well trained and with an ingrained sense of national mission. It was prepared to sacrifice for the progress of the country and felt a responsibility to succeed where civilians, despite their condescending attitude toward military men, had failed. Velasco managed civilian input carefully to keep the military institutions behind him. Such men as Guillermo Figallo and Benjamín Samanez frequently consulted with the top governing circle on agricultural matters, as did other nonmilitary adviser on affairs pertinent to their sectors. These civilians shared friendship, common life experiences, and ideological and policy preferences with their military contemporaries (perhaps more so than these military men did with their less adventurous comrades-in-arms) and offered specialized knowledge in return. The civilians helped to fill out the design of and implement the revolutionary polity, and could count on protection from the core coalition when they came under attack, as Samanez frequently was. But the reason they could not be considered full-fledged members of the core coalition was that they were consulted only on those policy matters that concerned their sectors. The job of synthesizing political demands and calculating opportunities across the board was the guarded reserve of the core military coalition, which admitted no civilian presence.[14]

The barring of civilians from the innermost sanctuaries helped to maintain the support coalition relatively intact. By not merging with civilian political elites, the regime could preserve its distinctive military flavor and cushion itself more easily against accusations of neglecting its institutional heritage and mandate.[15] The regime chose its internal battles with care.

14. A clear example of the sensitivity of the core coalition to civilians speaking in its name occurred in the case of Augusto Zimmerman, Velasco's confidant and press secretary. In March 1975, Ismais Frías, editor of *Ultima Hora*, was Zimmerman's main obstacle in his effort to control the government-created newspaper union. Zimmerman made the mistake of saying that his policies were personally supported by Velasco. Hearing of this excessive usurpation of authority, Velasco sent a message of denial to the next meeting. The message, read by his opponents, embarrassed Zimmerman and ended his attempt to control the Peruvian press personally.

15. Interpretations vary on why the core coalition did not act to prevent Morales Bermúdez from executing his coup, which he declared in Tacna on August 31, 1975. One is that Jorge Fernández Maldonado, Leonidas Rodríguez, Enrique Gallegos, and Rafael Hoyos were concerned that the Misión faction, headed by Javier Tantaleán, was gaining too much power, and they felt that Morales was a preferable alternative who would continue the broad outlines of the revolution. Another is that the core coalition, together with junior officers, was waiting for Maldonado to take the initiative, and that they would have resisted the coup with the aid of the Rodríguez-commanded Lima military garrison. Whether because of lack of courage or because of his personal friendship with Morales, Maldonado failed to act and the opportunity was lost. A final version is that the move was a total surprise, coming as it did in the middle of a Third World conference being held in Lima. While some of these

When conflict rose above precarious levels, it relied on military commissions to examine the facts, as in the small farmers' controversy. The procedure neutralized opposition and conserved the support, albeit conditional, of doubting military officers. Velasco recognized the importance of these considerations because, as military governments go, his regime was radical. To continue its experiments, he needed to generate all the trust he could from within the armed forces, trust that could be translated into freedom of action. The core coalition created a mystique around the idea of a unified armed forces carrying out a revolution in Peru, as a way of postponing manifest disagreement over policy issues until broad popular support could be secured. Naturally, the contradiction in this approach was that the military regime had difficulty gaining support from a larger segment of the population as long as it ostracized civilians from high-level political roles and conceded to conservative officers who refused to countenance a mobilization of the Peruvian masses.

By the time Velasco fell from office, the army was divided by seven years of maneuvering, not only in political interaction with civil society but also within the ranks over promotions and appointments. To strengthen his minority position, Velasco encouraged the army to move along more quickly those officers who were committed to the goals of the revolution. As discussed in Chapter 1, this favoritism often boiled down to personalism; senior officers within the core or support coalition lobbied in favor of junior officers whose performance in the civilian bureaucracy or ideological banter was found to be praiseworthy. Such nontraditional criteria for military promotions provoked jealousies also in the navy and air force, but

---

factors may have played a part, it is most likely that the core coalition recognized that it had insufficient control of army, navy, and air force commands to mount effective resistance, and Velasco, because of his illness and arbitrary decisions, had become a liability to their cause rather than its legitimate leader. Thus they negotiated the best deal they could with Morales at the time of the coup, and abandoned their personal allegiance to Velasco. After the coup, Velasco was reported to feel especially bitter toward Rodríguez, who he felt had betrayed him at the crucial moment. The analysis in the next paragraphs was enriched by conversations with Alfred Stepan during Cleaves's 1976 visiting fellowship at Yale University.

to a lesser degree. Within each of the armed forces, factions had emerged that were in disagreement over the political and moral value of the Velasco experiments. Tantaleán and his cohorts in La Misión felt that the revolution should continue under an aggressive form of corporatism. The army institutionalists felt that embroilment in politics was undermining the armed forces' traditional coherence and strength. The progressive wing of the core coalition was sympathetic to the needs of the lower classes, but it refused to break its links with the army and ally itself irrevocably with their interests. Finally, the rivalry between the navy and army had heightened as a result of the firing, as head of the navy, of Luis Vargas Caballero and the submissiveness of one of his successors to humiliating army directives. When Morales Bermúdez assumed power, the unity of the armed forces had given way to bickering and even overt struggle. Instead of using a symbol of unity to proceed with confidence, Morales had to tone down these disputes and re-build a spirit of cooperation among institutions that, in the last analysis, were responsible for the physical protection of the national territory.[16]

Third, in October 1968 the traditional political groups were in disarray. The term "oligarchy" had been incorporated into the country's political vocabulary with very unsavory connota-tions. Although it was always difficult to identify precisely the members of the oligarchy, the pervasive revulsion against the term permitted Velasco to move against many of the country's political, economic, and social elites with little resistance sim-ply by referring to them as the "oligarchy." APRA's antioligar-chic stance had been discredited by its coalition with the UNO during the Belaúnde years, resulting in a loss of prestige that Velasco exploited when countering APRA influence in the sugar cooperatives, the teachers' union, the Lima Bar Associa-tion, and other unions and professional groups under APRA leadership. Simultaneously, although deeply anticommunist himself, Velasco formed a tactical alliance with the Communist

16. Thus Morales Bermúdez moved quickly to reassure other branches of the armed forces of their fundamental importance to the nation. See Alfonso Baella, *El poder invisible* (Lima: Editorial Andina, 1976), p. 393.

Party, as had many populist Latin American presidents before him.

Morales Bermúdez had fewer possibilities of conjuring up animosity toward the "oligarchy," which theoretically Velasco had swept away. Moreover, those interest groups that had suffered under the pressures of Velasco's policies and police had developed a garrison mentality. Their leadership, under perpetual threat of arrest or deportation and battle-hardened in extreme opposition to the regime, was mostly of rightist persuasion. It was this array of militant interest groups and opposition party leaders that Morales Bermúdez faced when he assumed office. They moved to the offensive with a vengeance, challenging the military to return almost immediately to electoral democracy. This thrust did not bear fruit, however. They then turned their attention to securing the dismissal of all remaining Velasco men in the upper ranks of government and a reevaluation of his reforms. Finally, they joined forces with conservative military men to break the coalition with the Communist Party, which passed into the opposition.

This shift to the Right was precipitated by the forth factor, a change in the country's economic situation. Although funds from international lending agencies dried up soon after Velasco's ascent to power, his government was able to transform the country's rich fish, mineral, and—apparently—oil resources into a steady stream of investment and credits by private sources in Europe and the United States. This economic flexibility permitted his policy makers to increase food imports, build up the country's economic infrastructure, and moderate their concern about a low rate of internal savings. By 1975, however, the economic situation was dismal. Commodity prices were depressed, anchoveta production was in hiatus because of ecological factors and overfishing, the hopes for a large oil income were damped by a depressing string of dry wells, and high interest and principle payments were decimating the foreign currency reserves. To add to the debacle, the large public-sector enterprises were running severe deficits. Morales Bermúdez inherited a nearly bankrupt economy, which reduced his political and economic options enormously. His approach was to spur local savings and investment, and to drop

Velasco's anti-imperialistic rhetoric in order to qualify for foreign loans. The economic situation thus favored conventional restrictive financial policies and helped to explain Morales Bermúdez's suppression of the same workers' movement that Velasco had tried to coddle.

Fifth, in 1968 Peru's geopolitical situation was conducive to more radical policies with less risk than in 1975. Velasco was a *cause célèbre* when he nationalized the IPC in October 1968. Within two years, however, international attention was focused elsewhere. In Chile, Allende was confirmed as the first Marxist president in South America. In Bolivia, General José Torres assumed power supported by leftist military, miners, peasants, and students, and pursued an anti-imperialist foreign policy. In Argentina, Juan Perón returned from a long exile abroad in the midst of widespread uncertainty about his government's intentions. In Ecuador, Guillermo Rodríguez Lara deposed José María Velasco Ibarra and promised social reforms *a la peruana*. This series of events bolstered Peru's feelings of military security vis-à-vis its traditional rivals, Chile and Ecuador, which appeared to have like-minded governments, and for three years Velasco was not distracted by issues of national defense. It was Brazil, even with the solicitous attention of the United States, that was odd man out. The more radical political posture of the region also lessened Peru's visibility. If the United States was worried about leftist governments in Latin America, Chile was a more significant threat to be dealt with than Peru.

Within a short time, however, these conditions turned around almost completely. Torres was deposed by a right-wing uprising headed by Hugo Banzer.[17] Perón died. Allende fell in a bloody coup. The Ecuadorian government turned out to be less radical than first suspected. Peru's visibility increased markedly, and suddenly it was surrounded by regimes unsympathetic with its leaders' social philosophy. Tension over the granting of Bolivia's corridor to the sea heightened its sense of vulnerability.[18] Peru would have been severely disadvantaged

17. And later murdered by unidentified assailants in Buenos Aires in 1976.
18. Before the War of the Pacific (1879–81) Bolivia possessed the port of Antofagasta and Peru the region of Arica. After its victory, Chile retained Antofagasta and Arica, thus converting Bolivia into a landlocked country granted

in any conflict with its three neighbors. When Morales Bermúdez assumed power, his options for manipulation of international affairs to Peru's net benefit were circumscribed. Indeed, even before his coup, he met with Chilean and Bolivian commanders in an effort to relieve tensions and, through conciliatory gestures, moved toward extricating Peru from a potentially disastrous situation in the first year of his administration.[19]

Sixth, Velasco entered power with a mandate to advance on a number of fronts. The country's intellectual and military leadership were almost unanimously in favor of the nationalization of the IPC, the agrarian reform, and the increased role of the state in planning the economy. As the government's intentions took shape, it seemed to many as if Peru were emerging from the dark ages of public policy. This inclination toward change, euphoric in some quarters, gave Velasco the momentum to move beyond the original plan in the realms of industrial organization, expropriations, foreign policy, press reform, property relations, and mass mobilization. These latter policies came to be known as the Peruvian "experiment." They kept the political atmosphere in Peru in a state of perpetual excitement, and Velasco took pleasure in keeping uncertainty at high levels during much of his presidency.

By the time of the Morales Bermúdez coup, the country was suffering from psychological weariness. The deep desire of many sectors for a moratorium on new initiatives played into the hands of those who wished to suppress disruptive groups. The fact that almost everything conceivable had been tried

liberal access to the Antofagasta port facilities. Border tensions occurred periodically because the Bolivians pressured through diplomatic channels for a corridor to the Pacific Ocean, and the Peruvian army never fully accepted that Arica was no longer Peruvian territory. In 1974 Chile and Bolivia began negotiations to provide Bolivia with a corridor, but the discussions caused alarm in Lima because the area ceded would pass through Peru's former territory, which was forbidden by treaty unless the settlement was ratified by Peru. Aside from institutional and national pride, the Peruvians were worried that a Bolivian outlet would be used as the Pacific port for the Brazilian fleet, given the close ties between Brazil and Bolivia at the time.

19. Both the Peruvians and Chileans continued to equip their armed forces, however, to prepare for any eventuality resulting from the corridor issue.

under Velasco dampened the imagination of Morales Bermúdez's advisers, who satisfied themselves with sifting
through Velasco's hope chest of reforms in search of those that
would mesh well with new priorities. Adherents of some of
Velasco's more comprehensive programs—such as social
property—were forced into hasty retreat to await more propitious times.

These six conditions, which changed drastically from 1968
to 1980, set parameters for both Velasco and Morales Bermúdez. By most standards, however, the behavior of Morales
Bermúdez's government was more "predictable" than that of
Velasco's. Morales Bermúdez responded to the power of the
country's economic elites, the continuing lack of effective organization of the lower classes, international financial concerns, and geopolitical realities in steering the course he did.
The policies pursued displayed a low level of state autonomy,
and, although variously described as pragmatic, intelligent and
realistic, in no way could his government be termed exceptional in a theoretical sense.

Velasco, too, seemed to fall within standard constrictures
during the first months of his regime. He assumed power during a period of disarray of the bourgeoisie, comparable perhaps
to the period of Bonapartism in nineteenth-century France.[20]
His first public acts, such as nationalization and agrarian reform, appeared to be in the long-term interests of industrialists
and middle-sized farmers, just as Gutelman suggests. Later,
however, his policies shifted to the detriment of private-sector
elites. No objective factors compelled the Velasco regime to
move in the direction it did. Unlike the Cuban revolution, it
was not forced to take one path because another was blocked. A
token payment for the IPC could have soothed relations with the
international financial community, which otherwise felt no ill
will toward Peru.[21] Workers and peasants were not so

20. See Karl Marx, *The Eighteenth Brumaire of Louis Bonaparte* (New York:
International Publishers, 1963).
21. The Greene Agreement of February 1974 resolved the outstanding claims
of U.S. companies against Peru, including the IPC. The terms provided that
Peru would pay $76 million into a trust fund to be dispensed by the U.S.
government as compensation to expropriated U.S. firms, and another $74 mil-

mobilized as to oblige a leftist course. Middle- and upper-middle-class elements did not, at the beginning, withhold their support or declare their open hostility to Velasco. It could be argued that, had the 1968 government taken the path of least resistance, it would have followed the Brazilian model. The reason it did not was that the outlook of the core coalition, nurtured during years spent in military intelligence, was at odds with the creation of a military–industrialist–foreign capitalist alliance. A structural interpretation of social ills, compassion for lower-class groups, mistrust of the patriotism (or lack of it) of national entrepreneurs, and desire for international respect molded the tone and content of the 1968–75 Peruvian polity.

The Velasco group was conscious of the precariousness of the revolution, and banked on three factors to minimize the risks of failure. Each of these precautions failed, the first because of uncontrollable adversity, the other two because of faulty logic.

To assure the continuity of national leadership in the hands of those committed to the revolution, the Velasco group institutionalized the norm that the highest ranking army officer would occupy the prime minister's post. The prime minister was next in line to the presidency, but had to retire thirty-five years after graduating from the Chorrillos Military School.[22] In accordance with this norm (which did not apply to Velasco himself), Generals Ernesto Montagne and Edgardo Mercado Jarrín (neither of whom was in the core coalition) reached the prime ministership, and subsequently retired. Morales Bermúdez, as the top-ranking member of his graduating class, succeeded to the prime ministry on February 1, 1975, and was due to retire on December 31, 1977. After his retirement, the next officers in line would have been Leonidas Rodríguez, Enrique Gallegos, and Rafael Hoyos, all members of the core coalition. Political considerations in the promotion of junior officers

---

lion directly to Cerro Corporation, W. R. Grace and Company, Star-Kist Foods, Inc., and Cargill, Inc.

22. The military regime has not published the decrees establishing promotion and succession procedures, but Baella (*El poder invisible*, pp. 103, 110, 304) refers to them.

complemented this strategy as insurance for future years. Its success depended on Velasco's maintaining his health and governing capacity at least until Morales Bermúdez could be discarded late in 1977. Unfortunately for the overall plan, Velasco's aneurism in 1974 marked the beginning of his physical decline, which impaired his judgment and gradually loosened his grip on political reality.[23] The governing group could not have foreseen that Velasco's health would be the Achilles' heel of the revolution.

On the basis of 1970 trends, the military and civilian planners projected that exports of fish meal, minerals, and sugar would reap $6.8 billion from 1971 to 1975, and that imports would be $7.5 billion or less during the same period.[24] By increasing its foreign debt by $564 million, the government could maintain its balance of payments at a reasonable level while creating the necessary infrastructure in the extractive industries to finance, in the late 1970s and beyond, other aspects of the polity, including educational reform, social property, and the gearing up of the agrarian cooperatives to full production. The disappearance of anchovetas and the economic recession in the rich countries, which depressed commodity prices, dealt a heavy blow to these plans. The investments in economic infrastructure proved to be more expensive than imagined. Moreover, many of the regime's policies distorted the country's economy. Incentives for industrialization permitted large imports of capital machinery, which did little to alleviate unemployment or redistribute income. Freezing the sol–dollar exchange rate despite inflation reduced exports, made imported food artificially inexpensive, and undermined the profit-making ability of agrarian cooperatives. These miscalculations, which Morales Bermúdez failed to correct while he was finance minister, meant that Peru's export earnings over the period

23. After the coup, thinking in retrospect about the last months of his rule, Velasco denied he had lost touch with reality. His wife, Consuelo González de Velasco, daughter of an APRA party leader in Arequipa, asserted that he had, and that she had told him so in so many words at the time. Approximately seventeen months after the coup, Velasco began writing his memoirs, but died on December 24, 1977, before completing them.

24. Presidencia de la República, *Plan nacional, 1971–1975*, vol. 1: *Plan Global* (Lima: Instituto Nacional de Planificación, 1971), pp. 21–22.

were only $5.8 billion, and the country had to increase its external debt by $2.1 billion.[25]

The government's policies in agriculture, education, industrial communities, and property were comprehensive attempts to increase the economic and social position of the Peruvian lower classes. Although the regime's methods were occasionally heavy-handed, especially when it tried to displace APRA influence in the sugar cooperatives and to outflank the Communist Party in the labor sector, they were not necessarily cynical attempts to pander to and demobilize the masses. If so, Velasco could not have maintained his bewilderment at his reforms' incapacity to generate widespread support for his administration. This absent support was one element of the "survival" plan that was poorly conceived. These revolutionary reforms were the brainstorms of the government's political advisers, and did not percolate up from the lower classes themselves. While the formers' objectives may have been charitable, they completely misread what would and not animate the Peruvian masses. Our discussions of member support for cooperatives uncovered some of these incongruencies. The haughtiness and paternalism of some officials compounded the problem, because SINAMOS and presidential rhetoric had increased these classes' awareness of their self-worth.

The issue here was hardly simple, because the military establishment would not tolerate any attempt to radicalize the masses. Without such radicalization, these nonhegemonic elements could not struggle for the desired reforms, protect their gains, and associate the continuation of the revolution with their aspirations for the future. An increase in popular support would also have provided the regime with a cushion of legitimacy and the opportunity to seek greater consistency in its governing philosophy, the functions of national institutions, and bureaucratic behavior. Velasco was unwilling to break his bonds with the military establishment in order to represent the popular sectors. Thus he was not able to count on the backing of workers and peasants during his administration, but he did provide the impetus for political organization in urban and

25. *Andean Report*, no. 4 (October 1975), p. 1.

rural areas which seemed to exist independent of government tutelage. Had he remained in power longer, it is possible that the contradictions of the situation, prompted by such organizations as the Communist Party and Vanguardia Revolucionaria, would have reached sufficient proportions to have assisted a furtherance (*profundización*) of the revolution by Rodríguez or a like-minded presidential successor.

Economic stability, a healthy president, and gradually increasing popular support were the pinions of the revolution. A slightly different outcome in these factors would have helped to prolong the Peruvian experiment. The Velasco government, however, did not conceive of a development model that was sufficiently congruent with social and economic patterns in Peru to guarantee institutional succession and continuity. At the nadir of the Peruvian revolution, these failures were manifest in economic depression, an unstable agrarian sector, a divided military, and a bureaucracy devoid of performance standards appropriate to the country's social complexity. Velasco attempted to suppress the oligarchy and neutralize the middle classes in order to integrate the popular sectors into national life. The social consequence of the revolution, however, was to raise the relative status of the middle class, including professionals, bureaucrats, independent farmers, and the military itself. Peru will need to await another turn of the wheel for a leader to emerge who will renew the mission that Velasco left pending.

*Appendix*

# Notes on the Interviews

The data for this book came from government documents, legal codes, newspapers, speeches, official statistics, memoirs, secondary sources, and interviews. We conducted interviews with major and minor figures inside and outside of government who had direct knowledge of the subjects under study.

A list of potential interviewees was prepared for each chapter. We made contact with them usually be telephone, briefly described the research project, and identified our institutional affiliations. Some background research on the interviewee preceded each conversation, though this step became less necessary as the project matured. Informal, open-ended questions were prepared for each interviewee. Initial discussion of each subject elicited general information on the course of events and helped to alert us to important data that required further investigation. Later, the respondent was encouraged to discuss specific actions, events, or processes of which he or she had direct knowledge. Typical questions were: "Who did what, when, and how? Why do you think they did it that way? Why did you do what you did? How did you assume they would react? Why? Other people have told me such-and-such. How accurate a statement is that?"

We promised all of the interviewees that their conversations would be confidential and that information provided would not be attributed to them. We took extensive notes during the meetings and did not rely on mechanical recording devices. Immediately after the interview, the text was typed as faithfully as possible. All comments were included, no matter how irrelevant they may have seemed at the time. Fifteen minutes of interview resulted in approximately one single-spaced typewritten page of notes. The date, length of the interview, and respondent's affiliation were placed on the first page of the interview, but not his or her name, which remained confidential. A copy of the interview was then sent to the respondent by certified mail with a letter of thanks.

The first interview for this work took place in July 1970 in the context of another research project.[1] The last was recorded in March 1977. Information from these necessarily anonymous interviews sheds light on Peruvian politics during this period beyond the narrative contained in this book, and may be made available to professional historians and bona fide scholars of the country. The full schedule of interviews is listed below, with an indication of whether they were conducted and written up by Cleaves (PSC) or by Scurrah (MJS).

| Number | Date | Length of interview (minutes) | Interviewer | Affiliation or occupation of interviewee |
|--------|------|-------------------------------|-------------|-------------------------------------------|
| 1 | July 1970 | 30 | PSC | Newspaper editor |
| 2 | July 1970 | 120 | PSC | Budget officials |
| 3 | July 1970 | 75 | PSC | Planning official |
| 4 | July 1970 | 60 | PSC | Ministerial budget official |
| 5 | July 1970 | 60 | PSC | Government financial executive |
| 6 | April 1973 | 45 | MJS | EPSA official |
| 7 | April 1973 | 45 | MJS | EPSA official |
| 8 | May 1973 | 30 | PSC | Law researcher |
| 9 | May 1973 | 30 | PSC | Legal consultant to government |
| 10 | June 1973 | 30 | PSC | Agrarian Tribunal justice |

1. See Naomi J. Caiden and Aaron B. Wildavsky, *Planning and Budgeting in Poor Countries* (New York: John Wiley, 1973).

| Number | Date | Length of interview (minutes) | Interviewer | Affiliation or occupation of interviewee |
|--------|------|-------------------------------|-------------|------------------------------------------|
| 11 | June 1973 | 50 | PSC | Agriculture Ministry lawyer |
| 12 | June 1973 | 75 | PSC | Agrarian Tribunal administrator |
| 13 | June 1973 | 75 | PSC | Agrarian Tribunal administrator |
| 14 | June 1973 | 105 | PSC | Agrarian Tribunal justice |
| 15 | July 1973 | 60 | MJS | EPSA administrator |
| 16 | July 1973 | 90 | MJS | EPSA administrator |
| 17 | July 1973 | 60 | MJS | EPSA administrator |
| 18 | July 1973 | 30 | MJS | EPSA administrator |
| 19 | July 1973 | 55 | MJS | EPSA administrator |
| 20 | July 1973 | 45 | MJS | EPSA administrator |
| 21 | August 1973 | 30 | MJS | EPSA administrator |
| 22 | August 1973 | 20 | MJS | EPSA administrator |
| 23 | August 1973 | 90 | MJS | EPSA administrator |
| 24 | August 1973 | 30 | MJS | EPSA administrator |
| 25 | August 1973 | 120 | MJS | EPSA official |
| 26 | August 1973 | 150 | MJS | EPSA official |
| 27 | September 1973 | 55 | MJS | EPSA official |
| 28 | September 1973 | 60 | MJS | EPSA administrator |
| 29 | September 1973 | 45 | MJS | EPSA administrator |
| 30 | September 1973 | 75 | MJS | EPSA administrator |
| 31 | October 1973 | 60 | MJS | EPSA administrator |
| 32 | October 1973 | 40 | MJS | EPSA administrator |
| 33 | November 1973 | 75 | PSC | Former land judge |
| 34 | November 1973 | 75 | PSC | Agrarian Tribunal justice |
| 35 | November 1973 | 105 | PSC | Former land judge |
| 36 | November 1973 | 75 | PSC | Agrarian Tribunal justice |
| 37 | November 1973 | 75 | PSC | Land judge |
| 38 | November 1973 | 75 | PSC | Adviser, Ministry of Agriculture |
| 39 | November 1973 | 75 | PSC | Agrarian Tribunal justice |
| 40 | November 1973 | 45 | MJS | EPSA official |
| 41 | March 1974 | 90 | PSC | COFIDE officials |
| 42 | March 1974 | 60 | PSC | INP administrator |
| 43 | April 1974 | 60 | PSC | INAP administrator |
| 44 | April 1974 | 90 | PSC | Ministry of Energy and Mines administrator |
| 45 | April 1974 | 75 | PSC | Ministry of Housing administrator |
| 46 | April 1974 | 40 | PSC | INAP official |

(continued)

| Number | Date | Length of interview (minutes) | Interviewer | Affiliation or occupation of interviewee |
|--------|------|-------------------------------|-------------|------------------------------------------|
| 47 | April 1974 | 50 | PSC | Military general, Ministry of War |
| 48 | April 1974 | 90 | PSC | Planning executive, Production Ministry |
| 49 | April 1974 | 60 | PSC | Agriculture Ministry official |
| 50 | June 1974 | 60 | MJS | EPSA upper-middle-level manager |
| 51 | October 1974 | 60 | MJS | Ministry of Commerce economist |
| 52 | October 1974 | 80 | MJS | Agriculture official |
| 53 | November 1974 | 60 | MJS | INP high official |
| 54 | November 1974 | 45 | MJS | Regional Agriculture official |
| 55 | November 1974 | 90 | MJS | Agriculture project engineer |
| 56 | November 1974 | 45 | MJS | Irrigation official |
| 57 | November 1974 | 90 | MJS | Irrigation official |
| 58 | November 1974 | 60 | MJS | Chira-Piura project official |
| 59 | November 1974 | | | Agriculture marketing official |
| 60 | November 1974 | 60 | MJS | Former hacendado, Piura |
| 61 | November 1974 | 45 | MJS | Regional agronomy official |
| 62 | November 1974 | 45 | MJS | Regional Agriculture official |
| 63 | November 1974 | 60 | MJS | Regional project manager |
| 64 | November 1974 | 30 | MJS | Former hacendado, Piura |
| 65 | November 1974 | 30 | MJS | Former hacendado, Piura |
| 66 | November 1974 | 15 | MJS | High official, Piura Department |
| 67 | November 1974 | 30 | MJS | Peasant leader, Piura Department |
| 68 | November 1974 | 120 | MJS | Former Piura interest-group leader |
| 69 | April 1975 | 60 | PSC | Agrarian Reform official |
| 70 | April 1975 | 70 | PSC | Agrarian Reform official |
| 71 | April 1975 | 60 | PSC | Agrarian Reform official |

(continued)

| Number | Date | Length of interview (minutes) | Interviewer | Affiliation or occupation of interviewee |
|--------|------|------|------|------|
| 72 | April 1975 | 110 | PSC | Agrarian Reform official |
| 73 | April 1975 | 60 | PSC | Agriculture official |
| 74 | April 1975 | 170 | PSC | Agrarian Reform official |
| 75 | April 1975 | 45 | PSC | Military general |
| 76 | May 1975 | 35 | PSC | Military general |
| 77 | May 1975 | 70 | PSC | Agriculture official |
| 78 | May 1975 | 90 | PSC | Agriculture official |
| 79 | May 1975 | 40 | PSC | Agrarian Reform official |
| 80 | May 1975 | 30 | PSC | Agrarian Reform administrator |
| 81 | June 1975 | 30 | PSC | Agrarian Reform official |
| 82 | June 1975 | 60 | PSC | Housing Ministry official |
| 83 | June 1975 | 60 | PSC | Agrarian Reform official |
| 84 | June 1975 | 120 | PSC | Agriculture official |
| 85 | June 1975 | 135 | PSC | Agriculture official |
| 86 | July 1975 | 70 | PSC | Leader of small and middle-sized farmers |
| 87 | August 1975 | 45 | PSC | Regional Agrarian Reform official |
| 88 | August 1975 | 40 | PSC | Officials of Piura Agrarian Federation |
| 89 | October 1975 | 60 | MJS | CNA high official |
| 90 | October 1975 | 90 | MJS | CNA technical adviser |
| 91 | November 1975 | 90 | MJS | CNA technical adviser |
| 92 | November 1975 | 30 | MJS | Head, agricultural interest group |
| 93 | November 1975 | 105 | MJS | CNA high official |
| 94 | November 1975 | 120 | MJS | CNA high official |
| 95 | January 1976 | 45 | PSC | Education Ministry official |
| 96 | February 1976 | 45 | PSC | Education Ministry official |
| 97 | January 1976 | 30 | PSC | Education Ministry official |
| 98 | February 1976 | 30 | PSC | Education Ministry official |
| 99 | May 1976 | 60 | PSC | Agrarian Bank manager |

(continued)

| Number | Date | Length of interview (minutes) | Interviewer | Affiliation or occupation of interviewee |
|--------|------|------|------|------|
| 100 | February 1976 | 45 | PSC | Anthropology researcher |
| 101 | May 1976 | 120 | PSC | Campesino Support Agency official |
| 102 | May 1976 | 60 | PSC | Campesino Support Agency official |
| 103 | May 1976 | 75 | PSC | Food Ministry administrator |
| 104 | May 1976 | 30 | PSC | Food Ministry administrator |
| 105 | May 1976 | 75 | PSC | SINAMOS official |
| 106 | June 1976 | 90 | PSC | SINAMOS official |
| 107 | June 1976 | 45 | PSC | Anthropology researcher |
| 108 | June 1976 | 20 | PSC | Peasant leader |
| 109 | June 1976 | 75 | PSC | Campesino Support Agency provincial administrator |
| 110 | June 1976 | 45 | PSC | Campesino Support Agency provincial official |
| 111 | June 1976 | 90 | PSC | Agrarian Bank provincial official |
| 112 | June 1976 | 60 | PSC | Anthropology researchers |
| 113 | June 1976 | 40 | PSC | Director, Regional CNA Federation |
| 114 | June 1976 | 20 | PSC | Land judge, Agrarian Court System |
| 115 | June 1976 | 60 | PSC | Cooperative manager |
| 116 | June 1976 | 40 | PSC | Peasant leader on cooperative |
| 117 | June 1976 | 60 | PSC | SINAMOS provincial official |
| 118 | June 1976 | 60 | PSC | Food Ministry provincial official |
| 119 | June 1976 | 61 | PSC | Sociology researcher |
| 120 | July 1976 | 60 | PSC | Agrarian court administrator |
| 121 | September 1976 | 60 | PSC | Military officer, adviser to prime minister's office |
| 122 | September 1976 | 60 | MJS | CNA peasant leader |
| 123 | September 1976 | 120 | MJS | CNA peasant leader |
| 124 | September 1976 | 60 | MJS | Agriculture Ministry official |
| 125 | October 1976 | 75 | MJS | EPSA finance official |

(*continued*)

| Number | Date | Length of interview (minutes) | Interviewer | Affiliation or occupation of interviewee |
|--------|------|-------------------------------|-------------|------------------------------------------|
| 126 | October 1976 | 75 | MJS | EPSA manager |
| 127 | October 1976 | 90 | MJS | EPSA official |
| 128 | October 1976 | 30 | MJS | Agrarian Bank official |
| 129 | October 1976 | 45 | MJS | Agrarian Bank manager |
| 130 | October 1976 | 20 | MJS | EPSA assistant manager |
| 131 | October 1976 | 30 | MJS | EPSA manager |
| 132 | March 1977 | 90 | MJS | Former SINAMOS official |
| 133 | March 1977 | 60 | MJS | Former Education Ministry official |
| 134 | March 1977 | 60 | MJS | Former Education Ministry official |

# Bibliography

Books, Monographs, and Theses

ADAMS, ROBERT McC. *The Evolution of Urban Society: Early Mesopotamia and Prehispanic Mexico.* Chicago: Aldine, 1966.

ALBERTI, GIORGIO, and ENRIQUE MAYER, eds. *Reciprocidad e intercambio en los Andes peruanos.* Lima: Instituto de Estudios Peruanos, 1974.

———— and RODRIGO SÁNCHEZ. *Poder y conflicto social en el valle del Mantaro.* Lima: Instituto de Estudios Peruanos, 1974.

ALEGRÍA CAMPOS, MARIO. *Poder judicial: Reforma urgente.* Lima: Chiabra, 1972.

ALEXANDER, ROBERT J., ed. *Aprismo: The Ideas and Doctrines of Victor Raúl Haya de la Torre.* Kent, O.: Kent State University Press, 1973.

APTER, DAVID E. *The Mythic Factor in Developmental Ideologies.* Forthcoming.

ARGYRIS, CHRIS. *Integrating the Individual and the Organization.* New York: Wiley, 1964.

ARORA, RAMESH K. *Comparative Public Administration.* New Delhi: Associated Publishing House, 1972.

ARTOLA AZCÁRATE, ARMANDO. *Subversión.* Lima: Editorial Jurídica, 1976.

ASTIZ, CARLOS A. *Pressure Groups and Power Elites in Peruvian Politics.* Ithaca: Cornell University Press, 1969.

AVENDAÑO V., JORGE. *Seminario de propiedad social: Materiales para el trabajo de clase.* Lima: Pontificia Universidad Católica, 1976.

————. *La propiedad en el Perú*. Forthcoming.

BAELLA TUESTA, ALFONSO. *El poder invisible*. Lima: Editorial Andina, 1976.

BARNARD, CHESTER I. *The Functions of the Executive*. Cambridge: Harvard University Press, 1938.

BASADRE, JORGE. *Historia de la República del Perú*. 6th ed. 11 vols. Lima: Editorial Universitario, 1968–70.

BAUDIN, LOUIS. *L'empire socialiste des Inka*. Paris: Université de Paris, 1928.

BAYER, DAVID L. *Descapitalización del minifundio y formación de la burguesía rural*. Lima: Universidad Nacional Agraria, 1975.

BÉJAR, HÉCTOR. *Peru 1965: Notes on a Guerrilla Experience*. Trans. William Rose. New York: Monthly Review Press, 1970.

BENNIS, WARREN G., ed. *Interpersonal Dynamics: Essays and Readings on Human Interaction*. Homewood, Ill.: Dorsey Press, 1964.

BLANCO, HUGO. *Land or Death: The Peasant Struggle in Peru*. Trans. Naomi Allen. New York: Pathfinder Press, 1972.

BLAU, PETER. *Exchange and Power in Social Life*. New York: John Wiley, 1967.

BOLTON, RALPH, and ENRIQUE MAYER, eds. *Andean Kinship and Marriage*. Washington, D.C.: American Anthropological Association, 1977.

BONILLA, HERACLIO, and KAREN SPALDING, eds. *La independencia en el Perú*. Lima: Instituto de Estudios Peruanos, 1972.

BOURRICAUD, FRANÇOIS. *Poder y sociedad en el Perú contemporáneo*. Buenos Aires: Editorial Sur, 1967.

————. *Power and Society in Contemporary Peru*. Trans. Paul Stevenson. London: Faber & Faber, 1970.

BOWSER, FREDERICK P. *The African Slave in Colonial Peru, 1524–1650*. Stanford: Stanford University Press, 1974.

BRAIBANTI, RALPH, ed. *Political and Administrative Development*. Durham, N.C.: Duke University Press, 1969.

BRASS, PAUL R. *Factional Politics in an Indian State: The Congress Party in Uttar Pradesh*. Berkeley: University of California Press, 1965.

BUCHANAN, JAMES M., and GORDON TULLOCK. *The Calculus of Consent: Logical Foundations of Constitutional Democracy*. Ann Arbor: University of Michigan Press, 1969.

BURGA, MANUEL. *De la encomienda a la hacienda capitalista: El Valle del Jequetepeque del siglo XVI al XX*. Lima: Instituto de Estudios Peruanos, 1976.

BUSTAMENTE, ALBERTO. *Legislación sobre reforma agraria y cooperativas agrarias*. Lima: DESCO, 1974.

————. "Las alternativas en la ideología jurídica prevaleciente." Thesis, Pontificia Universidad Católica del Perú, 1975.

CAIDEN, NAOMI J., and AARON B. WILDAVSKY. *Planning and Budgeting in Poor Countries.* New York: John Wiley, 1973.

CARAVEDO MOLINARI, BALTAZAR. *Burguesía e industria en el Perú, 1933–1945.* Lima: Instituto de Estudios Peruanos, 1976.

CARDOSO, FERNANDO HENRIQUE. *Autoritarismo e democratização.* Rio de Janeiro: Paz e Terra, 1975.

CELESTINO, OLINDA. *Migración y cambio estructural: La comunidad de Lampían.* Lima: Instituto de Estudios Peruanos, 1972.

CHALMERS, DOUGLAS A., ed. *Changing Latin America: New Interpretations of Its Politics and Society.* New York: Academy of Political Science, Columbia University, 1972.

CHANDLER, TERTIUS, and GERALD FOX. *Three Thousand Years of Urban Growth.* New York: Academic Press, 1974.

CHANG-RODRÍGUEZ, EUGENIO. *La literatura política de González Prada, Mariátegui, y Haya de la Torre.* Mexico City: Andrea, 1957.

CHAPLIN, DAVID, ed. *Peruvian Nationalism: A Corporatist Revolution.* New Brunswick, N.J.: Transaction Books, 1976.

———— and HUGO VEGA. *A Glossary of Peruvian Land Tenure and Rural Labor Organization Terminology.* Madison, Wis.: Land Tenure Center, 1972.

CLEAVES, PETER S. *Bureaucratic Politics and Administration in Chile.* Berkeley: University of California Press, 1974.

COLE, JOHN P. *Geografía urbana del Perú.* Publication no. 10. Lima: Instituto de Etnología y Arqueología, 1955.

COLLIER, DAVID. *Squatters and Oligarchs: Authoritarian Rule and Policy Change in Peru.* Baltimore: Johns Hopkins University Press, 1976.

CORNEJO K., ROBERTO. *El presupuesto gubernamental por programas.* Lima: Editorial Universitaria, 1970.

CORNELIUS, WAYNE A., and ROBERT VAN KEMPER, eds. *Metropolitan Problems and Governmental Response in Latin America.* Latin American Urban Research, vol. 6. Beverly Hills, Calif.: Sage, 1977.

COTLER, JULIO. *Clases, estado y nación en el Perú.* Lima: Instituto de Estudios Peruanos, 1978.

COUTU, ARTHUR J., and RICHARD A. KING. *The Agricultural Development of Peru.* New York: Praeger, 1969.

CROZIER, MICHEL. *The Bureaucratic Phenomenon.* Chicago: University of Chicago Press, 1964.

DAVIES, THOMAS M., JR. *Indian Integration in Peru: A Half Century of Experience, 1900–1948.* Lincoln: University of Nebraska Press, 1974.

DAVIS, STANLEY M., and LOUIS WOLF GOODMAN, eds. *Workers and Managers in Latin America.* Lexington, Mass.: D. C. Heath, 1973.

DEGREGORI, CARLOS, and JÜRGEN GOLTE. *Dependencia y desintegración estructural en la comunidad de Pacaraos.* Lima: Instituto de Estudios Peruanos, 1973.

DE LA PUENTE UCEDA, LUIS F. La Reforma del Agro Peruano. Lima: Ensayos Sociales, 1966.

DELGADO, CARLOS. Problemas sociales en el Perú contemporáneo. Lima: Instituto de Estudios Peruanos, 1971.

———. Revolución peruana: Autonomía y deslindes. Lima: Libros de Contratiempo, 1975.

DEPROSPO, ERNST R., JR. "The Administration of the Peruvian Land Reform." Ph.D. dissertation, Pennsylvania State University, 1967.

DEW, EDWARD. Politics in the Altiplano: The Dynamics of Change in Rural Peru. Austin: University of Texas Press, 1969.

DOBYNS, HENRY E., and PAUL L. DOUGHTY. Peru: A Cultural History. New York: Oxford University Press, 1976.

DOMÍNGUEZ, JORGE. Cuba: Order and Revolution. Cambridge: Harvard University Press, 1979.

DORE, RONALD P. Land Reform in Japan. London: Oxford University Press, 1959.

DOS SANTOS, THEOTONIO, et al. La crisis del desarrollismo y la nueva dependencia. Lima: Instituto de Estudios Peruanos, 1969.

DOWNING, THEODORE E., and McGUIRE GIBSON, eds. Irrigation's Impact on Society. Tucson: University of Arizona Press, 1974.

DUMONT, RENÉ. Cuba ¿Es socialista? Caracas: Tiempo Nuevo, 1970.

DUNCAN, KENNETH, and IAN RUTLEDGE. Land and Labor in Latin America: Essays in the Development of Agrarian Capitalism in the Nineteenth and Twentieth Centuries. London: Cambridge University Press, 1978.

EATON, JOSEPH, ed. Institution Building and Development: From Concepts to Application. Beverly Hills, Calif.: Sage, 1972.

EBERHARD, WOLFRAM. Conquerors and Rulers: Social Forces in Medieval China. 2d ed. Leiden: E. J. Brill, 1965.

EGUREN LÓPEZ, FERNANDO. Reforma agraria, cooperativazación, y lucha campesina: El valle Chancay-Huaral. Lima: DESCO, 1975.

ESCOBAR, GABRIEL. Sicaya: Cambios culturales en una comunidad mestiza andina. Lima: Instituto de Estudios Peruanos, 1973.

ESCULIES LARRABURE, OSCAR, et al. Comercialización de alimentos: Quienes ganan, quienes pagan, quienes pierden. Lima: DESCO, 1977.

FAVRE, HENRI, CLAUDE COLLIN-DÉLAVAUD, and JOSÉ MATOS MAR. La hacienda en el Perú. Lima: Instituto de Estudios Peruanos, 1964.

FAYOL, HENRI. General Industrial Management. London: Isaac Pitman, 1949.

FIORAVANTI, EDUARDO. Latifundio y sindicalismo agrario en el Perú: El caso de los valles de La Convención y Lares, 1958–1964. 2d ed. Lima: Instituto de Estudios Peruanos, 1976.

FITCHETT, DELBERT A. "Defects in the Agrarian Structure as Obstacles to Economic Development: A Study of the Northern Coast of Perú." Ph.D. dissertation, University of California, Berkeley, 1963.

FITZGERALD, E. V. K. The State and Economic Development: Peru since 1968. Cambridge: Cambridge University Press, 1976.

FORD, THOMAS R. *Man and Land in Peru.* Gainesville: University of Florida Press, 1959.

FOX, ROBERT W. *Urban Growth in Peru.* Washington: Inter-American Development Bank, 1972.

FRENCH, WENDALL. *The Personnel Management Process: Human Resources Administration.* 2d ed. Boston: Houghton Mifflin, 1970.

FUENZALIDA, FERNANDO, et al. *Estructuras tradicionales y economía del mercado: La comunidad de indígenas de Huayopampa.* Lima: Instituto de Estudios Peruanos, 1968.

GÁLVEZ VEGA, JOSÉ M. *El Fuero Privativo Agrario en el Perú.* Ayacucho: Bolivariana, 1971.

GARCÍA HURTADO, FEDERICO. *Tierra o muerte: La revolución agraria del Perú.* Havana: Centro de Documentación sobre América Latina, 1964.

GARCILASO DE LA VEGA, INCA. *Comentarios reales de los Incas.* Lima: Librería Internacional, 1959; first published 1609.

GARLAND ALEJANDRO. *El Perú en 1906.* Lima: La Industria, 1907.

GERTH, H. H., and C. WRIGHT MILLS, eds. *From Max Weber: Essays in Sociology.* New York: Oxford University Press, 1946.

GIDDENS, ANTHONY. *The Class Structure of the Advanced Societies.* New York: Barnes & Noble, 1973.

GIESECKE SARA-LAFOSSE, ALBERTO. "Bases para el estudio del estado y la burocracia en el Perú." Thesis, Pontificia Universidad Católica del Perú, 1971.

GOMEZ, MICHAEL A. "The Role of International Technical Cooperation in the Interregional Development of Peru." Ph.D. dissertation, Ohio State University, 1962.

GONZÁLEZ PRADA, MANUEL. *Anarquía.* Santiago: Ercilla, 1936.

_____. *Horas de lucha.* Lima: Futuro, 1964.

GOODSELL, CHARLES T. *American Corporations and Peruvian Politics.* Cambridge: Harvard University Press, 1974.

GRAHAM, LAWRENCE S. *Portugal: The Decline and Fall of an Authoritarian Order.* Beverly Hills, Calif.: Sage, 1975.

GREENSTEIN, FRED I., and NELSON W. POLSBY, eds. *Handbook of Political Science.* 9 vols. Reading, Mass.: Addison-Wesley, 1975.

GRINDLE, MERILEE S. *Coalition and Clienteles: Bureaucracy and Public Policy in Mexico.* Berkeley: University of California Press, 1977.

GROENNINGS, SVEN, et al. *The Study of Coalition Behavior.* New York: Holt, Rinehart & Winston, 1970.

GUTELMAN, MICHEL. *L'agriculture socialisée à Cuba: Enseignements et perspectives.* Paris: François Maspero, 1967.

_____. *Réforme et mystification agraires en Amérique latine: Le cas du Mexique.* Paris: François Maspero, 1971.

_____. *Structure et réformes agraires: Instruments pour l'analyse.* Paris: François Maspero, 1974.

HANDELMAN, HOWARD. *Struggle in the Andes: Peasant Mobilization in Peru.* Austin: University of Texas Press, 1975.

HARTH-TERRÉ, EMILIO. Negros e indios: Un estamento social ignorado del Perú colonial. Lima: Juan Mejía Baca, 1973.

HAYA DE LA TORRE, VICTOR RAÚL. Por la emancipación de América latina. Buenos Aires: M. Gleizer, 1927.

―――― Construyendo el Aprismo: Artículos y cartas desde el exilio, 1924–1931. Buenos Aires: Claridad, 1933.

――――. Política aprista. Lima: Amauta, 1967; first published 1933.

――――. El imperialismo y el Apra. 4th ed. Lima: Amauta, 1972.

HEADY, FERREL, and SYBIL L. STOKES, eds. Papers in Comparative Administration. Ann Arbor: Institute of Public Administration, University of Michigan, 1962.

HERBOLD, CARL F. "Developments in the Peruvian Administrative System, 1919–1939: Modern and Traditional Qualities of Government under Authoritarian Regimes." Ph.D. dissertation, Yale University, 1973.

HINTON, WILLIAM. Fanshen: A Documentary of Revolution in a Chinese Village. New York: Monthly Review Press, 1966.

HIRSCHMAN, ALBERT O. Development Projects Observed. Washington: Brookings Institution, 1967.

――――. El comportamiento de los proyectos de desarrollo. Mexico City: Siglo XXI, 1969.

HORTON, DOUGLAS E. Land Reform and Reform Enterprises in Peru. 2 vols. Madison, Wis.: Land Tenure Center, 1974.

――――. "Haciendas and Cooperatives: A Study of Estate Organization, Land Reform, and New Reform Enterprises in Peru." Ph.D. dissertation, University of Wisconsin, 1976.

HURTADO G., HUGO. Formación de las comunidades campesinas en el Perú. Lima: Tercer Mundo, 1974.

ILCHMAN, WARREN I., and NORMAN P. UPHOFF. The Political Economy of Change. Berkeley: University of California Press, 1969.

JAGUARIBE, HELIO, et al. La dependencia política-económica de América latina. Mexico City: Siglo XXI, 1969.

JAQUETTE, JANE S. The Politics of Development in Peru. Ithaca: Cornell University Dissertation Series, 1971.

JELICIC, JORGE. La reforma agraria y la ganadería lechera en el Perú. Lima: Minerva, 1978.

JIMÉNEZ CASTRO, WILBURG. Administración pública para el desarrollo integral. Mexico: Fondo de Cultura Económica, 1971.

KANTOR, HARRY. The Ideology and Program of the Peruvian Aprista Party. Berkeley: University of California Press, 1953.

――――. El movimiento aprista peruano. Buenos Aires: Pleamar, 1964.

KAPSOLI, WILFREDO. Los movimientos campesinos en Cerro de Pasco, 1800–1963. Huancayo: Instituto de Estudios Andinos, 1975.

KAUFMAN, ROBERT R. The Politics of Land Reform in Chile, 1950–1970: Public Policy, Political Institutions, and Social Change. Cambridge: Harvard University Press, 1972.

KILTY, DANIEL R. *Planning for Development in Peru*. New York: Praeger, 1966.

KLARÉN, PETER F. *Formación de las haciendas azucareras y orígenes del APRA*. 2d ed. Lima: Instituto de Estudios Peruanos, 1976.

KNIGHT, PETER T. *Perú: ¿Hacia la autogestion?* Buenos Aires: Proyección, 1974.

KRIESBERG, MARTIN, ed. *Public Administration in Developing Countries*. Washington: Brookings Institution, 1965.

KUCZYNSKI, PEDRO-PABLO. *Peruvian Democracy under Economic Stress: An Account of the Belaúnde Administration, 1963–1968.* Princeton: Princeton University Press, 1977.

LANDSBERGER, HENRY A., ed. *Latin American Peasant Movements*. Ithaca: Cornell University Press, 1966.

LARSON, MAGALI SARFATTI, and ARLENE EISEN BERGMAN. *Social Stratification in Peru*. Berkeley: Institute of International Studies, 1969.

LASKI, HAROLD J. *The State in Theory and Practice*. London: Allen & Unwin, 1935.

LEACH, EDMUND. *Pul Eliya*. Cambridge: Cambridge University Press, 1961.

LECAROS, FERNANDO. *Propiedad Social: Teoría y realidad*. Lima: Rikchay Perú, 1975.

LEHMANN, DAVID, ed. *Peasants, Landlords, and Governments: Agrarian Reform in the Third World*. New York: Holmes & Meier, 1974.

LENIN, VLADIMIR I. *State and Revolution*. New York: International Publishers, 1932.

LETTS COLMENARES, RICARDO. *Reforma agraria: Conferencia y debate*. Lima: Compañía de Impresiones y Publicidad, 1962.

LINDBLOM, CHARLES E. *The Intelligence of Democracy: Decision Making through Mutual Adjustment*. New York: Free Press, 1965.

LONG, NORMAN, and BRYAN R. ROBERTS, eds. *Peasant Cooperation and Capitalist Expansion in Central Peru*. Austin: University of Texas Press, 1978.

LORSCH, JAY W., and PAUL R. LAWRENCE, eds. *Studies of Organization Design*. Homewood, Ill.: Richard D. Irwin, 1970.

LOVEMAN, BRIAN. *Struggle in the Countryside: Politics and Rural Labor in Chile, 1919–1973*. Bloomington: Indiana University Press, 1975.

LOWENTHAL, ABRAHAM F., ed. *The Peruvian Experiment: Continuity and Change under Military Rule*. Princeton: Princeton University Press, 1975.

McCLINTOCK, CYNTHIA. *Self-Management and the Peasant: Aspirations and Realities in the Peruvian Cooperatives*. Princeton: Princeton University Press. Forthcoming.

MACLEAN Y ESTRENÓS, ROBERTO. *La reforma agraria en el Perú*. Mexico City: Instituto de Investigaciones Sociales, Universidad Nacional Autónoma, 1965.

Maisch von Humboldt, Lucrecia. Comentarios a la ley de propiedad social. Lima: Justo Valenzuela, 1975.

Malloy, James M., ed. Authoritarianism and Corporatism in Latin America. Pittsburgh: Pittsburgh University Press, 1977.

Malpica S. S., Carlos. Los dueños del Perú. Lima: Ensayos Sociales, 1968.

Marett, Robert H. K. Peru. London: Benn, 1969.

Mariátegui, José Carlos. Siete ensayos de interpretación de la realidad peruana. Lima: Amauta, 1929.

_____. Seven Interpretative Essays on Peruvian Reality. Trans. Marjory Urquidi. Austin: University of Texas Press, 1971.

Martín, Luis. The Kingdom of the Sun: A Short History of Peru. New York: Scribner, 1974.

Martínez-Alier, Juan. Los huacchilleros del Perú: Dos estudios de formaciones sociales agrarias. Lima and Paris: Instituto de Estudios Peruanos and Ruedo Ibérico, 1973.

Marx, Karl. The Eighteenth Brumaire of Louis Bonaparte. New York: International Publishers, 1963.

Matos Mar, José. Yanaconaje y reforma agraria en el Perú. Lima: Instituto de Estudios Peruanos, 1976.

Mayer, Enrique, Sidney W. Mintz, and G. William Skinner. Los campesinos y el mercado. Lima: Pontificia Universidad Católica, 1974.

Mayo, Elton. The Human Problems of an Industrial Civilization. Boston: Graduate School of Business Administration, Harvard University, 1946.

Mejía, José M., and Rosa Díaz S. Sindicalismo y reforma agraria en el Valle de Chancay. Lima: Instituto de Estudios Peruanos, 1975.

Middlebrook, Kevin J., and David Scott Palmer. Military Government and Political Development: Lessons from Peru. Beverly Hills, Calif.: Sage, 1975.

Millones Santagadea, Luis. Minorías etnicas en el Perú. Lima: Pontificia Universidad Católica, 1973.

Mitchell, William C. Public Choice in America: An Introduction to American Government. Chicago: Markham, 1971.

Moncloa, Francisco. Perú: ¿Qué pasó? Lima: Horizonte, 1977.

Montoya Rojas, Rodrigo. A propósito del carácter predominantemente capitalista de la economía peruana actual. Lima: Teoría y Realidad, 1970.

_____ et al. La SAIS Cahuide y sus contradicciones. Lima: Universidad Nacional Mayor de San Marcos, 1974.

Moreno, Federico. Las irrigaciones de la costa. Lima, 1900.

Murphy, Walter, and C. Herman Pritchett. Court, Judges, and Politics. 2d ed. New York: Alfred A. Knopf, 1974.

Murra, John V. "The Economic Organization of the Inca State." Ph.D. dissertation, University of Chicago, 1956.

————. *Formaciones económicas y políticas del mundo andino.* Lima: Instituto de Estudios Peruanos, 1975.

NEYRA, VÍCTOR. *Elementos de administración participante.* Lima: SINAMOS, 1974.

NUÑEZ BARREDA, ANGEL. *Los recursos humanos en el sector público peruano.* Lima: Instituto Nacional de Administración Pública, 1974.

OCHOA R., GABRIEL, et al. *Estudio diagnóstico sobre funcionamiento organizacional de la administración pública peruana según análisis de tres casos observados.* Lima: Instituto Nacional de Administración Pública, 1974.

O'DONNELL, GUILLERMO. *Modernization and Bureaucratic-Authoritarianism: Studies in South American Politics.* Berkeley: Institute of International Studies, 1973.

ORLOVE, BENJAMIN S. *Alpacas, Sheep, and Men: The Wool Export Economy and Regional Society in Southern Peru.* New York: Academic Press, 1977.

OSTROM, VINCENT. *The Intelligence Crisis in American Public Administration.* University: University of Alabama Press, 1973.

OSZLAK, OSCAR. *Capitalismo del estado: ¿Alternativa o transición?* Caracas: CLAD, 1974.

————. *Formación y evolución histórica del estado en América latina.* Buenos Aires: CEDES, 1979.

OWENS, R. J. *Peru.* London: Oxford University Press, 1963.

PAIGE, JEFFREY M. *Agrarian Revolution: Social Movements and Export Agriculture in the Underdeveloped World.* New York: Free Press, 1975.

PALMER, DAVID SCOTT. *Revolution from Above: Military Government and Popular Participation in Peru, 1968–1972.* Ithaca: Cornell University Dissertation Series, 1973.

PÁSARA, LUIS. *Reforma agraria: Derecho y conflicto.* Lima: Instituto de Estudios Peruanos, 1978.

PEASE GARCÍA, HENRY. *El ocaso del poder oligárquico: Lucha política en la escena official, 1968–1975.* Lima: DESCO, 1977.

————. *Los caminos del poder: Tres años de crisis en la escena política.* Lima: DESCO, 1979.

———— and OLGA VERME INSÚA. *Perú 1968–1973: Cronología política.* 2 vols. Lima: DESCO, 1974.

———— et al. *Estado y política agraria.* Lima: DESCO, 1977.

PETRAS, JAMES. *Politics and Social Structure in Latin America.* New York: Monthly Review Press, 1970.

PHILIP, GEORGE D. E. *The Rise and Fall of the Peruvian Military Radicals, 1968–1976.* London: Athlone Press, 1978.

PIGORS, PAUL J. W., and CHARLES A. MYERS. *Personnel Administration: A Point of View and a Method.* New York: McGraw-Hill, 1947.

PIKE, FREDRICK B. *The Modern History of Peru.* New York: Praeger, 1967.

———, ed. The New Corporatism: Social and Political Structures in the Iberian World. South Bend, Ind.: University of Notre Dame Press, 1974.

POBLETE TRONCOSCO, MOISÉS. Condiciones de vida y trabajo de la población Indigena del Perú. Study no. 28. Geneva: International Labor Office, 1938.

POULANTZAS, NICOS. Fascisme et dictature: La III<sup>e</sup> Internationale face au fascisme. Paris: François Maspero, 1970.

———. Political Power and Social Classes. Trans. Timothy O'Hagan. London: NLB, 1973.

———. Les classes sociales dans le capitalisme aujourd'hui. Paris: Editions du Seuil, 1974.

———. Classes in Contemporary Capitalism. Trans. David Fernbach. London: NLB, 1975.

POWELL, JOHN D. Political Mobilization of the Venezuelan Peasant. Cambridge: Harvard University Press, 1971.

PRESSMAN, JEFFREY L., and AARON B. WILDAVSKY. Implementation. Berkeley: University of California Press, 1973.

PYE, LUCIAN W. Politics, Personality, and Nation-Building: Burma's Search for Identity. New Haven: Yale University Press, 1962.

QUIJANO OBREGÓN, ANÍBAL. Nacionalismo, neoimperialismo, y militarismo en el Perú. Buenos Aires: Periferia, 1971.

RIGGS, FRED. Administration in Developing Countries: The Theory of Prismatic Society. Boston: Houghton Mifflin, 1964.

———, ed. Frontiers of Development Administration. Durham, N.C.: Duke University Press, 1970.

ROCA, SANTIAGO. Las cooperativas azucareras del Perú: Distribución de ingresos. Lima: ESAN Campodónico, 1975.

RODRÍGUEZ, ALFREDO, GUSTAVO RIOFRÍO, and EILEEN WELSH. De invasores a invadidos. Lima: DESCO, 1973.

RODRÍGUEZ PASTOR, HUMBERTO. Caqui: Estudio de una hacienda costeña. Lima: Instituto de Estudios Peruanos, 1969.

ROMERO, EMILIO. Geografía económica del Perú. Lima: Politécnico Nacional "José Pardo," 1961.

ROSEN, GEORGE. Democracy and Economic Change in India. Berkeley: University of California Press, 1966.

ROTH, GUENTHER, and CLAUS WITTICH, eds. Max Weber: Economy and Society: An Outline of Interpretive Sociology. 2 vols. Berkeley: University of California Press, 1978.

SAAVEDRA, JUAN BAUTISTA. El Ayllu. Santiago: Nascimento, 1938.

SALMÓN DE LA JARA, PABLO. Desarrollo económico, desarrollo agricola, y reforma agraria. Lima: P. L. Villanueva, 1963.

SANDERS, WILLIAM T., and BARBARA PRICE. Mesoamerica: The Evolution of a Civilization. New York: Random House, 1968.

SCHMITTER, PHILIPPE C. Interest Conflict and Political Change in Brazil. Stanford: Stanford University Press, 1971.

SCHNEIDER, BENJAMIN. *Staffing Organizations*. Pacific Palisades, Calif.: Goodyear, 1976.

SCOTT, JAMES C. *The Moral Economy of the Peasant*. New Haven: Yale University Press, 1976.

SCOTT, ROBERT E. *Mexican Government in Transition*. Urbana: University of Illinois Press, 1959.

SCURRAH, MARTIN J. "What's Wrong with the Universities? Some Organizational Structural Determinants of Student Protest in U.S. Universities and Colleges." Ph.D. dissertation, Cornell University, 1972.

SELZNICK, PHILIP. *TVA and the Grass Roots*. Berkeley: University of California Press, 1949.

SEOANE CORRALES, EDGARDO. *Surcos de paz*. Lima: Industrial Gráfica, 1903.

SHAFER, ROBERT J. *Mexico: Mutual Adjustment Planning*. Syracuse: Syracuse University Press, 1966.

SHARP, DANIEL A., ed. *United States Foreign Policy and Peru*. Austin: University of Texas Press, 1972.

SHARPE, KENNETH E. *Peasant Politics: Struggle in a Dominican Village*. Baltimore: Johns Hopkins University Press, 1978.

SILVERT, KALMAN H., ed. *Expectant Peoples: Nationalism and Development*. New York: Random House, 1963.

————. *Man's Power: A Biased Guide to Political Thought and Action*. New York: Viking Press, 1970.

————. *The Reason for Democracy*. New York: Viking Press, 1977.

———— and LEONARD REISSMAN. *Education, Class, and Nation*. New York: Elsevier Scientific, 1976.

SOLÍS, ABELARDO. *Ante el problema agrario peruano*. Lima: Perú, 1928.

SPALDING, KAREN. *De Indio a campesino*. Lima: Instituto de Estudios Peruanos, 1974.

STEIN, STANLEY J., and BARBARA STEIN. *The Colonial Heritage of Latin America: Essays on Economic Dependence in Perspective*. New York: Oxford University Press, 1970.

STEIN, WILLIAM W. *Countrymen and Townsmen in the Callejón de Huaylas: Two Views of Andean Social Structure*. Buffalo: SUNY, 1974.

STEPAN, ALFRED C. *The Military in Politics: Changing Patterns in Brazil*. Princeton: Princeton University Press, 1971.

————. *The State and Society: Peru in Comparative Perspective*. Princeton: Princeton University Press, 1978.

STEWART, WATT. *Chinese Bondage in Peru: A History of the Chinese Coolie in Peru, 1849–1874*. Durham, N.C.: Duke University Press, 1951.

STRIKON, ARNOLD, and SIDNEY GREENFIELD, eds. *Structure and Process in Latin America: Patronage, Clientage, and Power Systems*. Albuquerque: University of New Mexico Press, 1972.

SUNKEL, OSVALDO. El marco histórico del proceso de desarrollo y de subdesarrollo. Santiago: Instituto Latinoamericano de Planificación Económica y Social, 1967.

SWERDLOW, IRVING. The Public Administration of Economic Development. New York: Praeger, 1975.

TAI, HUNG-CHAO. Land Reform and Politics: A Comparative Analysis. Berkeley: University of California Press, 1974.

TANNENBAUM, FRANK. The Mexican Agrarian Revolution. Hamden, Conn.: Archon Books, 1968; first published 1928.

TAYLOR, FREDERICK W. Shop Management. New York: Harper, 1912.

THOMPSON, JAMES D. Organizations in Action: Social Science Bases of Administrative Theory. New York: McGraw-Hill, 1967.

THORNDIKE, GUILLERMO. El año de la barbarie: Perú 1932. Lima: Nueva América, 1969.

————. No, Mi General. Lima: Industriagráfica, 1976.

THORP, ROSEMARY, and GEOFFREY BERTRAM. Peru, 1890–1977: Growth and Policy in an Open Economy. New York: Columbia University Press, 1979.

THURBER, CLARENCE E., and LAWRENCE S. GRAHAM, eds. Development Administration in Latin America. Durham, N.C.: Duke University Press, 1973.

TORRES Y TORRES LLOSA, CARLOS. La empresa de propiedad social: El modelo empresarial peruano. Lima: Asesor Andina, 1975.

TRIMBERGER, ELLEN KAY. Revolution from Above: Military Bureaucrats and Development in Japan, Turkey, Egypt, and Peru. New Brunswick, N.J.: Transaction, 1976.

TULLIS, F. LA MOND. Lord and Peasant in Peru: A Paradigm of Political and Social Change. Cambridge: Harvard University Press, 1970.

VALDERRAMA, MARIANO. Siete años de reforma agraria peruana, 1969–1976. Lima: Pontificia Universidad Católica, 1976.

VAN DEN BERGHE, PIERRE L., ed. Class and Ethnicity in Peru. Leiden: E. J. Brill, 1974.

VAN EDWIN, ROTHROCK. "The Autonomous Entities of the Peruvian Government in Perspective." D.B.A. dissertation, Indiana University, 1969.

VAN GINNEKEN, PIETER. El desarrollo del cooperativismo y la educación cooperativa. Lima: Centro de Estudios de Participación Popular, SINAMOS, 1974.

VARGAS PRADA, JULIO. Destierro: Cartas a los peruanos. Lima: Atlántida, 1976.

VARGAS UGARTE, RUBÉN. Historia general del Perú. 10 vols. Lima: C. Milla Batres, 1966–71.

VÁSQUEZ, MARIO C. Hacienda, peonaje, y servidumbre en los Andes peruanos. Lima: Estudios Andinos, 1961.

VILLANUEVA, VICTOR. El militarismo en el Perú. Lima: Scheuch, 1963.

————. ¿Nueva mentalidad militar en el Perú? Lima: Juan Mejía Baca, 1969.

————. *Cien años del ejército peruano: Frustraciones y cambios.* Lima: Juan Mejía Baca, 1971.

————. *El CAEM y la revolución de la fuerza armada.* Lima: Instituto de Estudios Peruanos, 1972.

WACHTEL, NATHAN. *Sociedad y ideología: Ensayos de historia y antropología andinas.* Lima: Instituto de Estudios Peruanos, 1973.

WALDO, DWIGHT. *The Administrative State: A Study of the Political Theory of American Public Administration.* New York: Ronald Press, 1948.

————, ed. *Temporal Dimensions of Development Administration.* Durham, N.C.: Duke University Press, 1970.

WAMSLEY, GARY L. *The Political Economy of Public Organization: A Critique and Approach to the Study of Public Administration.* Lexington, Mass.: Lexington Books, 1973.

WARRINER, DOREEN. *Land Reform in Principle and Practice.* New York: Oxford University Press, 1969.

WEBB, RICHARD, and ADOLFO FIGUEROA. *Distribution del ingreso en el Perú.* Lima: Instituto de Estudios Peruanos, 1975.

WEIL, THOMAS, et al. *Area Handbook for Peru.* Washington: Government Printing Office, 1972.

WESTACOTT, GEORGE H. *La confianza interpersonal en el Perú: Estudio psicosocial de campesinos y obreros.* Lima: ESAN, 1975.

WHYTE, WILLIAM FOOTE. *Organizational Behavior: Theory and Application.* Homewood, Ill.: Richard D. Irwin, 1969.

———— and GIORGIO ALBERTI. *Power, Politics, and Progress: Social Change in Rural Peru.* New York: Elsevier, 1976.

WIARDA, HOWARD J., ed. *Politics and Social Change in Latin America: The Distinct Tradition.* Amherst: University of Massachusetts Press, 1974.

WITTFOGEL, KARL. *Oriental Despotism: A Comparative Study of Total Power.* New Haven: Yale University Press, 1957.

WOODBURY, RICHARD B., ed. *Civilizations in Desert Lands.* Salt Lake City: Department of Anthropology, University of Utah, 1962.

ZALD, MAYER N., ed. *Power in Organizations.* Nashville: Vanderbilt University Press, 1970.

ZIMMERMAN ZÁVALA, AUGUSTO. *Objetivo: Revolución peruana.* Lima: El Peruano, 1974.

ZÚÑIGA TRELLES, WASHINGTON. *Perú: Agriculture, reforma agraria, y desarrollo económico.* Lima: Amauta, 1970.

*Articles*

ABRAVANAL, ALLAN R. "Defensores de Oficio: An Analysis of Rural Legal Services in Peru." *International Legal Center Newsletter* 12 (June 1974), 13–14.

ABUSADA-SALAH, ROBERTO. "Propiedad social: Algunas consideraciones económicas." *Documentos de Trabajo* CISEPA. Lima: Pontificia Universidad Católica del Perú, October 1973.

ALBERTI, GIORGIO. "The Breakdown of Provincial Urban Power Structure and the Rise of Peasant Movements." *Sociologia Ruralis* 12:3/4 (1972), 315–33.

ALLRED, WELLS M. "System of Government in Peru." *Philippine Journal of Public Administration* 4:1 (January 1960), 46–60.

ASH, ROBERT. "Economic Aspects of Land Reform in Kiangsu, 1949–52 (Part 1)." *China Quarterly* 66 (June 1976), 261–92.

ASTIZ, CARLOS A., and JOSÉ Z. GARCÍA. "The Peruvian Military: Achievement, Orientation, Training, and Political Tendencies." *Western Political Quarterly* 25:4 (December 1972), 667–85.

BAER, WERNER, ISAAC KERSTENETZKY, and ANNIBAL V. VILLELA. "The Changing Role of the State in the Brazilian Economy." *World Development* 1:11 (November 1975), 23–24.

BARRACLOUGH, SOLON L. "Agricultural Policy and Strategies of Land Reform." *Studies in Comparative International Development* 7:8 (1968–69), 167–201.

_____. "Agricultural Policy and Land Reform." *Journal of Political Economy* 78:4 (July–August 1970), 906–47.

_____ and ARTHUR L. DOMIKE. "Agricultural Structure in Seven Latin American Countries." *Land Economics* 42:4 (November 1966), 391–424.

BONEO, HORACIO. "Algunas problemas administrativos y organizacionales de la Empresa Minera del Peru." Lima, MINEROPERU, January 1973.

BRENNER, MICHAEL J. "Functional Representation and Interest Group Theory." *Comparative Politics* 2:1 (October 1969), 111–34.

BRIDGES, AMY BETH. "Nicos Poulantzas and the Marxist Theory of the State." *Politics and Society* 4:2 (Winter 1974), 161–90.

CABALLERO, JOSÉ MARÍA. "Reforma agraria y capitalismo del estado: Discusión de algunas tesis sobre reforma agraria militar en el Perú." Lima: Department of Economics, Pontificia Universidad Católica, June 1976.

CÁCERES S. M., BALDOMERO. "Opiniones de profesores universitarios de ciencias agrarias sobre la problemática del campo." Publicaciones CISE. Lima: Universidad Nacional Agraria, January 1976, pp. 1–21.

CARROLL, THOMAS. "Land Reform in Peru." *AID Spring Review*, Country Paper SR/LR/C-6. Washington: Agency for International Development, 1970.

CAVAROZZI, MARCELO. "El rol de los partidos gobernantes y las organizaciones públicas en la generación de políticas de industrialización." Technical Paper Series no. 2. Austin: Institute of Latin American Studies, University of Texas, 1976.

CHONG SÁNCHEZ, JUAN. "El proceso de planificación social en el Perú." *Estudios Andinos* 3:1 (1973), 29–55.

CHURCHWARD, L. G. "Contemporary Soviet Theory of the Soviet State." *Soviet Studies* 12:4 (April 1961), 404–19.

CLEAVES, PETER S. "Peruvian Policymakers and the New Development Concept." Paper, American Society for Public Administration, Syracuse, N.Y., May 1974.

———. "The Implementation of the Educational and Agrarian Reforms in Peru." Technical Paper Series no. 8. Austin: Institute of Latin American Studies, University of Texas, 1977.

——— and MARTIN J. SCURRAH. "State Society Relations and Bureaucratic Behavior in Peru." SICA Occasional Papers. Hayward, Calif.: American Society for Public Administration, February 1976.

COFFREY, JOSEPH D. "Impact of Technology on Traditional Agriculture: The Peru Case," *Journal of Farm Economics* 49:2 (May 1967), 450–57.

COLLIER, DAVID. "Industrial Modernization and Political Change. A Latin American Perspective." *World Politics* 30:4 (July 1978), 593–614.

COTLER, JULIO. "The Mechanics of Internal Domination and Social Change in Peru," *Studies in Comparative International Development* 3:12 (1967–68), 229–46.

———. "Bases del corporativismo en el Perú." *Sociedad y Política* 1:2 (October 1972), 3–11.

CUNNINGHAM, FRANK. "Marxism and the State." *Revolutionary World* 6 (1974), 21–30.

DE GRÉ, GERALD. "Realignments of Class Attitudes in the Military and Bourgeoisie in Developing Countries: Egypt, Peru, and Cuba." *International Journal of Comparative Sociology* 15:1–2 (March–June 1974), 35–46.

DELER, JEAN-PAUL. "Croissance accelerée et formes de sous-développement urbain à Lima," *Cahiers d'Outre-Mer* 23:89 (January–March 1970), 73–94.

DELGADO, CARLOS. "SINAMOS: La participación popular en la revolución peruana." *Participación* 2:2 (February 1973), 6–25.

DEL RISCO S., FERNANDO E. "Elementos para la definición del rol del sector agrario del Perú." *Revista Interamericana de Planificación* 9:34 (June 1975), 16–35.

DENEVAN, WILLIAM M. "Campa Subsistence in the Gran Pajonal, Eastern Peru." *Geographical Review* 61:4 (October 1971), 496–518.

DEWIND, ADRIAN. "From Peasants to Miners: The Background of Strikes in the Mines of Peru." *Science and Society* 39:1 (Spring 1975), 44–72.

DORNER, PETER, and DON KANEL. "Group Farming Issues and Prospects: A Summary of International Experience." *Land Tenure Center Newsletter* 49 (July–September 1975), 1–16.

DYE, RICHARD W. "Peru, the U.S., and Hemispheric Relations." *Inter-American Economic Affairs* 26:2 (Autumn 1972), 69–87.

ECKSTEIN, HARRY. "Authority Patterns: A Structural Basis for Political Inquiry." *American Political Science Review* 67:4 (December 1973), 1142–61.

ESTIVALS, PIERRE, FRANCIS HENIN, and PHILIPPE TILLOUS-BORDE. "Cooperatives et systèmes traditionnels sur l'altiplan péruvien en 1972 (étude de cas)." Développement et Civilisations 52–53 (April–September (1973), 80–140.

FABREGA, HORACIO, JR., and PETER K. MANNING. "Health Maintenance among Peruvian Peasants." Human Organization 31:3 (Fall 1972), 243–56.

FERNANDEZ PEREDA, VÍCTOR M. "Situación de la agricultura, la planificación agraria, y la participación campesina en el Perú: Crítica y perspectivas." Publicaciones CISE. Lima: Universidad Nacional Agraria, April 1976.

FERNER, ANTHONY. "Dominant Classes and the State: The Problem of Relative Autonomy." Seminar discussion paper, University of Liverpool, March 1976.

FIGALLO A., GUILLERMO. "El marco jurídico de la reforma agraria." Participación 2:3 (August 1973), 35–43.

FIORAVANTI-MOLINIÉ, ANTOINETTE. "Tendances actuelles de la communauté rurale péruvienne." Sociologie du Travail 16:2 (April–June 1974), 174–92.

FLANNERY, KENT V. "The Cultural Evolution of Civilizations." Annual Review of Ecology and Systematics 3 (1972), 399–426.

FLORES CISNEROS, WILFREDO, JOSÉ MAGUERIRA AFA, JAMES VARGAS, and RAÚL SOTOMAYOR ÁLVAREZ. "Diagnóstico integral y perfil de estrategia de la Empresa Tiendas Afiliadas EPSA S.A. (AEPSA)." Seminar discussion paper, ESAN, 1976.

FREDERICKSON, H. GEORGE. "The Lineage of New Public Administration." Administration and Society 9:1 (May 1977).

GABLENTZ, OTTO HEINRICH VON DER. "Staat und Gesellschaft." Politische Vierteljahresschrift 2:1 (March 1961), 2–23.

GAITZSCH, ANDREA. "Hemmende Faktoren bei der Modernisierung der peruanischen Agrarstruktur: Ergebnisse einer Fallstudie in der Pampa de Anta, Cuzco." Dritte Welt 2:2 (1973), 235–50.

GALL, NORMAN. "Peru's Educational Reform: I, II, III (More Schools, Escape from Poverty, Dialogue of the Deaf)." Fieldstaff Reports (American Universities Field Staff) 21:3–5 (1974).

GOODMAN, LEO A., and WILLIAM H. KRUSKAL. "Measures of Association for Cross Classification." Journal of the American Statistical Association 49:268 (December 1954), 732–64.

GOODSELL, CHARLES T. "That Confounding Revolution in Peru." Current History 68:20 (January 1975), 20–23.

GRAEFF, PETER. "Two Approaches to the Legislation and Administration of Agrarian Reform in Peru." Seminar discussion paper, Department of Political Science, University of Wisconsin, May 1972.

GUILLET, DAVID. "Migration, Agrarian Reform, and Structural Change in Rural Peru." Human Organization 35:3 (Fall 1976), 295–302.

HAMMERGREN, LINN A. "Corporatism in Latin American Politics: A

Reexamination of the 'Unique' Tradition." *Comparative Politics* 9:4 (July 1977), 443–61.

HAVENS, A. EUGENE, and ALFONSO CERRATE VALENZUELA. "A Socio-Economic Diagnostic of the Peruvian Small Farm Sector with Particular Reference to the Production of Starchy Corn in Cajamarca, Ancash, and Cuzco." Mimeo. Lima, 1976.

HOPKINS, JACK W. "Comparative Observations on Peruvian Bureaucracy." *Journal of Comparative Bureaucracy* 1 (1969), 301–20.

HUIZER, GERRIT. "Community Development, Land Reform, and Political Participation." *American Journal of Economics and Sociology* 28:2 (April 1969), 159–78.

JAQUETTE, JANE S. "Revolution by Fiat: The Context of Policy Making in Peru." *Western Political Quarterly* 25:4 (December 1972), 648–66.

JAWORSKI, HELÁN. "El desarrollo social en el Perú y la política pública en el sector agrícola." Paper, Seminar on Planning and State Enterprises in Latin America, CEPAL-ILPES-ILDES, Lima, August 28–30, 1978.

JØRGENSEN, EDWARD. "The Peruvian Social Property Law." *Harvard International Law Journal* 16:1 (Winter 1975), 132–55.

KASSEM, M. SANI. "Organization Theory: American and European Styles." *International Studies of Management and Organization* 6:3 (Fall 1976), 46–59.

KLITGAARD, ROBERT E. "Observations on the Peruvian National Plan for Development, 1971–1975." *Inter-American Economic Affairs* 25:3 (Winter 1971), 3–22.

LAFER, CELSO. "Sistema politico brasileiro: Balanço e perspectivas." Mimeo. Rio de Janeiro: Fundação Getulio Vargas, 1973.

LEHMANN, DAVID. "Political Incorporation versus Political Stability: The Case of the Chilean Agrarian Reform, 1965–1970." *Journal of Development Studies* 7:4 (July 1971), 365–95.

LEÓN, FEDERICO. "El rol de miembro del Consejo de Administración en las Cooperatives Agrarias de Producción de la costa peruana." Mimeo. Lima: ESAN, January 1977.

LEVINE, CHARLES H., and LLOYD G. NIGRO. "The Public Personnel System: Can Juridical Administrators and Manpower Management Coexist?" *Public Administration Review* 35:1 (January–February 1975), 98–107.

LINCOLN, JENNIE KAH. "The Politics of a Developing Bureaucracy and Its Implementation of Agrarian Reform in Peru: The Impact of Regime Change." Dissertation prospectus, Ohio State University, Fall 1974.

McCLINTOCK, CYNTHIA. "Self-Management and Political Participation in Peru, 1969–1975: The Corporatist Illusion." Paper, Latin American Studies Association, Houston, November 1976.

———. "Socio-Economic Status and Political Participation in Peru:

The Impact of Agrarian Cooperatives, 1969–1975." Sage Monograph Series. Beverly Hills, Calif., 1978.

MALENGREAU, JACQUES. "Solidarité et antagonismes dans un district rural des andes péruviennes: Conditions d'organisation collective." Cultures et Développement 4:4 (1972), 755–84.

MALLON, RICHARD D. "Reform of Property Ownership and Income Distribution in Peru." Mimeo. Lima, December 1972.

MANN, FRED L., JOHN HUERTA, DENNIS MORRISEY, et al. "Preliminary Analysis, Agrarian Reform Law No. 17,716." Iowa-Peru Mission Program Reports, no. T-4. Lima, January 30, 1970.

MARTÍNEZ, HÉCTOR. "Tres haciendas altiplánicas: Chujuni, Cochela, y Panascachi." Perú Indígena 26 (1967), 96–162.

————. "Peru: Educación en las comunidades indígenas." América Indígena 33:2 (April–June 1973), 539–60.

MASPÉTIOL, ROLAND. "L'apport à la téorie de l'Etat des mèthodes phénoménologiques et structuralistes." Archives de Philosophie du Droit (1970), 269–86.

MAYHEW, LEON H. "Society." In International Encyclopedia of the Social Sciences 14, 577–86. 17 vols. Ed. David L. Sills. New York: Free Press, 1968.

MEANS, PHILIP AINSWORTH. "Social Conditions in the Piura-Tumbes Region." Scientific Monthly (November 1918), 385–99.

MEJÍA VALERA, JOSÉ. "El comportamiento del obrero peruano." Aportes 24 (April 1972), 101–15.

MITCHELL, WILLIAM P. ·"The Hydraulic Hypothesis: Reappraisal," Current Anthropology 14:5 (December 1973), 532–34.

MONTGOMERY, JOHN D. "Allocation of Authority in Land Reform Programs: A Comparative Study of Administrative Processes and Outputs." Administrative Science Quarterly 17:1 (March 1972), 62–74.

MOORE, CLEMENT HENRY. "Authoritarian Politics in Unincorporated Society: The Case of Nasser's Egypt." Comparative Politics 6:2 (November 1974), 193–218.

MORALES FLORES, ACRON. "El problema administrativo de la empresa comercial del Estado." Proyección 3 (June 1976), 12–15.

MORRIS, THOMAS D. "Merit Principles in Military Officers' Personnel Administration." Public Administration Review 34:5 (September–October 1974), 445–50.

MOSELEY, M. EDWARD. "Subsistence and Demography: An Example of Interaction from Prehistoric Peru." Southwest Journal of Anthropology 28:1 (Spring 1972), 25–49.

O'BRIEN, P. "The Emperor Has No Clothes: Class and State in Latin America." Paper, Conference on the State in Latin America, Cambridge University, December 1976.

O'DONNELL, GUILLERMO. "Acerca del 'corporativismo' y la cuestion del Estado burocrático-autoritario." Documento CEDES. Buenos Aires, August 1975.

――――. "Reflexiones sobre las tendencias generales de cambio en el Estado burocrático-autoritario." Documentos CEDES. Buenos Aires, August 1975.

――――. "Estado y alianzas en la Argentina, 1956–1976." Documentos CEDES. Buenos Aires, October 1976.

OMAN, CHARLES. "Problems of Peruvian Agricultural Development and Possibilities for Ford Foundation Assistance." Report, Ford Foundation. Lima, 1973.

PANICH, LEO. "The Development of Corporatism in Liberal Democracies." Mimeo. Department of Political Science, Carlton University, 1976.

PARSONS, TALCOTT. "Suggestions for a Sociological Approach to the Theory of Organization." *Administrative Science Quarterly* 1:1–2 (June–September 1956), 63–85, 225–39.

PÁSARA, LUIS. "Propiedad social: La utopía y el proyecto." Documentos de Trabajo CISEPA. Lima: Pontificia Universidad Católica del Perú, October 1973.

PAULSTON, ROLLAND G. "Education and Community Development in Peru: Problems at the Cultural Interface." *Council on Anthropology and Education Newsletter* 2:2 (1971), 1–8.

PAZ SILVA, LUIS J. "La política de precios en la planificación del desarrollo agrario del Perú." *Revista Interamericana de Planificación* 9:34 (June 1975), 16–35.

PETERS, B. GUY. "The Problem of Bureaucratic Government." Paper, Southern Political Science Association, Atlanta, November 1976.

POULANTZAS, NICOS. "The Capitalist State: A Reply to Miliband and Laclau." *New Left Review* 95 (January–February 1976), 63–83.

PRICE, BARBARA J. "Prehispanic Irrigation Agriculture in Nuclear America." *Latin American Research Review* 6:3 (Fall 1971), 3–60.

QUISPE, JUAN. "La deuda agraria: Un escollo para los reformistas." *Debate Socialista* 4 (November 1974), 2–26.

REYNOLDS, CLARK W. "Reforma social y deuda externa: El dilema peruano." *Trimestre Económico* 45:3 (July–September 1978), 643–68.

RINGLIEN, WAYNE R. "Some Economic and Institutional Results of the Agrarian Reform in Peru." *Land Tenure Center Newsletter* 38 (October–December 1972), 5–14.

ROBERTS, BRYAN, and CARLOS SAMANIEGO. "La reforma agraria en la sierra del Perú: El caso de Cahuide." *Problemas de Desarrollo* 6:25 (February–March 1976), 61–88.

SAMANIEGO, CARLOS, and BERNARDO SORJ. "Articulaciones de modos de producción y campesinado en América latina." Publicaciones CISE. Lima: Universidad Nacional Agraria, January 1976.

SANDERSON, JOHN. "Marx and Engels on the State." *Western Political Quarterly* 16:4 (December 1963), 946–55.

SANTISTEVAN, JORGE. "El régimen laboral en el anteproyecto del decreto ley de propiedad social." *Derecho* (Pontificia Universidad Católica del Perú, Lima) 31 (1973).

SARTORI, GIOVANNI. "Concept Misinformation in Comparative Politics." *American Political Science Review* 64:4 (December 1970), 1033–53.

SCOTT, CHRISTOPHER D. "Peasants, Proletarianization, and the Articulation of Modes of Production: The Case of Sugar Cane Cutters in Northern Peru, 1940–69." *Journal of Peasant Studies* 3:3 (April 1969), 321–41.

SCOTT, WILLIAM G., and DAVID K. HART. "The Moral Nature of Man in Organization: A Comparative Analysis." *Academy of Management Journal* 14:2 (June 1971), 241–55.

SCURRAH, MARTIN J. "Neither Capitalist nor Communist: Authoritarianism and Participation in Peru." Mimeo. Lima: ESAN, November 1973.

——— and MOSHE SHANI. "PPBS versus Conventional Budgeting in a Simulated Educational Organization." *Educational Administration Quarterly* 10:3 (Autumn 1974), 63–79.

SHEPHERD, GEOFFREY. "¿Son los márgenes del mercadeo de frutas y hortalizas demasiado amplios?" Iowa and North Carolina State Universities Mission to Peru, February 1967.

——— et al. "Política de comercialización y precios para las menestras en el Perú." Iowa and North Carolina State Universities Mission to Peru, June 1969.

SORJ, BERNARDO. "The Socio-Economic Structure of the Peruvian Public Enterprise Sector." Mimeo. Faculty of Social Sciences, Universidade de Minas Gerais, 1976.

SOTELO, I. "Los militares en el Perú: Continuidad y cambio de su función política." *Trabajos de Sociologia* 2 (1974), 79–114.

SPRINGER, J. FRED. "Empirical Theory and Development Administration: Prologues and Promise." *Public Administration Review* 36:6 (November–December 1976), 636–41.

TAPIA-VIDELA, JORGE I. "Understanding Organizations and Environments." *Public Administration Review* 36:6 (November–December 1976), 631–36.

TRAZEGNIES G., FERNANDO DE. "¿Existe la propiedad social?" *Derecho* (Pontificia Universidad Católica del Perú, Lima) 31 (1973).

TWOMEY, MICHAEL. "Ensayo sobre la agricultura peruana." *Cuadernos del Taller de Investigación Rural* (Pontificia Universidad Católica del Perú, Lima) 4 (1972).

VÉLIZ, CLAUDIO. "Centralism and Nationalism in Latin America." *Foreign Affairs* 47:1 (October 1968), 68–83.

WARREN, BILL. "The State and Capitalist Planning." *New Left Review* 72 (March–April 1972), 3–29.

WATKINS, FREDERICK M. "State: The Concept." In *International Encyclopedia of the Social Sciences* 15, 150–57. 17 vols. ed. David L. Sills. New York: Free Press, 1968.

WEICHELT, WOLFGANG. "Das Wesen des sozialistischen Staates." *Staat und Recht* 23:10 (October 1974), 1629–47.

WEISS, G. "Campa Organization." *American Ethnologist* 1:2 (May 1974), 379–404.

WIARDA, HOWARD J. "Toward a Framework for the Study of Political Change in the Iberic-Latin Tradition: The Corporative Model." *World Politics* 25:2 (January 1973), 206–35.

WINKLER, J. T. "Corporatism." *Archives Européennes de Sociologie* 17:1 (1976), 100–136.

ZALDÍVAR, RAMÓN (pseud). "Elementos para un enfoque general de la reforma agraria peruana." *Cuadernos Agrarios* 1 (August 1971).

ZENTNER, HENRY. "The State and the Community: A Conceptual Clarification." *Sociology and Social Research* 48·4 (July 1964), 414–27.

ZUCKER, ROSS. "The Relative Autonomy of the State." Seminar discussion paper, Department of Political Science, Yale University, 1975.

Documents

BONILLA, F., ed. *Ley orgánica del poder judicial.* Lima: Mercurio, 1972.

*Características del empleo estatal, 1970–1975: Investigación final del Censo II.* Lima: CPND, INP-UNI, OIC-IPL, May 1978.

CIAP. *El esfuerzo interno y las necesidades de financiamiento externo para el desarrollo del Perú.* Washington: Organization of American States, 1973.

CIDA. *Tenencia de la tierra y desarrollo socio-económico del sector agrícola: Perú.* Washington: Pan American Union, 1966.

Congreso de Irrigación y Colonización del Norte. *Anales del primer congreso de irrigación y colonización del norte.* 4 vols. Lima: Torres Aguirre, 1929.

*D.L. 17,734.* Lima: Ministerio de Agricultura, 1969.

*D.L. 21,356.* Lima: Ministerio de Agricultura, 1974.

Fondo Monetario Internacional, Banco Interamericano de Desarrollo, and Centro de Estudios Monetarios Latinoamericanos. *Manual de presupuestos por programas y por realizaciones.* Mexico: CEMLA, 1968.

Frente Nacional de Abogados para la Defensa de la Reforma Agraria. *Reforma Agraria Peruana.* Lima: Editorial Gráfica Labor, 1971.

*General Education Law D.L. No. 19,326.* Unofficial translation. Lima: Agency for International Development, March 1972.

International Bank for Reconstruction and Development. *Current Economic Position and Prospects of Peru.* Washington: International Development Association, 1973.

International Engineering Company. *Estudio de planificación: Aprovechamiento de agua de las cuencas Piura y Chira y estudios de factibilidad Valle de`Chira desarrollados.* Lima: Instituto Nacional de Planificación and Ministerio de Fomento y Obras Públicas, 1967.

Iowa Universities Mission to Peru. *Peruvian Macro-Economic and Agricultural Prospects and Strategy.* Lima: Agency for International Development, 1967.

MARTINEZ, G. S., ed. *Legislación de reforma agraria: Texto único del D.L. 17,716 y reglamentos y disposiciones conexas.* Lima: Martínez, 1971.

Partidos Políticos AP-DC, UNO, APRA, FLN, and CCP. *Reforma agraria peruana: Cinco proyectos de ley.* Lima: Tesis, 1963.

Peru, Banco Central de Reserva. *Memoria anual, 1972.* Lima: Ministerio de Economía y Finanzas, 1973.

——. *Cuentas nacionales del Perú, 1960–1973.* Lima: Ministerio de Economía y Finanzas, 1974.

Peru, Comisión para la Reforma Agraria y la Vivienda. *La reforma agraria en el Perú: Exposición de motivos y proyecto de ley.* Lima: Villanueva, 1960.

Peru, EPSA. *Memoria 71–72.* Lima: Oficina de Relaciones Públicas, 1973.

——. *EPSA 20:1* (January 1974).

Peru, Fuero Privativo Agrario. *Memorias del Presidente del Tribunal Agrario.* Lima: Oficina de Relaciones Públicas del Tribunal Agrario, 1969–75.

Peru, Instituto Nacional de Administración Pública. *Procesos Administrativos.* Lima: Dirección Nacional de Personal, 1977.

Peru, Ministerio de Agricultura. *Ley orgánica de la Empresa Pública de Servicios Agropecuarios, D.L. 17, 734.* Lima: EPSA, July 4, 1969.

——. *Diagnóstico sector Alto Piura ZAI.* Piura: Zona Agraria I, 1972.

——. *Diagnóstico sectores Medio y Bajo Piura ZAI.* Piura: Zona Agraria I, 1972.

——. *Proyecto integral de irrigación Chira-Piura.* Lima: Dirección Ejecutiva del Proyecto Especial Chira-Piura, 1973.

——. *Proyecto Chira-Piura: Planta de bombeo Montenegro.* Lima: Dirección Ejecutiva del Proyecto Especial Chira-Piura, 1974.

——. "La reforma agraria en cifras." Lima: Dirección General de Reforma Agraria, December 1975.

Peru, Ministerio de Economía y Finanzas. *Presupuestos generales de la República.* Lima: Dirección General de Presupuesto Público, 1960–75.

——. *Síntesis del presupuesto del sector público nacional.* Lima: Dirección General de Presupuesto Público, 1974.

Peru, Ministerio de Trabajo. *Censo de servidores civiles de 1967.* Lima: CEMO, 1970.

Peru, Oficina Nacional de Reforma Administrativa. *Administración pública peruana: Diagnóstico y propuestos de reforma.* Lima: ONRAP, 1965–68.

Peru, Presidencia de la República. *Plan nacional de desarrollo para 1971–1975.* Vol. 1: Plan global. Lima: Instituto Nacional de Planificación, 1971.

————. Compendio de leyes orgánicas de la Presidencia de la República y sectores de actividad pública. Lima: Instituto Nacional de Planificación, 1972.

————. "Comentarios acerca de la participación del sector público en la economía peruana, 1968–1975." Report no. 036–76. Lima: Instituto Nacional de Planificación, July 1976.

————. "Concentración de la producción y estructura de propiedad." Report no. 040-76. Lima: Instituto Nacional de Planificación, July 1976.

————. "Patrón de crecimiento de la economía peruana." Report no. 041-76. Lima: Instituto Nacional de Planificación, July 1976.

Peru, SINAMOS. Primer curso de entrenamiento en servicios para gestión empresarial. Lima: Centro de Estudios de Participación Popular, 1973.

————. Red de instituciones externas relacionadas con las Cooperativas Agrarias de Producción azucarera. Lima: Centro de Estudios de la Participación Popular, April, 1974.

————. Investigación sobre la integración de las CAPs azucareras al desarrollo regional. Lima: Centro de Estudios de la Participación Popular, November 1975.

————. Cooperativismo y participación. Lima: Centro de Estudios de la Participación Popular, 1976.

Plan Inca: o, Plan de Gobierno Revolucionario de la Fuerza Armada del Perú. Lima: C. L. Cabrera V., 1974.

"Principales Funcionarios de la Administración Pública." Peru. Lima: Latinoamericano, 1963.

United Nations. Problemas relativos a la organización y administración de empresas públicas en el sector industrial. New York: U.N. Technical Assistance Administration, 1958.

————. Demographic Yearbook. New York: Department of Economic and Social Affairs, Statistical Office, 1960–75.

————. Production Yearbook. Rome: Food and Agricultural Organization, 1960–76.

————. Aspectos administrativos de la planificación. New York: CEPAL, 1968.

VALDIVIA RODRÍGUEZ, ANGEL EDUARDO, ed. Guía judicial de Lima. Lima: AEME, 1972.

Velasco: La voz de la revolución. Lima: SINAMOS, 1972.

# Index

# AGRICULTURE, BUREAUCRACY, AND MILITARY GOVERNMENT IN PERU

Designed by G. T. Whipple, Jr.
Composed by The Composing Room of Michigan, Inc.
in 10 point VIP Melior, 2 points leaded,
with display lines in Melior.
Printed offset by Thomson/Shore, Inc.
on Warren's Number 66 text, 50 pound basis.
Bound by John H. Dekker & Sons, Inc.
in Holliston book cloth
and stamped in All Purpose foil.

*Library of Congress Cataloging in Publication Data*

CLEAVES, PETER S
    Agriculture, bureaucracy, and military govern-
ment in Peru.

    Bibliography: p.
    Includes index.
    1. Land reform—Peru.    2. Agriculture and
state—Peru.    3. Peru—Politics and government—
1968–    II. Scurrah, Martin J., joint author.
II. Title.
HD556.C56        333.3'1'85        80-14687
ISBN 0-8014-1300-1